Fundamentals of
Library Organisation
and Administration

By the same author

Public Library Finance and Accountancy
The Public Library and its Control (*AAL*)
Librarianship as a Career (*Sunday Times*)
Introduction to Librarianship (*James Clarke*)
Photo-charging (*James Clarke*)

etc

EDMUND V. CORBETT
MA FRSA FLA

Fundamentals of Library Organisation and Administration

A
PRACTICAL
GUIDE

The Library Association
1978

The Library Association
7 Ridgmount Street, London WC1E 7AE

First published 1978

© Edmund V Corbett 1978

British Library Cataloguing in Publication Data
Corbett, Edmund Victor
  Fundamentals of library organisation and
  administration.
  1. Library administration   2. Libraries—
  Great Britain
  1. Title   2. Library Association
  658′. 91′02100941   Z678.8.G/ .

boards: 85365 540 5

paperback: 85365 840 4

Designed and produced by
Mechanick Exercises, London

set in 10 on 12pt. Monotype Plantin
and printed in Great Britain by
Latimer Trend & Company Ltd Plymouth
and bound by Mansell, Witham, Essex

Contents

Preface   vii

Acknowledgements   ix

1 The Library Background in Britain   1

2 Types of Library and Their Parent-Bodies   16

3 Management by Committees   37

4 Goals, Objectives, Functions and Standards   60

5 Organisation of the Library System   79

6 Finance—Estimates   100

7 Finance—Control; Audit; Charges   121

8 Personnel   136

9 Library Stock—Selection; Acquisition; Records   172

10 Security—Circulation Control; Care of Stock; Library Rules   205

11 Library and User—Arrangement and Guidance; Co-operation; Public Relations   236

Appendix I   267

Appendix II   269

Index   273

Preface

The emphasis throughout this book has been on the discussion of library organisation and management in simple and practical terms, avoiding the theory and language of so-called 'scientific' management which has taken over in recent years. It makes no pretence of being a manual of library practice for all kinds of library. The complexity of libraries nowadays, the numerous types of library (especially those embraced by the word 'special') and the differing needs of the library users make this quite impracticable for any one person to attempt. The aim, rather, has been to concentrate on certain fundamental factors which are common to all kinds of library. While, as a general principle, each fundamental has been discussed in the context of all kinds of library, it is inevitable that major consideration has been given in each case to those kinds which best illustrate the point. Public, university and national library practices predominate in the examples; but other kinds of library have not been neglected.

Although the student should understand management theory it tends to gloss over the vast difference between the organisation and management of industry and that of a library. The profits of the latter have to be measured, not in real monetary terms, but in the promotion of the individual, the improvement of society, fostering better standards and better understanding both nationally and internationally, and in some cases in assisting the profitability of industry or commerce: all such profits are, however, 'intangible' rather than 'tangible'.

After introductory chapters describing the background and the 'national' library service of the United Kingdom, the book proceeds to deal with such fundamentals as the relationship between the library and its parent organisation and the way this is dictated from above, either by central government, local government, or by the parent body itself; this is followed by the consideration of the use of committees for control; library objectives; the fundamental structure of the library system; the vital issue of finance; the need to acquire staff in the right numbers and of the required calibre and to provide job satisfaction; stock building policy and acquisition; security of library materials and care of stock, and finally the book concludes with a very wide discussion of the over-riding premise that libraries are for users, and that public relations in its many aspects is the key to the efficient library service.

While the book is slanted towards library students generally, it should also be part of the library of more mature librarians for its up-to-date survey of the library scene in the United Kingdom and the many references to library legislation and official reports. At the same time its principles are common to libraries and librarians the world over and it should therefore be of value to anyone interested in a simple analysis of library organisation and management *as it is in practice.*

E. V. CORBETT

August 1977

Acknowledgements

Many good friends have helped me in various ways in the writing and production of this book and my gratitude is expressed to: Dr H. T. Hookway, Deputy Chairman and Chief Executive of the British Library for permission to quote from his address to the International Federation of Library Associations conference in 1974, and to use publicity material of the British Library, and to the Director of Publishing, Her Majesty's Stationery Office for authority to use extracts from relevant Acts of Parliament and other government publications. Mr R. Eatwell, Librarian of the University of Surrey kindly supplied me with material and information about university libraries, and gallantly read the whole manuscript, and Mr H. A. Chessyre likewise helped on polytechnic libraries and devoted time to checking of the related parts of the manuscript. On finance I had the expert assistance of Mr J. Wakely, Deputy Secretary and Accountant of the University of Surrey and Mr R. J. Nichols, Chief Finance Officer of the British Library. Mr M. A. Scoones, Head of Library Administration, Shell International gave very valuable help about libraries in his field, and Mr Alan Longworth, County Librarian of Lancashire and Mr G. Smith, County Librarian, Leicestershire provided details about 'agency arrangements' in their respective counties. Mr P. Curtis of Automated Library Systems Ltd, and Mr P. A. Armitage of Plessey Telecommunications were most generous in the supply of literature about their respective automated book charging systems. Several librarian members of WANDPETLS assisted by sending copies of their own libraries' publicity material, including, Miss B. R. Graves, Miss F. Solomonz, Mrs R. J. Lovell, Miss N. M. Morgan, Miss C. S. Ker, and Messrs J. Clarke, F. D. Staples, and C. J. Fellowes. Miss P. Meyer, Pauline Hunt, and other members of the West Hill Reference Library, Wandsworth, were extremely helpful in providing me with necessary books, reports and articles. To Mr Bruce Coward and the staff of the publications department of The Library Association I should like to extend thanks for the efficient way in which they have dealt with publication and the encouragement they have provided throughout, also to their assessor, Mr O. S. Tomlinson, Assistant County Librarian, North Yorkshire, for his kindly criticisms and suggestions, most of which have been incorporated. I must also pay tribute to Laurie Taylor, librarian of The LA library for his recently published *A Librarian's Handbook* in which he has collected together invaluable statutes, reports, and statements related to libraries. Unfortunately it came too late for my initial task, but at the revision stage it saved an enormous amount of work by enabling me to find so much of this vital material between the covers of one volume.

Finally, I would like to thank my wife for her patience while the writing was in progress, and for reading the drafts of the manuscript and checking the proofs.

E V C

1

The Library Background
in Britain

I t is generally claimed that Britain has the finest library system in
the world, and although such a thesis might be argued against in
view of the rapid developments in other countries, notably
Scandinavia, in recent years, it can still justifiably be claimed that
Britain has the most extensive library system in the world both in its
variety of libraries and their coverage. Furthermore in contrast to the
newer libraries of many other countries of the western world, the
library habit was established centuries ago in Britain, and the richness
of its collections is thereby considerably enhanced.

The earliest libraries in Britain can be said to date back to the collections of manuscripts built up in the monasteries and other ecclesiastical institutions. The Chapter Library of Canterbury Cathedral
and the monastic libraries of Jarrow and Wearmouth date back to
the seventh century. The Dean and Chapter Library of Durham
Cathedral dates from 998 AD; Hereford Cathedral Library was established before the Norman Conquest, and that of Wells before 1298.
Lambeth Palace Library, the historic library of the archbishops of
Canterbury 'was founded as a public library of Archbishop Bancroft
in 1610'.[1]

The libraries of our universities and colleges also originated several
centuries ago. The university library of Oxford dates from the bequest
of Bishop Cobham in 1327, and Merton and Balliol libraries, established in the second half of the thirteenth century, are even earlier.
The university library of Cambridge was founded *circa* 1400, and in
Scotland, that of St Andrews goes back to 1411, and Edinburgh's to
1580. Other academic libraries of significance with a long history include The Warden and Fellows Library, Winchester College (four-
teenth century), and Sion College Library (*circa* 1631) a copyright
library during the eighteenth century.

Also some learned society libraries have a long history: that of the

Royal Society dates from 1660, and the much older library of the Royal College of Physicians from 1518. The libraries of the legal world too have their place in history, for instance Lincoln's Inn (*circa* 1474), the Inner Temple (*circa* 1507), Gray's Inn (*circa* 1555) and the Middle Temple (1641).

Forerunners of the public library emerged in the seventeenth century, usually as a result of public philanthropy, in Norwich, Leicester, Ipswich and elsewhere but failed to survive for long through inadequate funds. A similar fate overtook several small parish libraries but the idea of *the collective provision of books* gained a firm hold and helped the provision of public libraries in due course. One of the early seventeenth century forerunners of the public library does, in fact, survive to this day: namely the Humphrey Chetham Library in Manchester, opened in 1653, though its modern emphasis is on local history and bibliography. The eighteenth century also witnessed the rise of the subscription library in London and elsewhere. Though most of these have, perforce, long-since closed their doors, the famous London Library, founded by Thomas Carlyle and his contemporaries in 1841, survives in spite of a succession of financial storms. An even earlier library of this kind which continues to function is the Leeds Library, established in 1768.

Nationally, the British Museum Library (now the Reference Division of the British Library) was established by an Act of 1753 which set up a Trust to acquire the library of Sir Hans Sloane in accordance with a wish he expressed in his will. The Trust bought this collection for the nation together with the Harleian manuscripts and the Cotton manuscripts and assembled them in Montagu House as a national library.

The idea of collective provision, referred to earlier, was again in evidence in 1850, this time with much greater support and firmer foundations. In that year an Act was passed which gave birth to public libraries throughout England and Wales. Niggardly in its financial provisions and ignoring the need to buy books, the Act permitted any town of over 10,000 population to set up a library service, although the library had to be paid for out of the product of a mere half-penny rate—little wonder that there was no great rush to adopt the Act! Subsequent legislation in 1855 permitted the purchase of books and raised the rate limit to one penny. (Its other main point, the reduction of the population limit to 5,000 was a step in the wrong direction.) It was not until 1919 that a new Act abolished the rate limit and extended library services to the counties (see Chapter 2). Meanwhile, Scotland and Northern Ireland had their own legislation, though it generally lagged behind that of England and Wales.

In fact it was not until after the programme of rehabilitation following the Second World War that fresh legislation was passed by Parliament which provided the solid basis for a reasonably good standard of library service: namely the Public Libraries and Museums Act, 1964, relating only to England and Wales. (This had been pressed for, for many years by public librarians, foremost among whom was Lionel McColvin.) This promoted a meteoric improvement in library services as compared with the previous half century. Its impetus was aided by London government reorganisation in 1965 and by similar reform elsewhere in England and Wales in 1974. This was followed by reform in Scotland in 1975. A reorganisation of library authorities in Northern Ireland just preceded events in England and Wales. This is dealt with in the next chapter, and others as applicable.[2]

The post-war period witnessed a colossal growth of libraries of every kind, particularly in the field of higher education. In the 1960s no fewer than sixteen new universities were founded, making a total of forty-four in Britain (thirty-three in England, eight in Scotland, two in Northern Ireland and one in Wales). In addition the Open University, demanding no specific entry qualifications, was established in 1969 for mature students working on their own. In 1976 the first independent, fee-paying, students enrolled at University College at Buckingham. These universities collectively cater for over 250,000 students at undergraduate and postgraduate levels.

The development of university libraries was given further stimulus in 1967 by the publication of the Parry Committee Report,[3] which underlined the statement made by the University Grants Committee as far back as 1921, that: 'the character and efficiency of a university may be gauged by its treatment of its central organ—the library. We regard the fullest provision for library maintenance as the primary and most vital need in the equipment of a university.' Indeed, it has been a feature of university teaching in recent years to place more and more emphasis on very extensive reading and hence on increased use of libraries. This has in turn confronted librarians with additional problems of administration.[4]

Parallel with the growth of university facilities has been the creation (1964) of the non-university degree awarding body, the

Council for National Academic Awards and the emergence, and subsequent expansion, of the polytechnics which in many cases have been created from an amalgamation of existing technical, commercial, art, and other types of college. They are controlled by the local authorities and offer a diversity of educational facilities for people over the age of eighteen. The courses provided are for graduates and undergraduates and are geared to CNAA degrees, as well as professional and vocational qualifications. The latter are aimed at the examinations of the professional associations and at higher certificates and diplomas. Local authorities are also responsible for many other academic institutions, including colleges of higher education, colleges of education, technical colleges, colleges of further education and agricultural colleges. The library in all these is an essential part of the academic framework.

In addition to university, polytechnic, and local authority colleges, libraries are provided in voluntary colleges, and special colleges such as those of librarianship or law, the Police College, or the Administrative Staff College. Then most large state schools have their own library, many of them in the charge of a qualified librarian or a tutor-librarian. The independent schools, too, have their libraries, although staffing seems more often to be in the hands of a teacher rather than a professional librarian.

Other libraries financed from public funds include those in hospitals where the services vary from collections of recreational reading only, distributed by voluntary helpers, to first-class stocks of well-selected fiction and non-fiction, administered by professional librarians. In some cases the hospital library includes a library for both medical and nursing staff. Sometimes the service is organised by the hospital authorities and in others it may be administered, wholly or in part, by the public library, most likely on a per capita basis, but in some cases free. Many other institutions such as prisons, detention centres and approved homes also have their own libraries, again usually run by the public library in return for a government grant. Locally the public library will provide a library service to its old people's homes and to handicapped persons.

There are thousands of so-called 'special libraries' which promote trade or industry within firms or associations. In the case of libraries of government departments these have a function of serving the needs of the Minister and his senior staff. Usually both private firms and government departments are willing to help *bona-fide* researchers

4

other than those in their own employ; in fact some government department libraries do provide a public reference service without restriction. Naturally no such library will give outsiders access to confidential materials, and in some cases they may well require an introduction from another library. Many of these libraries also help others through various inter-lending schemes.

Finally, to complete this brief survey of the kinds of library found in Britain (they are dealt with in some detail in the next chapter), we come to the national libraries, namely the National Library of Scotland, the National Library of Wales, and the British Library. Important as are the first two of these and immense as are their resources (see pp 19–20) it is the British Library we think of when we speak of *the* national library. Until 1973 there was, strictly speaking, no national library with a leading national rôle to play in overall library services and co-ordination although the British Museum Library was the one people thought of when the word 'national' was mentioned. It was, however only national in the sense of being a repository of the nation's literary heritage, and as the leading centre for research material—the library where research workers were expected to go only as a last resort. However, following on the report of the Parry Committee which although basically concerned with the libraries of universities and colleges of advanced technology and central institutions, included a section in its report on the requirements of a national library the Dainton Committee was established and only published its *Report of the National Libraries Committee*[5] in 1969. As a result the government issued a White Paper in 1971 setting forth its intentions with regard to a national library. Thus the British Library Act, 1972, was passed which unified the British Museum Library (including its National Reference Library of Science and Invention), the National Lending Library for Science and Technology, the National Central Library, and the British National Bibliography. The functions of the former Office of Scientific and Technical Information (OSTI) were also transferred to the Research and Development Department.

It is, thus, evident that libraries in Britain have a long and proud history. Library services of different kinds provide for every conceivable type of reader through a multiplicity of agencies. It should also be added that through the most extensive systems of co-operation (many of them voluntary) among libraries both at home and abroad, few demands for serious literature go unsatisfied. With the advent of the British Library in the rôle of a very active national library, operating at several key levels, we have what can truthfully be called a national library service.

The concept of 'national' as applied to the library service has, however, different interpretations in various parts of the world, and it is necessary, therefore, to examine closely the rôles of both central government and the British Library in assessing what we in Britain mean by the term national library service. Accordingly, before describing in some detail the functions and controlling bodies of the different types of library, it is useful to investigate the part that the central government now plays, and its influence, direct and indirect, on libraries generally.

The 'national' library service

While it is generally accepted that the library service of any individual country should be based on national as well as international objectives, the pathways to the various national patterns are diverse. It must also be appreciated that it is much simpler to develop a country's entire library service as an integrated whole, in a developing country starting from scratch, than it is in a country where many types of library have been established under the auspices of a host of organisations and institutions over the centuries.

At the conference of the International Federation of Library Associations (IFLA) in Washington in 1974 the subject of national library and information services was the key theme. Four speakers from different countries described their own national library services: the gulf between them was striking. The Russian outlook regarded the library as an appendage of the State, a view aptly summed up by the speaker, N. M. Sikorsky: 'The activity of Soviet libraries is based on clear-cut ideological and organisational principles, which were largely developed by Lenin. The most vital of these principles is the state character of librarianship in a socialist society.' Then there was a paper describing the relatively recent, and very successful, Jamaica Library Service. Although this was labelled a national library service, as yet it is severely limited, being to all intents and purposes confined to public libraries. A third paper was given by Stanley McElderry of the United States. There is virtually no direct national control of libraries in that country. The local authorities are responsible for the support of schools, libraries and other institutions, with some support

6

from the State and Federal governments in equalising opportunity and improving standards. In spite of the American love of independence however, there is a great deal of co-operation between libraries. The need for further pooling of resources leads American librarians to look closely at British methods of co-operation, particularly at regional and local levels. In particular it has led to the establishment of the National Commission on Libraries and Information Science with a view to exploring ways of improving information services on a national basis and improved methods of co-operation through regional and national programmes: to quote Stanley McElderry: 'The ultimate solution is seen as a more systematic national approach, designed to optimise available resources in order to achieve more rationally defined goals. . . . A strong leadership rôle by the federal government seems mandatory for establishing and maintaining a comprehensive, higher quality information service.'

The fourth paper was delivered by Dr H. T. Hookway, Deputy Chairman and Chief Executive of the British Library Board, who spoke about 'national library planning' in Britain. The title of this paper must have been chosen after considerable thought; it is very apt indeed for while we cannot call the British library service 'nationally controlled' there is a great deal of national planning involved, both of an obvious and less obvious a nature. A large percentage of our libraries is also supported, in whole or in part, with public funds. Dr Hookway discussed the ways in which British libraries had grown up piecemeal, and said that although it was tempting to produce a detailed, comprehensive and systematic plan for the closely articulated development of all these services to meet national goals, 'many activities are better regulated in response to local needs, rather than within the constraints imposed by the operation of a central plan. . . . National planning should focus on a limited range of crucial issues so that a flexible and responsive national system can evolve naturally over a reasonable period of time. These crucial issues are related mainly to the provision of appropriate legislative, institutional and manpower needs.' This is a masterly summing-up. *While we do not have a completely centrally controlled library service, we have in recent years in particular, gone a long way towards a nationally planned system.* It is a system planned largely around financial controls and government policies, engineered through the Department of Education and Science, the University Grants Committee, the local authorities, and the Boards of national libraries.

The libraries of industrial and commercial firms, societies and associations, certain academic institutions, and others not supported with public funds remain independent of any direct government influence, except possibly research grants. However, although there are many such libraries, most of them are relatively small. On the other hand the remainder are mostly large, comprising as they do, the national libraries, public libraries, and those of universities, polytechnics and colleges, government departments, public corporations and nationalised industries. All are subject, directly or indirectly, to a great deal of government control and influence.

Control can originate for example in the initial legislation which establishes the library or libraries. For instance, the British Library through the British Library Act, 1972, and public libraries through both library and local government laws, eg in England and Wales the Public Libraries and Museums Act, 1964, and the Local Government Act, 1972. The legislation places a duty (ie a statutory requirement) upon public library authorities to provide a 'comprehensive and efficient service'. Moreover the same legislation makes a Minister responsible for ensuring that the service of each authority comes up to certain, though ill-defined, standards. (See p. 63)

The very pattern of control of the public library service has also been fashioned by government-supported committees which have suggested appropriate management structures for local authorities. The result is that in England and Wales and particularly in Scotland, many public libraries have been linked with leisure or recreation services. In Northern Ireland on the other hand, the library has been regarded as a regional service and linked with education. The government provides over sixty per cent of the income of local authorities in England and Wales through the Rate Support Grant. Any reduction in this amount can have a devastating effect on local authority services, and the public library has to bear its share (often more) of the reduction. The libraries of colleges controlled by local authorities also suffer similarly. Capital expenditure is also dictated by the amount of money the government is prepared to allocate to local authorities, both for education and in the non-essential sector. Where this is inadequate the authority will be unable to press ahead with plans for new central libraries, branches, mobiles, etc, or for new college libraries and extensions. Then again in times of financial stringency government policies, or merely recommendations, can well result in economies being made in library staffing, book-funds, hours of opening, periodical purchases, audio-visual funds, or even the closure of some service points (this has been very evident in non-metropolitan counties in 1976 and 1977). Where public money is being spent the accounts will be inspected by government auditors, and although no criticism can be made of this practice which is in the interests of all concerned with public spending, it is a further indication of government supervision. All types of library supported by public funds can be affected by government economies.

In England and Wales* the Department of Education and Science, through its Minister and his staff, is responsible for the promotion of library services in the public sector. It has two advisory councils to assist in this work, one for England and the other for Wales. These councils are required to deliberate and report upon any matter submitted to them by the Minister and in turn may make their own suggestions to him for the investigation of anything affecting the library service. This Department operates through its Arts and Libraries Branch, and has a policy responsibility in relation to all kinds of library. It has been involved in a wide range of activities: man-power planning and the library schools; census of library staffs; establishment of library schools; research into public library staffing; research into co-operation between different types of library; charges in public libraries; Public Lending Right; inspection of public libraries; grant-in-aid to national and university libraries and others; library statistics; organisation of the British Library; National Libraries ADP Feasibility Study; the libraries of colleges of education in the light of reorganisation; and approval of college of education building projects; to name but a few.

As the Chief Executive of the British Library has said, the basic objective of the British national library service is: 'to try to ensure that, within the resources available, the libraries and information services of the country, taken as a whole aim to collect and store all information likely to be needed, to provide access to it as rapidly as necessary and to arrange its supply in the most useful form where it will be most effectively employed'.[6] The key words in this statement are 'within the resources available' and it has become evident in recent years that the government will strive through the agency of the Department of Education and Science and the British Library, as well as through pressure on the University Grants Committee and local authorities, to ensure economy in library expenditure on build-

* See note on p 29.

ings, bookstock, and otherwise, through library co-operation. Traditionally, co-operation between libraries has been voluntary but hard-pressed finances will inevitably lead to inescapable and compulsory co-operation though it might not be openly labelled as such. Examples of recent thought in this direction include the research project of the DES which resulted in the Sheffield Report[7] on co-operation among all types of library, and the proposals of the UGC's Working Party[8] (known as the Atkinson Committee) on capital provision for university libraries (see pp 90–1). These latter proposals, which would require the university library to discard a large part of its stock every year, like a public library, and send that which might only be required occasionally to the British Library Lending Division at Boston Spa, indicate gross interference with library policy in order to meet the government's policy of reducing capital expenditure on university building to an impossible level. The suggestion that all the lesser used volumes may be housed at BLLD is also an interference with the national library and assumes an unlimited capacity for storage.

In terms of library staff and library schools the Department of Education and Science exercises considerable influence over the training of librarians, their length of training, qualifications required for admission to library schools, and the numbers to be admitted at various levels, the number of library schools and their standards, and proposals for postgraduate courses. As the government provides a very large part of the money which finances the schools and also the grants which most students receive, such controls are not unreasonable but are quoted just to underline how government influence permeates so much of library activities.

In matters of research the government is able to *support* many projects which should be for the benefit of librarianship generally. This is all to the good but at the same time it has to be appreciated that apart from the funds available through the British Library there is very little finance to be obtained from other sources. Thus the British Library virtually has a monopoly, and it means in effect that it is the government which decides which research project shall be carried out. (To be fair, however, the British Library is always prepared to consider outside applications for funds for specific research projects and has been very generous to-date.) This inevitably gives central government, indirectly at least, a great deal of power in determining the usefulness of technical and other possible innovations, and of minimising any it wishes. At the same time the results of research or of working party deliberations within the DES need never be accredited with outright government acceptance: eg the Bourdillon Report on public library standards,[9] published in 1962 and widely hailed at that time as a significant landmark. Although the recommendations were for minimum standards they were never accorded any higher status than of being 'for guidance only'. Similarly, the LAMSAC report (see p 64) on the Staffing of Public Libraries[10] (published after a two-year delay), although sponsored by DES, received only lukewarm support from the Department itself, presumably in case any authority might think the government was interfering in its business, or encouraging it to employ more staff. Thus, while central government has the means for actively improving the library service, it can also prevaricate if the political climate so demands.

In the academic world although the universities have always been proud of their autonomy, state influence is again evident, for autonomy with financial strings attached is only half autonomy at best. The tradition of independence has been eroded over the years as the government has ploughed more and more millions of pounds into higher education. Outwardly it was concealed by the establishment, in 1919, of the University Grants Committee 'to act as a buffer between the government and the universities, interpreting the one to the other, and enabling public funds to flow into universities without direct government intervention'.[11] Intervention or no intervention, as the recent financially restrictive years have shown, government attitudes towards university education have had considerable impact upon university spending. The examples of the Atkinson Report already referred to, and the White Paper *Education: a framework for expansion, Cmnd 5174*, published in 1972 demonstrate this point. Again as 'it seems that the UGC distributes grants according to a formula, based on student enrolments'[12] and as the government also controls the number of students, this can directly affect library resources.

Another significant example of government influence in the university field came about in 1968 when universities were required to make their books and records available for inspection by the comptroller and Auditor-General. Furthermore, Joel Hurstfield was in no doubt about the subordination of the universities to the government when he wrote to the effect, 'the transfer of the universities to the

Department of Education and Science was a significant stage in reducing the relative independence of the universities. Imperceptibly but cumulatively, the power of decision was passing from the academics to the government and administration.'[13] Finally, even if the universities seek a partial solution to some of their problems through more extensive channels of co-operation it is very expensive to set up national and international networks, and only the government could supply the necessary funds.

Similarly, government influence is to be seen in the polytechnics and other institutions of higher and further education. Government policies affect the numbers of colleges and their status, the variety of courses offered and the numbers of students. All these factors have a bearing on the required standards and volume of library provision. In this respect the White Paper, Cmnd 5174 already referred to, the DES Circular 7/73, and the government's policy statement of November 1976, show only too well the results of government's deliberations. Both the creation of the polytechnics some years ago and the more recent reorganisation of the various colleges provided by the local authorities and in particular the colleges of education, have had the effect of building up very substantial libraries in the polytechnics, and of closing down some colleges and their libraries, or amalgamating them with others. In turn such reorganisation has had a very marked effect on librarians: some have been made redundant or have been encouraged to take early retirement; some have been transferred, and some on the other hand, have been promoted. Again, though these types of library are under the control of the local authority the central government largely controls the purse-strings, and adverse economic conditions can be reflected in less money for the colleges and their libraries. Many of the polytechnics still have to operate inefficiently without a central library building and school libraries have suffered drastic financial cuts.

Apart from these major controls, DES exerts various strong influences over colleges, and these often affect library provision. They include such matters as staff/student ratios, standards for books and equipment, local authority representation on the governing bodies of polytechnics, and notes for guidance on the design of libraries.

At national level the legislation specifies the functions of the national libraries and special privileges such as copyright receipt which they enjoy. It places control of the national library under a Board of Trustees. The major control of finance, once more, lies with the government and progress therefore depends on its policies to a very great extent. To take an outstanding example—for years it has been recognised on all sides that a new library building is necessary to replace the former British Museum Library. With its incorporation into the broader framework of the British Library Reference Division the need is that much greater and more urgent. For years, however, the building has been deferred pending various decisions at top level and especially, whether to build again in Bloomsbury or on a new site in Camden. Although the decision has been made in favour of the latter, it will still be some time before any building operations can commence. Meanwhile, costs continue to escalate, and government can always make temporary savings by putting off a start date.[14]

Although the British Library makes no claim to be the fountainhead from which springs the direction of all other publicly financed libraries in Britain, it is justifiably claimed by its Chief Executive to be the hub of the nation's library services. The British Library Act, 1972, supports this claim in its very wide remit of functions. S.1(3) reads:

The Board shall make the services of the British Library available in particular to institutions of education and learning, other libraries and industry; and (a) it shall be within the functions of the Board, so far as they think it expedient for achieving the objects of this Act and generally for contributing to the efficient management of other libraries and information services, to carry out and sponsor research; and (b) the Board may contribute to the expenses of library authorities within the meaning of the Public Libraries and Museums Act 1964, or of any other person providing library facilities, whether for members of the public or otherwise.

Thus, the British Library has the authorisation to go much further than the provision of central library facilities for it also has the legal right to act as the government's agent in the promotion of more efficient and productive library and information services generally.

Apart from the nation-wide reference function of the Reference Division and its importance as a final referral centre, the major impact of the British Library on all types of library is through the work of its Lending Division. With its large financial resources which permit it to purchase all significant serials and reports in all languages, as well as all English language monographs, and, with its claim of speed and cheapness, this library could develop into a service planned at government level to reduce expenditure by libraries in the public fields on books and periodicals. The idea that it might save very considerable expenditure on university stack accommodation has already been advanced (see pp 90–1). In turn provision at this level and on this scale could in time herald the demise of some or all of the regional library systems. Whether the BLLD could carry such a burden seems doubtful, and its claim of cheapness is already being questioned in some quarters.

Another field in which the British Library undoubtedly affects all types of library, a field in which this national help and initiative is very much appreciated, is that of bibliographical services. It has long been recognised that the production of bibliographies and catalogues should be undertaken nationally rather than be repeated time and time again by hundreds of individual libraries. Without doubt this service represents one of the greatest advantages to be derived from government's interest in libraries.

Thus, while the British Library can be a tower of strength to libraries and librarians and is so organised that it can get expert advice through its advisory committees it must be recognised that much of the forward thinking in British librarianship will in future be done, not so much through the individual librarians and the professional associations but by a quasi-governmental body. While this will facilitate progress and make possible investigations hitherto beyond the means of the profession, it must be appreciated that automatically some freedom will be sacrificed to government thinking and policy. In fact the surrender goes much further than this: as national representatives attend international conferences of government representatives including librarians, and there subscribe to certain decisions, the direction of British librarianship is consequently often subtly changed.

To sum up therefore, it is fair to say that in Britain today the existing system of largely independent libraries (though the majority are financed from public funds) revolves round the British Library, and this permits the system to work to the best of advantage. The national library provides a generating station or a 'think-tank' which has for so long been missing; and it aims to weld the several parts of the country's library and information services (excluding the privately or commercially owned sectors) into a loosely integrated whole but without any superimposed overall administrative structure. By investigation, research and co-operation, the opportunity is there for all librarians to work to a common end in a national library service in which individualism and autonomy will still have a part to play. With the government (both central and local) responsible for so much of the financial support of libraries in the many public sectors however, one can foresee that the library service could fall a victim to politics and economics. It therefore behoves the professional associations and librarians individually to continue to take a very active interest in current developments and, above all, to ensure that the library service never becomes part of the state political machine as in some other countries.

References

1   *Libraries, museums and art galleries year book*, 1971, p 350.
2   For a full account of public library legislation and progress see: Morris, R. J. B. *Parliament and public libraries*, Mansell, 1977.
3   University Grants Committee. *Report of the committee on libraries*, HMSO, 1967, p 9.
4   McAnnally, A. M. and Downes, R. B. 'Changing role of the university librarian'. *College and research libraries*, Vol 34, No 2, March 1973.
5   Report of the national library committee, HMSO, Cmnd 4028, 1969.
6   IFLA conference, Washington 1974.
7   University of Sheffield. 'Postgraduate school of librarianship', *Local library co-operation*. 1974, 2 vols.
8   University grants committee. *Capital provision for university libraries: report of the working party*, HMSO, 1976.
9   Ministry of Education. *Standards of public library service*, HMSO, 1962.
10 Department of Education and Science. *The staffing of public libraries*, 3 vols, HMSO, 1976.
11 Thompson, J. *An introduction to university library administration*, 2nd ed, 1974, p 9.
12 *Times Higher Education Supplement*, 11 July 1975.
13 *The Listener*, 3 October 1974.
14 Authority to commence the building in 1979 was announced in April 1978.

2

Types of Library and their Parent Bodies

The preceding chapter has given an outline of the nation's library service. There are common links and shared objectives between the different types of library but there is no overall pyramidical unification. Libraries are the responsibility of the institution or organisation which provides them and which can be called the 'parent-body' or 'parent-organisation' although the word 'authority' is often employed instead. This chapter examines more fully the different types of library, their background, functions, and management by the parent-body. The succeeding chapter will deal with a further stage in management employed in many organisations, ie management by committee.

National Libraries

THE BRITISH LIBRARY

The former British Museum Library is now the heart of the Reference Division of the British Library but it also includes the former National Reference Library of Science and Invention, housed separately in two parts at Bayswater and Holborn. The two together are now referred to as the Science Reference Library. A new building to house all sections of the Reference Division is planned for the 1980s. In addition to the Sloane Collection and the Harleian MSS, the former British Museum Library contains the Royal Library added by George II in 1757, and the Library of George III, presented by his son George IV in 1823 and known as the King's Library. The main Library has enjoyed the right to a copy of every book published in the United Kingdom since 1757 though before 1842, as Arundell Esdaile[1] has said, the supply was fitful and unfavourable. The total number of books is around 10 million. There are also extensive collections of Oriental and Western MSS, newspapers, maps, music, postage stamps, charters and other official documents. Accordingly, the Library is divided into three departments: Printed Books (including the Newspaper Library at Colindale), the Department of Manuscripts, and the Department of Oriental Manuscripts and Printed Books. Admission to the Reading Room is by ticket only. The Science Reference Library is used by 150,000 people annually who make two million consultations of books and other items and require a similar number of photocopies.

The Lending Division at Boston Spa, Yorkshire, is the largest lending library in the world and its loan service of books, periodicals, reports, etc, (or alternatively photocopies) extends to the whole of the United Kingdom and to many organisations abroad. It also acts as a clearing house for libraries wishing to dispose of little-used material, and provides short courses for information workers and a translation service from Russian and other Slavonic and some Oriental languages. The Lending Division is also the national centre for MEDLARS (Medical Literature Analysis and Retrieval System) which organises medical literature searches in the data bank maintained by the US National Library of Medicine.

Basically, the Lending Division is intended as a back-up service to individual libraries and other co-operative agencies. Its acquisition policy is now so extensive, however, that more and more requests go there direct from libraries rather than via the regional and other systems. This is particularly the case where time is of the essence; the BLLD's postal service aims at a twenty-four-hour delivery.

The Bibliographical Services Division is likely to revolutionise library routines and to provide greater uniformity of method; it is facilitating the adoption of computer based catalogues, issue methods, book order routines, etc, and is improving the means of communication of information between libraries and facilitating information retrieval. Further development of more national bibliographical records, particularly those of non-book material, will be expedited and the productions of this Division can be expected to add considerably to the individual library's ability to exploit its stock. The sponsorship of the Research Department has already been referred to on p 10, it should enable many individual libraries or groups of libraries to experiment with new methods and techniques. The total staff of the British Library is now more than 2,000.

Management of the BL is provided for in the British Library Act, 1972, which establishes a Board, known as the British Library

Board and specifies in S.2(1) that its membership should be: a chairman, appointed by the Secretary of State, and not less than eight nor more than thirteen other members, one of whom is to be appointed by the Queen, the remainder by the Secretary of State. At least one member (who may be the chairman) shall be a whole-time member, the others may be part-time and one of these shall be nominated by the Trustees of the British Museum. The Act specifies that: 'In selecting persons for appointment to be members of the Board, the Secretary of State shall give preference to those who appear to him to have knowledge and experience of library or university affairs, finance, industry, or administration' S.2(2). In actual practice the constitution of the Board is a part-time chairman, a full-time chief executive who is also deputy chairman, three other full-time members who have responsibility as executives for the three operational Divisions of the Library and report direct to the chief executive, and nine part-time members (one of whom is the appointee of the Queen with special responsibility for the Library of King George III).

The Library Board in accordance with S.2(3) of the Act is assisted by an Advisory Council and Committees with responsibility for providing advice to the Board, or to any department of the British Library, on such matters as the Secretary of State, or the Board may determine from time to time. The British Library Act 1972 also provides for an annual grant-in-aid as approved by the Treasury to be paid by the Secretary of State and 'the Board shall act in accordance with such directions as may from time to time be given . . . by the Secretary of State'. (S.5(1).)

Within the limits of public accountability the British Library is neither a government department nor a civil service department but is autonomous like any other public corporation. The part-time chairman is Lord Eccles, at one time Minister for the Arts and Libraries; its deputy chairman and chief executive is Harry Hookway, a former civil servant with much experience in the arts and libraries branch of the DES; the three divisional directors are all professional librarians.

An unusual feature of the board's constitution is that the chief executive and his three divisional directors are all members. This is very difficult for a public librarian to appreciate, for in local authorities the chief librarian is never a member of the library committee, nor can he be a member of the council: he is always essentially a paid professional adviser (although moves for greater worker-participation in management might change this one day). The British Library is organised more like a university, where the librarian and sometimes the deputy too, are members of the library committee and senate, and have a similar standing to that enjoyed by other academics. Even here, however, the authority of the librarian will be subject to other committees of the university and the council. Another curious factor is that the full-time officers of the British Library are serving on the board alongside part-time lay members. Strange though the practice may seem to some, it is a tribute to professional expertise.

THE NATIONAL LIBRARY OF SCOTLAND

The library, situated in Edinburgh, was in the first place built as the Advocates' Library in 1682. It was granted legal deposit rights as far back as 1709, but the task of administering so large a library outgrew the means at its disposal and the governing body offered it to the nation in 1922. It was accepted three years later and by Act of Parliament it became the National Library of Scotland in 1925. The library's present building was opened by the Queen in 1956 and contains over three million books. It is particularly strong on Scottish literature and also has numerous special collections of books and manuscripts. Admission is by ticket for reference and research which cannot conveniently be carried out elsewhere. It has taken over the functions of the former Scottish Central Library, and took the lead in 1973 in establishing the Scottish Libraries Co-operative Automation Project (SCOLCAP) in conjunction with university and public libraries.

The National Library of Scotland is controlled by a board of trustees, appointed in terms of the Act of 1925. The Secretary of State for Scotland is an *ex-officio* member and there are thirty-three others. Of these five are appointed by the Crown on the recommendation of the Secretary of State; twelve including the Lord Advocate and the Lord Provost of major cities are *ex-officio* members; five represent the Faculty of Advocates; seven represent other interests including the Scottish universities; and five are co-opted. The chief executive is the librarian and secretary to the trustees. When all proposed developments have been completed the NLS will provide a range of services similar, though on a smaller scale, to those offered by the BL.

THE NATIONAL LIBRARY OF WALES

The Library is in Aberystwyth; it was founded by Royal Charter in

1907 and became operational on 1 January 1909. It is maintained by annual grant-in-aid from the Treasury and is entitled to most privileges under the Copyright Acts. It holds nearly two million printed works, thirty thousand volumes of manuscripts, about three and a half million deeds and documents, and large collections of maps, prints, drawings, and portraits. It is a general reference library and admission is by ticket. The library specialises in manuscripts and books relating to Wales and the Celtic peoples; it also has many other special collections. It is organised in three main departments: printed books; manuscripts; prints, drawings, and maps. It also houses the Bureau of the Welsh Regional Library System. Under its Charter the National Library is given authority to maintain a department of duplicates to meet the needs of individuals which cannot be satisfied by their local library; such loans however can only be made through the Regional Library System.

Government of the Library is prescribed by its Charter as through a president, vice-president, treasurer, a court of governors and a council. The court of governors is similar to that found in a university, being composed of local representatives of Welsh political, educational and administrative circles. As its membership is so large it elects a council of about thirty-five members as its executive body. The librarian is the chief executive.

Other Libraries

GOVERNMENT LIBRARIES

In addition to the three national libraries there are other government libraries which although not specifically designated as national have, nevertheless, acquired national significance. The two best-known both come under the control of the Department of Education and Science and both are in South Kensington, London, at the Science Museum and the Victoria and Albert Museum.

The Science Museum Library was first formed in 1883 and from 1908 occupied part of the Royal College of Science until moving to its new building in 1969. Its acquisition policy is based on the needs of both the Science Museum and the Imperial College of Science and Technology; thus it has always been geared to the needs of research and post-graduate users, and to that extent functions as a national reference library. Although it was not incorporated into the British

Library it nevertheless has important links with the Lending Division and offers a back-up service. It holds a comprehensive source collection of material on the history of science and technology which numbers about four hundred thousand items and has over eleven thousand periodicals of which five and a half are current. The Victoria and Albert Museum Library is a reference library for the study of the fine and applied arts of all periods and all countries. It is used extensively by art historians and researchers and by students and practising artists. The library has a stock of over four hundred thousand volumes, and a wide variety of art journals; it includes many foreign items and has a number of world-famous special collections. The major part of the stock is on closed access available on demand only.

Among other government libraries with a similar standing is the British Museum (Natural History) Library. Primarily, this serves the needs of the museum's staff but it is open to research workers in the field from all over the world. Since the British Museum Act, 1963, it has been autonomous with its own board of trustees. It has a stock of about half a million items and takes over seven thousand current journals; it is organised into a General Library and six Departmental Libraries each dealing with a particular subject. The libraries of the Imperial War Museum, the National Maritime Museum, the Commonwealth Institute and the Royal Botanic Gardens, Kew, among others, also have a national reputation and are generally willing to assist genuine research workers. Both the House of Commons and the House of Lords have their own very extensive libraries for the use of members. They are rich in works on parliament, law, history and statistics. Limited public use is granted.

The libraries of the major government departments are substantial and of great importance for their specialist collections; they will usually assist genuine enquirers. They include such libraries as that of the Department of Industry which operates through its Central Library (the former Board of Trade Library), open to the public by appointment, and its Statistics and Market Intelligence Library (open for public reference) and the Library of the Department of Education and Science which has over two hundred thousand books and pamphlets, primarily for its own large staff, but also used extensively by research workers in the field of education and allied subjects, including librarianship. Then there is the library of the Department of Health and Social Security with a stock of almost a hundred and twenty thousand items catering for a very wide range of workers in the fields of health and social welfare. The list of government libraries is far too lengthy to mention more than these few but full details can be obtained from the two publications listed below.[2] It is however opportune to remark how this ample provision of libraries within its several departments is evidence of central government's appreciation of the value of the library service and the need for ready access to information. It is also a source of gratification that the government employs professional librarians and is insistent that their work should be confined to professional duties only.

The parent body in the case of these libraries is, of course, the government department but it is difficult to lay down the precise control as there are variations. In some cases the library is part of the Information Division, in others it comes under the Establishment Officer or Director of the Department, and in a few instances under the Assistant Under-Secretary of State. Expenditure on books, periodicals and other publications is charged to Her Majesty's Stationery Office budget granted annually by Parliament. Library staff appointments to all national and government libraries are made by the Civil Service Commission.

SPECIAL LIBRARIES

The 'special' function of government department libraries is in the collection of completely comprehensive and highly organised stocks of material relevant to the work of the Department, in providing Ministers and officials with any information that may be needed in the minimum of time, and of anticipating need and bringing material to the notice of anyone in the Department who should be aware of it. The term 'special library' is also applied to a host of other libraries with a special function, eg the libraries of industrial or commercial firms, research associations and public corporations which have to cater for the needs of research and other specialist staff, where the material has a limited subject coverage but must be acquired in depth. The librarian's function is not only to ensure the satisfactory provision of library material and information on demand but to go further than this and pursue an active rôle by anticipating need and keeping his clients informed of new material which might prove useful to their work. Thus he contributes to the development and profitability of the organisation. In such a library the librarian will be responsible to the head of the research department, the information department, the administration department, or sales, or possibly direct to management. Some of the larger special libraries have a number of branches in different parts of the country, eg ICI, IBM, Shell International, BP Chemicals, UKAEA, and English Electric. Some have offshoots abroad, all of which will rely to a greater or lesser degree on the firm's, or authority's, central library and information department. In all special libraries it is, of course, essential that the librarian should keep himself fully informed of the objectives and programmes of the parent body. A perusal of the pages of the *Libraries, art galleries and museums year book* will readily reveal the great variety of special libraries and their resources.

The libraries of societies and professional associations make up another category of special library. In this case the specialism is the subject or activity interest of the parent body, eg the library of the Royal Institute of British Architects and that of the Institute of Chartered Surveyors, or the Royal Geographical Society. In instances such as these the library control is in the hands of members of the council of the association or society which may or may not work through a library committee. Unfortunately, more and more of these organisations are finding it increasingly difficult to maintain their libraries adequately because of rising costs, indeed many of the smaller ones have no professional staff and have a very poor fund for the purchase of new books.

The Library Association's own library was excellent and generously staffed as compared with many other association libraries but it was feared it could not be maintained at the desired standard, so that in 1975 it was transferred to the British Library. Fortunately it has remained in the same building and with its previous librarian and other members of the staff. (In fact this library enjoys even better support than before and members of The Library Association have been very fortunate.) Few, if any other such libraries can anticipate such a bright future.

UNIVERSITY LIBRARIES

Universities are financed by government funds and this applies of course to their libraries. While some universities have minor sources of independent income and some of the older ones in particular have quite considerable endowment incomes, the truly significant portion is derived from taxation (although from 1977 fees will provide a much increased income). The funds are voted on the Department of Education and Science through the intermediary of the University Grants Committee. This latter body was first established in 1919; its present terms of reference are 'To inquire into the financial needs of university education in Great Britain; to advise the government as to the application of any grants made by Parliament towards meeting them; to collect, examine and make available information relating to university education throughout the United Kingdom; and to assist, in consultation with the universities and other bodies concerned, the preparation and execution of such plans for the development of the universities as may from time to time be required in order to ensure that they are fully adequate to national needs.' Thus, one of the UGC's main functions is to assess the needs of the universities in terms of finance by examining the universities' estimates and future plans; the latter are obviously framed in accordance with government policies with regard to expansion or otherwise of university and higher education.

On its original inception a university is granted a royal charter which will set forth the objects of the university, its constitution and chief officers, and the responsibilities of the latter. The overall controlling body of the university is usually known as the Court. It consists of the officers of the university, members of the academic staff and certain members of convocation, representatives of the students' union and staff associations, and many people representative of local or national interests relevant to the university, including for instance, Her Majesty's lieutenants and deputy-lieutenants of the county, ecclesiastical dignitaries, the sheriff of the county and mayors and other leading representatives of local government, the local judiciary, representatives of relevant industries and professions, societies, trade's unions, and many others. Membership of the court is often numerous (it may exceed 150) so that *in practice its duties are very limited* probably to an annual meeting and very occasionally a special meeting. It will receive the accounts for the year, elect the chancellor and pro-chancellors should the occasion arise, elect its own representatives on the Council and receive the reports of the chancellor and vice-chancellor. Any member of the court will be able to ask questions. The court can also discuss any matter relating to the university and may express its views thereon to the Council and Senate.

The executive work of the university is usually vested in the council which is responsible for management and administration of the revenue and property of the university and has general control (in non-academic matters) of the affairs of the university. The council has a duty to ensure that any matter having academic implications is referred to the senate before being considered by the council. In turn the senate has a duty to ensure that any matter having financial implications or in any way affecting the general well-being of the university or its internal or external relations should be brought to the council.

The council's composition might be for example: the chancellor, pro-chancellors, vice-chancellor, pro-vice-chancellors, the treasurer, and the chairman of the academic assembly (as *ex-officio* members), plus members elected by the senate, two or three representatives of the local authority, two members of the court, two members of convocation not students at the university nor members of staff, about six representatives of local industry and commerce and one or two student representatives.

The library service is controlled by the decisions of the council with regard to finance, administrative procedures generally, and staffing but in terms of library policy, development, and regulations, and for making financial recommendations to the council the library is likely to be directly under the control of the senate.

The senate is the principal academic body of the university. The main part of its membership is made up of staff representing the academic departments including heads of departments and professors. Certain persons are likely to be *ex-officio* members, eg the Vice-Chancellor, the Pro Vice-Chancellors, the Academic Deans; nominations of council and the librarian. There will also be a number of members elected by the academic staff, one or two co-opted members and possibly one or more student representatives.

The terms of reference of the Senate in connection with the university library will be contained in the university statutes and may be stated in the broadest and simplest of terms, eg 'To be responsible for the general administration of the university library'. However, functions of more general application may also have bearing on the library and its control:

'to review from time to time the conditions of service of all members of the academic staff . . . and the staff of the university library, and to make recommendations thereon to the council';
'to determine the posts . . . appointment to which shall qualify a person to be a member of the academic staff';
'to recommend for appointment by the council the members of the academic staff';

35

'to recommend to the council, from time to time, the establishment of such posts on the academic staff . . . and the staff of the university library as the senate deems necessary to the adequate functioning of the university and to recommend the deletion of posts from the establishment as may be thought fit';

'to set up, with the council, joint committees as required, to make recommendations to the council for the appointment of the high officers of the university, and the university librarian'.

It is normal practice for the senate to set up a library committee. In some universities this is a joint committee of senate and council; it may also have a different title sometimes such as 'curators of the library'.

POLYTECHNIC AND COLLEGE LIBRARIES

The library is a central and indispensable feature of polytechnics and other local authority colleges. Many of these institutions will have been created by an amalgamation or federation of existing colleges and will thus still have to function in a number of separate buildings and will therefore be organised from a central point with branches like public libraries. In some cases even this may be impossible and centralisation will have to be confined to administration and technical processes. They are financed through the local authority, subject to a national equalisation pool but a very large part of the expenditure is reimbursed to the authority via the rate support grant. In general all these kinds of colleges are governed through the education committee of the local authority and a board of governors; the librarian being responsible to the director or principal. There is also likely to be an academic board of which the librarian should be a member and a library committee or sub-committee with the function of advising the librarian. In some colleges there is also a 'resources for learning committee' responsible for all matters concerned with learning resources. It does sometimes happen that there is an overall learning resources department which includes the library; in this case the librarian is likely to be subordinate to the head of the department, and may in this event not be a member of the academic board.

Some explanation of the rôles of the board of governors and the local authority is necessary but for the sake of brevity this will be confined to polytechnics. The local authority will draw up what is called an 'instrument of government for the polytechnic' which will set out the membership of the board of governors, which is rather similar in constitution but not in function to that of the court of a university. It is, however, considerably smaller. It prescribes for the appointment of a chairman and deputy; for the regulation of meetings and their frequency; provision for keeping minutes, for the calling of meetings by the chief education officer (perhaps once a term), and procedure for voting. It will then set out the method of government of the polytechnic in what may be called 'articles of government'. These will include the overall conduct of the polytechnic having regard to the Education Acts, regulations made by the Secretary of State for Education and Science, and the Instrument of Government. The articles will cover approval of new courses by both governors and the authority, consultation between the authority and the governors, and the provisions whereby the latter are responsible for the general running of the polytechnic. These will most likely include for: the submission of estimates by the governors to the authority while leaving the governors freedom to control expenditure within the ultimately agreed estimates; for consultation with industry and the professions; and, arrangements for members of the staff to submit their views to the governors if they so wish. The articles will include for the establishment of an academic board and set out its functions. These will be mainly concerned with such matters as planning courses, research, standards for admission, arrangements for examinations, and academic matters generally. They will give the academic board the power to establish committees and sub-committees and will also describe the responsibilities of the director and other senior administrative staff. The governors will determine the numbers and grades of teaching and non-teaching staff subject to the approval of the annual estimates by the authority and will be required to abide by financial regulations. The articles will also include the arrangements for the execution of building works, repairs, etc, as between the authority and the governors and for the appointment, suspension or dismissal of staff (generally this provides for initial processing by the governors but ultimate confirmation by the authority in respect of suspension or dismissal but, subject to general conditions of service as laid down by the authority, the governors would make staff appointments or delegate this function to the director). In the case of the appointment of the director and his deputy and perhaps some other very senior officers, the consent of the authority would first have to be obtained to the short list. (The foregoing account of the relationship between authority and governors is given as an example only, obviously there will be deviations—the position of polytechnics within the Inner London Education Authority for example.)

It will be seen that the librarian of a polytechnic works in a situation where there is a complexity of control, a situation which is a compound of parts of both the university and public library systems. There is a director, in a position rather akin to that of the chief executive of the local authority or the vice-chancellor of the university; a library sub-committee more like that of a university than of a public library; an academic board comparable to the senate of the university; a board of governors where the director represents the interests of the poly-technic; the education committee where the executive officer is the chief education officer; then finally, above this committee, is the full council of the local authority. In addition, there is also the Depart-ment of Education and Science.

PUBLIC LIBRARIES

The only libraries specifically established by Acts of Parliament are national libraries (viz the British Library Act, 1972) and public libraries (viz the Public Libraries and Museums Act, 1964). In the case of the latter the legislation very closely dictates the functions and method of control of the library. Moreover, this control is exerted not only by specific library legislation but also by local government law generally. In recent years changes in the legislation have had an immense effect on public library control, not only in England and Wales but also in Scotland and Northern Ireland.

The first law relating to public libraries in England and Wales was passed in 1850 as mentioned in Chapter 1.It was, to say the least, very modest in its proposals. Although a further Act of 1855 improved the finances of the libraries, there were only twenty-eight library authori-ties by 1860. However, thanks especially to Andrew Carnegie, and to a lesser degree to other public benefactors such as Passmore Edwards and Sir George Newnes, the numbers had increased to 352 by 1900, and within a year of the passage of the Public Libraries Act, 1919, in England and Wales, had risen to 551. This latter Act abolished the rate limitation entirely, it enabled county councils to adopt the Acts and existing library authorities, other than county boroughs, to hand over their library powers to the county council if they so wished. Thus, although the standards of today were still a long way off, particularly outside England and Wales, the Act of 1919 provided the essential ingredients for an adequate public library service—no arbitrary limit on expenditure; the provision of county as well as urban services; and, a voluntary means of getting rid of impoverished and completely inadequate small town libraries to the county. What was lacking was a means of coercing the backward authority to do better or enforcing any approved standards.

In the years following the Second World War there was a natural inclination to survey all the country's services and institutions; indeed the process was initiated *during* the war so far as the public library service was concerned when The Library Association prepared its own proposals for post-war development. Deliberations were detailed and sustained and in 1957 the long-desired breakthrough was achieved when the Minister of Education, Lord Hailsham, set up a committee to enquire into the structure of the public library service in England and Wales under the chairmanship of Sir Sydney Roberts. This committee's report was presented to Parliament in 1959.[3] Subsequently when two working parties, the one concerned with standards[4] and the other with co-operation,[5] had been set up and had reported to the Minister, a Bill was presented to Parliament which resulted in the Public Libraries and Museums Act, 1964. This Act repealed all previous public library legislation covering England and Wales. (These developments also triggered similar moves in Northern Ireland and Scotland.) The most important provisions of the Act were:

(i)   It became the duty of the Secretary of State to superintend and to promote the improvement of the public library service, and to secure the proper discharge by local authorities of their functions in relation to libraries as conferred by the Act. (S.1(1).)*

(ii)   Two library advisory councils were to be set up, one for England and one for Wales, to advise the Secretary of State upon library facilities, both on their own initiative and as referred to them by the Minister. (S.2(1).)

(iii)   Certain local authorities were specifically designated as library authorities. (S.4(1).) These have since been amended by local government reorganisation and are as follows: in England—the council of: a London borough, the City of London, a non-metro-

* From April 1978 responsibility for public libraries in Wales is to be transferred to the Secretary of State for Wales.

politan county, a metropolitan district, the Scilly Isles, and the joint board in the area the subject of a joint board order. In Wales—the council of: a county, or a district which has been constituted a library authority, or a joint board.

(iv)   Library authorities were given a specific duty (that is a statutory obligation, no longer *permission* as under previous legislation) to provide a comprehensive and efficient library service for all persons desiring to make use thereof, residing or working or receiving full-time education within the library area. (S.7(1).) The authorities were also given guidance in broad terms as to the interpretation of these duties, in respect of library facilities and range of services to be supplied, stocks of books and other materials, general and special services to children and adults, the encouragement of library use by various means, and the employment of co-operative methods with similar bodies. Unfortunately no specific compulsory standards were laid down in the report *Standards of public library service in England and Wales*, commonly referred to as the *Bourdillon Report* (see pp 63–4). They still remain as guidelines only. (S.7(2).)

(v)   The situation with regard to library charges was clarified. It was clearly laid down that no charge was to be made to an authorised borrower for the *loan* of a book, journal, pamphlet or similar article, or a reproduction made by photographic or other means of the whole or part of any such article. At the same time it laid down the services for which a charge *could* be made. (The failure of the Secretary of State to follow up the latter provisions with specific amounts to be levied for fines on overdue books and fees for reservations has unfortunately led many authorities to use them as a means of raising revenue and some of the charges are very high indeed.) (S.8.)

(vi)   A procedure was formulated for dealing with complaints brought against any library authority. (S.10.) When the Act was passed many thought this section to be a tremendous weapon to be used against recalcitrant library authorities who failed to live up to their obligations. In the light of economic difficulties facing the nation in 1975/7 it has, however, proved to be a very puny weapon indeed. While certain authorities made savage cuts in their library expenditure, appeals by The Library Association and others to the Minister for his intervention met with no substantial result, though in all fairness it must be admitted that appeals of this nature are not the same as 'complaints' from registered library users, as the Act envisages.

Briefly, S.10 of the Act reads to the effect that if a complaint is made to the Secretary of State that a library authority has failed to carry out its duties under the Act, or if the Secretary of State is of the opinion that an investigation should be made to establish whether any such failure on the part of the local authority has occurred, he can cause a local inquiry to be held into the matter, and if he is satisfied that there has been such a failure, he may make an order declaring the library authority to be in default. The local authority is then given a certain length of time to rectify the fault. If it fails to do so then the Secretary of State can exercise the ultimate sanction of withdrawing library powers from the authority and transferring them to himself, or elsewhere.

As mentioned previously, the Act designated those local authorities which were to be constituted as library authorities, but local government reorganisation amended these very considerably. It is worth recalling that the Public Libraries and Museums Act, 1964, was concerned that very small authorities should not be made library authorities and accordingly made 40,000 the minimum population for this purpose. Nevertheless, librarians generally were still of the opinion that this was too low a population to support an adequate public library service. They need not have worried however for as early as 1 April 1965, local government reorganisation in London reduced the number of library authorities from 83 to 33 and the minimum population of any of these was around 150,000 and the highest about 340,000. The Local Government Act, 1972, which came into effect on 1 April 1974, covered the remainder of England and Wales; it was this Act that abolished the very small local authorities and their library powers in the rest of the country outside London. The Act replaced the previous structure by six metropolitan counties (covering the major conurbations) and thirty-nine non-metropolitan counties in England, together with eight counties in Wales. The six metropolitan counties were: Tyne and Wear, Merseyside, Greater Manchester, West Midlands, South Yorkshire, and West Yorkshire. The populations of the metropolitan counties ranged from 1·2 million to 2·8 million, and of the non-metropolitan counties from 300,000 to 1·5 million.

The metropolitan counties were divided into thirty-six metropolitan districts with populations varying from about 175,000 in South Tyneside to well over 1,000,000 in Birmingham. Each of these metropolitan districts is responsible for libraries, and other duties prescribed under the Act of 1964. The non-metropolitan counties were also divided into districts with a wide range of populations but these do not have library powers; the non-metropolitan county councils are the library authorities. In Wales library powers have also been vested in four district councils in addition to the eight counties, they are: Cynon Valley, Merthyr Tydfil, Rhondda and Llanelli.

As a result of the Local Government Act, 1972, not only small local authorities lost their library powers but some very large provincial libraries found themselves transferred to the non-metropolitan counties, eg Bristol, Nottingham, Leicester, Southampton, Plymouth, Preston, Blackpool, and many others. S.101 and S.110 of the Local Government Act did however make provision whereby the county council could make arrangements with district councils within its area whereby the latter might have some voice in the library service in their particular districts. Guidance as to the kind of functions which might thus be delegated were given in the Department of the Environment *Circular 131/72 Annex 5*, and were elaborated in the Department of Education and Science *Circular 5/73*. We are informed by P. H. Sewell, former Senior Library Adviser to the DES, in *British library and information science, 1971–1975* that: 'On the basis of this guidance many non-metropolitan counties came to arrangements with constituent district councils for the delegation of certain functions and made arrangements for consultation in respect of those functions which had not been delegated . . . it can be said that a number of eminently workable arrangements have been concluded.' However, in another section of *BLIS* written by N. Tomlinson, a practising librarian, a different picture is painted, for he writes: 'there was a scheme whereby counties should offer some "agency powers" to the districts. In the majority of cases there was no effective substance in such "powers". . . . Annex 5 (to the Department of the Environment Circular 131/72) on libraries is worth reading as a fine example of tight-rope walking, lacking any effective guidance.'

It can be seen that opinion is very divided about the value of any *agency arrangements*. As library expenditure and basic policy-making must in any event remain with the principal authority, many librarians hold the view that the arrangements are mere lip-service. On the other hand if entered into in a spirit of mutual co-operation they do facilitate an expression of local opinion, and serve to ensure local support for the library in the area of a district council. At the same time it must be appreciated that it was a bitter blow for many provincial authorities when their splendid libraries became absorbed into the non-metropolitan county systems. It can, therefore, be taken for granted that agency arrangements will only work and be of some value where goodwill exists between the members and the staff of both county and district authorities. Lancashire has been quoted as a county in which the agency system works satisfactorily, and it has done so because the individuals concerned have gone out of their way to make it work. A copy of the Lancashire agreement is reproduced as an appendix at the end of this volume together with a report from the County Librarian of Leicestershire on the same subject which was considered and approved by the Libraries and Museums Committee, January, 1974.

Local government reorganisation has also had a tremendous impact upon the public library service in Scotland, but there the basic pattern has been different from that in England and Wales. Instead of generally placing libraries with the first tier or major group of local authorities, the opposite has happened very largely, due to the Wheatley Commission's Report in 1969 on local government reform. The Local Government (Scotland) Act 1973, S.163(1) reads: 'The local authority for the purpose of the Public Libraries (Scotland) Acts 1887 to 1955 in their application to libraries shall be an islands or district council, except that within the Highlands, Borders and Dumfries and Galloway regions, such authority shall be the appropriate regional council.' Thus while legislators in England and Wales seem to have been impressed by The Library Association pressure to have libraries aligned with the education authority, in Scotland the tendency has been to regard libraries as amenity services and hence the allocation of most of them to second tier authorities and very often the separation of the public library and school library service.

Currently in Scotland there are 33 district councils, 3 regional councils and the North East Scotland Library Service, and 3 Island Councils, which are library authorities. This is half the previous number with still, a large variation in populations served; caused by geography. These library authorities are responsible for exercising the library powers contained in the Public Libraries Consolidation (Scotland) Act, 1887, the Public Libraries (Scotland) Act, 1955 and the Local Government (Scotland) Act, 1973, together with other powers contained in miscellaneous legislation. S.163(2) of the Local Government (Scotland) Act, 1973, imposes on the library authorities the duty 'to secure the provision of adequate library facilities for all persons resident in their area'. Although this wording is cast in very much the same mould as the English legislation the word 'adequate' might justifiably be criticised as being even more nebulous than 'comprehensive and efficient'; it is also to be noted that the provision is confined to residents only although the main library Act of 1887 gives authority to extend provision to others. The Local Government (Scotland) Act, 1973, S.211 also provides a procedure for dealing with complaints made to the Secretary of State or any appropriate Minister in respect of a local authority having failed 'to do what is required of them' under the Act; it is similar in intent to S.10 of the Public Libraries and Museums Act, 1964.

Northern Ireland is very differently organised from England and Wales or Scotland, and it would not be unreasonable to suppose that the libraries have fared better. Although local government in Northern Ireland also came in for reorganisation under the Local Government (Boundaries) Act (Northern Ireland), 1971 and the Local Government Act (Northern Ireland), 1972, the massive change in the whole organisation of the public library service came about through the Education and Libraries (Northern Ireland) Order, 1972. This Order, which came into effect in October 1973, repealed the previous library Acts of 1855 to 1924 and established instead five area education and library boards to cover the whole of Northern Ireland and to replace sixteen former local authorities controlling libraries. Thus the libraries in Northern Ireland were divorced entirely from direct local authority control.

Under the Order, the boards have a duty, as in England and Wales, to provide a comprehensive and efficient service. The five boards are as follows: Belfast, South-Eastern, Southern, Western and North-Eastern. The Order sets out the membership of a board specifying that the maximum number of members shall be decided by the Minister and that it should include persons nominated by each district council in the area of the board, persons representing the interests of transferred schools in the area and those representing the interests of trustees of maintained schools in the area, and those thought suitable by reason of their interests in the service (ie the public library). The total of representatives of district councils and the number to be nominated by each council in the area are determined by the Minister but the total should be as nearly as possible equal to two-fifths (40 per cent) of the maximum number of members of the board and each council should nominate at least one member. The

34

number of persons representing transferred schools and trustees of maintained schools and their proportions are also laid down and those appointed by reason of interest in the services of the board must be as nearly as possible equal to seven-twentieths (35 per cent) of the maximum number of members; at least three of these persons must have a public library interest. The duties of the board are also prescribed and correspond closely with those of library authorities in England and Wales. Financing of the libraries is from grants made directly by the Minister based on the estimates prepared by the library committees. A library committee must be appointed by each board. A significant provision of the Order was for the establishment of a Commission to exercise general supervision of staff matters relating to the education and library boards; most of its recommendations need the approval of the Minister.

The chief officer of an education and library board is the chief education officer and although the chief librarian is appointed by the board and is the secretary to the library committee he has a lower status, and circumstances could arise where the chief education officer has the final power of decision or recommendation to the board. The power of the Ministry too must limit the independence of the board. Whether this national control allied with regional control is better than the purely local only the future can tell, but at least it provides for uniformity and common standards of service. As in England and Wales, and Scotland, provision is contained in the Order for inquiry into complaints lodged by or with the Ministry, and also provides default powers.

From this very cursory review of the British public library service since its inception to the present time, it can be seen that growth was slow until after the Second World War. However, in spite of the attention drawn to the service in several government-inspired reports and resultant legislation, there are still widely divergent patterns of control in the constituent countries of Great Britain. Perhaps the most significant factor is that although librarians thought that the Golden Age had arrived with the passing of the Public Libraries and Museums Act, 1964, the greatest changes in library organisation and services have come about not through library legislation but through local government reform thus demonstrating priorities in the mind of the law-makers. Though the local government legislation has been beneficial to libraries on the whole, they have lost a certain measure of independence in having to be regarded as just one of many departments run by a local authority rather than on their own merits. In some respects therefore the needs of the service may be seen to have been sacrificed to other considerations such as the principle of corporate management which has so frequently resulted in libraries becoming just part of an omnibus service. Their interests are now linked with those of education or recreation; they have become a financial pawn in the battle for local government subsidies from the government, and are afflicted by a welter of different management theories, which one may be excused for thinking were devised for the benefit of their propagators. In the midst of these and other factors, insufficient regard has been given by the politicians to the users of the public library and their requirements. The different treatments employed in England and Wales on the one hand, and in Scotland on the other, in the allocation of library functions to first or second tier authorities and the more radical creation of a library authority independent of the local councils in Northern Ireland, give much room for thought. The prospect of devolution in Scotland and Wales might conceivably lead to further reorganisation of local government on a regional pattern and might even bring with it an extension of the Northern Ireland system to the rest of the UK. In the immediate future, however, the pressure of economic circumstances, the clamour in some quarters for the introduction of charges for the use of library facilities, the call for more and more co-operation as a means of economy, and the further development of the British Library as the mainspring of the nation's library services, could bring startingly new changes in the service of public libraries, as might the ever-increasing commercial interest in the marketing of information and the development of highly sophisticated automated information services such as the Post Office's Viewdata.

References

1   Esdaile, A. *The British Museum Library*, Allen & Unwin, 1946.
2   Burkett J. *Government and related library and information services*, 3/e rev, LA 1974. Also *British Library guide to government department and other libraries*, 1976
3   Ministry of Education. *The structure of the public library service in England and Wales*, Cmnd 660, HMSO, 1959.
4   Ministry of Education. *Standards of public library service in England and Wales*, HMSO, 1962.
5   Ministry of Education. *Inter-library co-operation in England and Wales*, HMSO, 1962.

3

Management by Committee

Management through committee is a time-honoured practice throughout the world but nowhere is it employed more extensively than in Britain. Many organisations responsible for providing and maintaining libraries, manage them largely through a committee structure. In some cases, the parent body, ie the organisation responsible for the library *delegates* executive authority to the committee. This means that the committee not only deliberates upon the matters before it, but is then permitted to take action to put these decisions into operation; such a committee is called *executive*. If an executive committee is required to report back to the parent body on the action taken after its meetings it is sometimes referred to as a *reporting* committee. On the other hand, if a committee is not allowed to take action upon its decisions but can only make recommendations to the parent body, it is called *recommending*. Most committees have certain responsibilities delegated to them and can take action within these limits but in more important matters, usually those involving radical changes of policy, the expenditure of large sums of money, particularly if not included in the estimates, or those requiring large increases of staff, they are often required to make recommendations to the parent body. Thus, more often than not a committee has both an executive and a recommending rôle and in this connection the modern tendency is to give as much delegated authority to the committee as is consonant with the parent body's retaining control of finance and general lines of policy. The exact powers of the committee are normally contained in written terms of reference.

There are also other types of committee; one commonly found is the *advisory committee* which, as the name implies, is set up to give advice, usually between the users of the service and the body which offers or administers the service. In the case of a library this could be a committee representing borrowers, who use the committee channel to advise the librarian of the user's opinion of the library, its strengths and its weaknesses, with suggestions for its improvement or development. It is equally useful to librarian and user, as it also enables him to test opinion before taking some proposed action such as the introduction of a new issue method, introduction of fines, or reduced hours of opening.

All the foregoing types of committee are normally *standing committees,* that is to say they are set up on a permanent basis (although the term of office of members may be limited). They meet regularly, maybe once a month or once every three months, as necessary, but their meetings are programmed and the committee has specific terms of reference within which it acts. These can be printed in the Standing Orders of the parent body, as in the case of a local authority, or in the Ordinances of a university, or merely typed in sheet form for smaller organisations. In addition to standing committees there are also *ad hoc committees,* committees with a limited lease of life which are set up for a single specific purpose. For example an organisation might be in need of funds on a large scale and accordingly sets up an appeals fund; alternatively it might be going to build a new headquarters. A committee is set up for each of these purposes, possibly even for years, but once its objective is achieved it is dissolved.

Whatever the type of committee, it can be taken for granted that the parent body has a need for this method of management. It permits a small number of its members, usually those with appropriate experience, or at least enthusiasm, to meet as required, go into all relevant matters and take necessary action or make recommendations as the case may require. The essential value of the committee lies in detailed discussion which is only possible within a small gathering which combines expertise with enthusiasm, and is able to operate within a fixed time-scale. The governing body of many organisations is large and unwieldy. When we look at governing or parent bodies responsible for public libraries (ie the local authorities) we find that the council probably consists of 70 or more members, a number far too large to go into detailed discussion of the affairs of a department, and which in any case has far too many departments to look after for this to be possible. For instance, it may be responsible not only for libraries (probably a relatively small department) but also for social services, housing, roads, transport, education, staffing, works, and finance as well as others. It therefore sets up a series of committees, delegates much of its work to the committees, receives reports on action taken and at the same time receives recommendations on other matters on which the committee is not authorised to act. Similarly in a university the senate and council refer many matters to committees. On the other hand the purely advisory type of committee is more likely to be found in colleges and schools. The British Library also uses advisory committees to advise the board; they are made up of experts in special fields rather than just users. This topic is discussed at greater length in the pages which follow.

While one can readily understand the tendency of some librarians whose libraries are geared to committee procedure, being envious of their fellows in industrial libraries, for instance, who have no committees, the comparison is irrelevant. In the latter the librarian is the manager of a department in the same capacity as any other departmental manager (or he may have as an immediate superior the manager of a larger department like information or research in which the library is incorporated). The success or otherwise of the library depends upon the librarian; if the library adds nothing to the efficiency or profitability of the firm, both the library and the librarian will go. As opposed to this the librarians of a public or university library are responsible for providing a service to thousands of members of the public or the university. They have to please, not a board of directors motivated by profit, but every one of the library users whose requirements are almost unlimited and extremely varied. Quite rightly they are accountable to a committee which in the final analysis is representing library users. The committee, therefore, operates not only as a means of management, but perhaps even more important, as a channel of communication between library provider, library patron and the librarian. It is a two-way process which affords the librarian an excellent medium for the public relations exercise.

It is in the *management of public and university libraries* that the employment of a standing committee is so prevalent. In the case of the former the practice is backed up by legislation and the council's standing orders, in the university by its ordinances. Though management problems are usually slight in libraries of societies and associations the procedure of control through standing committees is usual and the following pages describe the committee background in all these three fields. In addition, polytechnics and college libraries also have library sub-committees of the academic board but these act more in an advisory capacity.

Public Libraries

The basic objectives, facilities and legal powers of public library authorities and the method of control of the libraries are laid down in legislation; this includes reference to management by committees. Different legislation governs England and Wales, Scotland, and Northern Ireland; though much of it is very similar, there are important differences:

APPOINTMENT OF COMMITTEES. ENGLAND AND WALES

The power of local authorities in England and Wales to appoint committees (including committees for libraries) is now contained in the Local Government Act, 1972 S.101(1) which gives the local authorities the power 'to arrange for the discharge of any of their functions: (a) by a committee, a sub-committee or an officer of the authority'. S.102(2) gives the committee itself, unless the local authority directs otherwise, the power to 'arrange for the discharge of any of these functions by a sub-committee or an officer', and furthermore, unless the local authority or the committee otherwise directs 'the sub-committee may arrange for the discharge of any of those functions by an officer of the authority'. The functions referred by a council to a library committee will be found in the council's standing orders and may be stated in very general terms such as 'The Libraries Committee shall have referred to them all matters relating to the regulation and management of the Council's libraries and all properties belonging thereto'. Such terms of reference however have to be qualified in the light of those duties allocated to other committees (see pp 45–6).

S.101(1b) of the Act also gives authority for the discharge of powers to be given to 'any other local authority' or under S.101(5) for two or more local authorities to discharge any of their functions jointly 'by a joint committee of theirs or by an officer of any one of them'. So far as libraries are concerned this seems unnecessary as S.5 of the Public Libraries and Museums Act, 1964 provides for the establishment of joint boards where two or more authorities so wish.

It should be noted that in contrast to previous legislation the term 'delegation' is now dropped in favour of 'arrange for the discharge of any of their functions'.

APPOINTMENT OF COMMITTEES. SCOTLAND

In Scotland authority is derived from the Local Government (Scotland) Act, 1973. S.56 is expressed in almost the same terms as the corresponding legislation for England and Wales, with the same exceptions with regard to determining a rate or borrowing money.

SIZE OF COMMITTEE. CO-OPTION. ENGLAND AND WALES; SCOTLAND

In England and Wales the Local Government Act, 1972 S.102(2) leaves the numbers of members of the committee and their term of office 'and the area within which the committee are to exercise their authority' to be fixed by the appointing authority, or in the case of a sub-committee by the appointing committee, and S.102(3) allows the co-option of non-council members to committees or sub-committees (except for the committee controlling the finance of the authority) but at least two-thirds of the committee (not the sub-committee) must be members of the Council. S.57 (2 and 3) of the Local Government (Scotland) Act, 1973 makes identical provisions for Scotland.

DISQUALIFICATION OF LIBRARY STAFF FROM MEMBERSHIP OF LOCAL AUTHORITY. ENGLAND & WALES; SCOTLAND

The librarian and his staff are disqualified from membership of the local authority which employs them, in England and Wales under S.80(1) of the Local Government Act, 1972 and from membership of any committee or sub-committee of the local authority by S.104(1). In Scotland S.31(1) and S.59(1) of the Local Government (Scotland) Act, 1973 are to similar effect.

COMMITTEES. NORTHERN IRELAND

In Northern Ireland the system of regional control of the public library by Education and Library Boards under the Education and Libraries (Northern Ireland) Order 1972 requires each board to appoint a library committee consisting of members of the board, and, that it must include those members of the board appointed by reason of their interest in the public library service. The functions of the committee were to be included in the scheme which had to be prepared and submitted to the Ministry on the initial establishment of each board. They included the preparation of estimates of expenditure from time to time, and the preparation of a development scheme for library services, as well as any revisions for which the Ministry might call.

Sub-committees of the library committee may be authorised for any purposes approved by the board and such sub-committees may include persons who are not members of either the committee or the board. The board can authorise a committee to take specific acts on its behalf (ie executive authority) but not a sub-committee. The order constitutes the chief librarian as secretary to the committee, but before the chief librarian may be appointed the Ministry has to be consulted about the qualifications and experience required and about the advertisement. When applications are received for any advertisement for the post of Chief Librarian they have to be sent to the Ministry with the proposed short-list, and Ministry approval must be obtained for the person appointed.

THE LIBRARY AND ITS CONTROLLING COMMITTEE

It will be seen from the foregoing that whereas the Education and Library Order of 1972 specifically requires the appointment of a committee to control public libraries and that it shall be solely a library committee, the Acts for England and Wales, and Scotland, merely permit the establishment of committees as thought fit by a local authority. There is no compulsion to appoint a committee to control libraries although it is common practice to allocate the function to a committee. Even so, there is no reason whatsoever for allocating library functions to a *library committee* as such. Until the end of the 1960s most municipalities allocated library control to a library committee, and most counties to a sub-committee of the education committee. However, local government reorganisation was of current interest (having taken place in London in 1965) and one by-product was the publication of certain government reports bearing on the management of local authorities. They included the Redcliffe-Maud Report (1967)[1] which, among other things, recommended a streamlining of council procedure, reducing committee work by giving more authority to the committees themselves, their Chairmen, and their Chief Officers, and by amalgamating two or more services, where appropriate, under a single committee. Thus, a number of authorities amalgamated such services as libraries, baths, entertainments, parks and the arts under one omnibus committee; some went even further, and appointed a director of the overall service to whom the librarian would be subordinate, unless he happened to be appointed director and still continue to take active charge of the library service. In some outer London boroughs the new link was with education. With the spread of local government re-organisation outside London in 1973 (and to Scotland in 1974), and in particular by the publication of the Bains[2] Committee Report which built upon the proposals of Redcliffe-Maud and suggested further telescoping of committees, the whole process was greatly accelerated. In Scotland the process was influenced by the report of the Wheatley Commission (1969)[3] which associated libraries with leisure, as distinct from education, and resulted in most libraries being linked with second tier authorities, and by the report of the Paterson Committee,[4] which was very similar to that of Bains.

Thus, in spite of the efforts of The Library Association, which throughout the pre-organisation period, had been stressing the educational rôle of public libraries and the need for a separate Libraries, or, Libraries and Arts Committee, a survey carried out in 1975 revealed that of the 160 library authorities (of a possible total of 166) who replied to a questionnaire, only a small proportion of the local authorities had adopted The Library Association's recommendation of a committee solely concerned with libraries or libraries and the arts. The figures were: in England 24; in Wales 2; in Scotland 6; in Northern Ireland 5 (all). The titles used to designate these committees varied: 'Libraries'; 'Arts', 'Cultural Services and Libraries'; and 'Halls, Entertainments and Libraries'. Under the umbrella of an Education Committee there were 20 authorities in England; 4 in Wales; and 5 in Scotland. There were also 2 libraries in England placed under a General Purposes Committee. All the remainder were functioning under some form of leisure committee, known variously as 'Leisure'; 'Amenities'; or 'Recreation'—there were as many as 20 different titles used to denote the same kind of committee. Of these 58 were in England; 5 in Wales; and 29 in Scotland. Thus, taking the United Kingdom as a whole, 60 per cent of libraries are classified as being part of a leisure, recreational, or amenity service. Moreover, in a very large number of these authorities a director has been appointed in overall control of the unified services. He often has no library experience whatsoever and in some cases no local government experience either.[1]

THE LIBRARIAN AND HIS COMMITTEE: (ENGLAND & WALES AND SCOTLAND)

The librarian (by whatever title he may be known) of a library authority in England and Wales, and Scotland, is, as has been shown, expressly disqualified from being an elected member of the local authority for whom he works. He is appointed by the authority as its servant and professional adviser. Whether he is the officer called upon to address the committee and explain various reports as required, as will usually be indicated by the chairman, depends on his exact status. If there is an overall director of an omnibus committee this officer may perform this function, but even then it is more likely that he will leave the librarian to answer questions and deal with points relevant to his section, though he may give support if he thinks it advisable. It should be pointed out that in the advice given by The Library Association to local authorities re the committee structure for libraries, the point was made that even if libraries were not placed under a separate committee the librarian should be the man to advise the committees and council on library matters. At management level if there is a director he is almost certain to leave the librarian to run his own section, merely expecting to be kept in touch, and co-ordinat- his whole department through regular meetings of his management team consisting of, for example, the librarian, the parks manager, the baths manager, the entertainments manager, and the administration officer. Reverting back to the committee procedure, although the paid officials give advice and information to enable the committee to reach decisions, they are not participant in the actual decision making. Their influence is obviously important and a sensible chairman and a sensible committee treat the advice of the professional staff with great respect. This is not to say, however, that they always act on it.

The committee will look to the librarian (perhaps through the director if there is one) to suggest new developments and new policies, and to submit reports on any matters required by the committee, eg: reduction in opening hours; provision of a picture loan service; the establishment of a home bindery, or library services to the dis-advantaged. At the same time the committee will not expect ad-ministrative matters, or relatively unimportant items to be brought before them. The librarian today is given a great deal of responsibility and is expected to shoulder it. He should be the best judge of whether or not something should be brought before the committee but if he is in any doubt the director of administration, or his equivalent, will soon tell him. The kind of items which should be placed before a committee for consideration include those involving finance beyond the financial powers of chief officers (though even in this instance it might well be within the powers of the chairman to authorise it and merely inform the committee at its next meeting and ask for approval); items involving policy; and new developments. The day-to-day running of the library and control of staff and expenditure within the approved estimates and financial regulations of the council will be within the jurisdiction of the librarian though he may be expected to make regular reports to the committee. Some authorities expect this at every committee meeting, but the tendency is declining and an annual report may suffice if a report is required at all.

Unlike the university librarian, the public librarian will not be responsible for preparing committee agendas or compiling minutes, this will be done by the staff of the department of the director of administration (this may still be called the town clerk's or clerk's department in some authorities). The librarian will be expected to attend all committee meetings and sometimes his deputy too. Where there are sub-committees of the committee controlling libraries perhaps the deputy or some other senior officer of the libraries attends instead. In addition, the librarian is usually expected to attend the meetings of the council (though this might not necessarily be the practice where there is an overall director). The supposed purpose of this is so that if any unexpected question about the library should arise, the librarian is there to help his chairman—a very rare occurrence indeed. The best that can be said for the practice of attendance (as all decisions have usually been made in advance by the majority party) is that it is good public relations and enables the librarian to know, and be known by, the council members. Where library business is discussed by any other committee eg establishment or finance then again the librarian or a senior member of his staff should be present. This is very necessary as committees not specially concerned with library matters may not fully understand some point under discussion; the presence of the librarian may ensure the successful passage of an item affecting his section which might otherwise have been rejected. The public relations angle is also very important at this level.

TERMS OF REFERENCE

As indicated on p 40 the council's terms of reference may give the committee responsible for libraries what appears to be 'carte blanche' control over them. These terms of reference, however, have to be interpreted in relation to those of other committees and in the light of powers reserved to the council. Thus, the council may have a separate establishment and resources committee which deals exclusively with staff and financial matters, quite possibly via two separate sub-committees for establishment and finance. The terms of reference of this committee may include the following: 'the appointment and dismissal, regulation of salaries, conditions of service, promotion, consultations with the trades unions . . . of the whole of the council's staff and employees'; 'all matters concerning the establishment of each and every department of the council'; 'the control and management of the finance and accounts of the council'; 'all matters relating to the council's superannuation fund'; 'the responsibility for the council's financial regulations'; 'regular audit of the council's accounts'; 'the responsibility for the council's central purchasing department'; 'all matters concerning the council's transport fleet'. The council cannot delegate responsibility for levying a rate or raising a loan and in addition it is almost certain to reserve other rights to itself such as new developments, new policies of significant importance, charges, membership of committees, and terms of reference.

It will be seen, therefore, that the terms of reference of the council and other committees considerably affect the interpretation of those allocated to the committee basically responsible for libraries. The major impact of this nature stems from those committees which have a responsibility ranging over the whole of the council's services (sometimes called 'pervasive' committees because their responsibilities pervade all departments) because it is essential in certain respects that all departments of a local authority act in the same way and in accordance with the same set of rules. The major examples of this relate to staffing and finance. It is important that all members of staff, regardless of department, should be treated equally, according to the same conditions of service interpreted by a common panel of councillors, ie by the same committee. If this were not so the staff in different departments would inevitably receive unequal treatment and a general state of dissatisfaction would soon creep in. Similarly with finance, it is essential that all departments play to the same set of rules: they must prepare their estimates in the same way; order goods and pay for them in a common way; abide by common financial regulations; be subject to a common audit system; and generally conform to a common procedure as laid down by the director of finance and his committee (this may be a separate finance committee or it may be combined with establishment as already indicated). To a lesser extent perhaps some other committees of the council may have responsibilities for some function relating to all departments, one such example would be a works committee which might be responsible for all council building works including both new buildings and maintenance and alterations to old buildings. This committee would, therefore, have an important part to play in the building of new libraries and the care of existing buildings.

Thus the chief officers of any department of the council, including the librarian, need to know just how the council and all its committees function before they can understand the exact powers and independence of their own particular committee.

CORPORATE MANAGEMENT

The general tendency now is for the local authority to employ corporate management methods whereby their chief officers of the individual departments work collectively as well as individually for the promotion of the council's services, and think in terms of the whole authority rather than a single department. Under the leadership of the chief executive they meet regularly (weekly or fortnightly) as a management team, sometimes called the 'board' to encourage, assist and advise members of the council, as well as officers, on policy formulation and implementation. One of the most important aims is to encourage inter-departmental relationships so that where one department is proposing a new policy, or a new service, which may have implications for other departments, the latter are represented right from the start of any discussions. In essence corporate management involves planning-programming-budgeting and a community approach to local government. Where the librarian is a chief officer he will be a member of the 'board', otherwise the library interests will have to be represented by the overall director who will of course have consulted the librarian in advance. It is axiomatic of corporate management that the requirements of any one department will have to be measured against those of others and in relation to the funds available. They will then have to take their place in the programme according to adjudged priorities, an example of this is when some major new development is being planned by the librarian, eg: complete computerisation of issue records, catalogue, book orders and management information. This is not only a costly venture but also involves a very considerable use of the staff and equipment of the council's computer section, especially in the early stages. A number of considerations are involved including, for instance: cost of equipment required in the libraries; cost of additional equipment which might be required by the computer section; more staff in both library and computer sections; the time factor; and whether such library use of the computer might prevent some other department from putting some of its processes on computer. Thus the decision is not one which should be decided solely on library needs and library finance, and it is common sense that board approval must be first obtained before the project even goes to the committees and council.

POLITICAL PARTIES

Finally, in considering the influence and rôles of other committees and cabals on the work of the committee responsible for libraries, mention should be made of the 'party' system. Practically all local authorities are now politically controlled and the party which has the majority representation on the council is in the position to get its own policies adopted: it will have a majority on the committees as well as on the council. The normal practice is for the parties to meet a few days before the council meetings and discuss how particular items on the agenda are to be handled, who is to lead and close the debate and the other selected speakers. All parties do this but the majority party does so in the knowledge that when a particular item is put to the vote, it must win it. The principle of party meetings is also employed before committees to come to a decision as to how to vote on important matters. All in all, therefore, where the party system is extensively employed it will be the party opinion which wins the day. It may seem rather useless for the minority parties to hold their own meetings but a common point of view is often thought to be necessary. The minority parties also like to have their views written up in the press; much of the sparring in both committee and council is for the benefit of the press: a euphemistic expression for the 'benefit of the party'.

CHAIRMAN OF COMMITTEE

It is usual for the chairman of a standing committee of the council to be elected from the majority party, and in spite of the charade of asking for nominations at the first committee meeting, the pre-selected party member inevitably is elected. (The same procedure frequently applies for the vice-chairman.) The chairman is, therefore, in a very strong position and this makes it very important that the librarian should consult him prior to a meeting of his committee. It is often necessary to consult the chairman before placing possibly contentious items on the agenda. The chairman is likely to know his party views

48

on certain topics or at least will be aware of possible objections to certain policies and can advise when an item should be left off an agenda, or alternatively when the most opportune time might be to include it. If the libraries are part of a larger department then perhaps all consultations with the chairman may be with the director, but that is a policy to be deplored.

THE COMMITTEE MEETING

The libraries committee (or its equivalent) will meet a week or two in advance of the scheduled council meetings which will be held not more than ten times a year and will be less in the counties. The agendas will be drawn up by the secretary to the committee, usually a member of the town clerk's department, or administration department, as it may now be called. The items to be included on an agenda come from a number of sources: there are probably some items from the previous meeting still requiring a further report; then the librarian may have some proposals and possibly the chairman or some other member of the committee. The architect may have to report on a new building or repairs to an existing building. If any major financial matter is to be considered then the director of finance would also be reporting, and so on.

At the meeting the chairman will take the reserved chair at the top or centre table, usually with his vice-chairman to one side and the librarian on the other. Also in attendance will be the secretary to the committee and senior officers of other departments as needed. Where there is a directorate system the director will sit next to the chairman and will probably have the librarian next to him. The heads of other sections, Baths, Parks, etc. will also be present as business dictates. Overleaf is a typical agenda for a meeting of a 'Libraries Committee'. (If it were a Recreation Committee the same items would appear but would be alongside those of other sections of the department.)

As will be seen, all the items on the agenda are matters of importance. The committee had asked at the previous meeting for a report from the librarian on the possibility of a book sale; they would obviously wish to see the plans of a new library and approve of them before finalisation; the librarian is concerned at heavy book losses and ought therefore to report these, at the same time he is suggesting expensive security installations which will involve additional and considerable expense; the matter of services to the disadvantaged was sufficiently

LIBRARIES COMMITTEE

Tuesday 14 June 1977 at 6 pm

AGENDA

1 Minutes of the Meeting held on 4 May 1977. To confirm and sign.

2 Matters arising from the minutes:
Librarian to report further on proposed book sale.

3 Hatton Branch Library—to reconsider plans of new branch library as revised by the architects, Messrs R. J. Jackson & Partners.   Paper 1160

4 Security—to consider report of Librarian *re* book losses from the Central Library and proposed security measures.   Paper 1161

5 Library services to the disadvantaged—to consider report of the sub-committee.   Paper 1162

6 Library charges—to consider proposals for increased charges as prepared by the Director of Finance and the Librarian. (All committees have been asked by the Finance Committee to review charges at this cycle of meetings.)   Paper 1163

important to warrant the setting-up of a special sub-committee which is now reporting; and the matter of library charges involves policy, it also has the finance committee's backing. A number of these items have financial implications and presumably no money has been allocated in the year's estimates. If approved they will have to be included in the next year's estimates; if expensive they may have to go into the development programme and take their turn. In due course Items 4, 5 and 6 are all likely to have financial implications which will require approval of the finance or equivalent committee, when the proposals were definite, and an implementation date agreed. Wherever any new proposal is likely to have repercussions on the public as for example Item 6, once approved a period of notice, say two months, is likely to be given before the new charges come into operation. One sometimes finds on an agenda a final item under the heading 'Any other business' but many councils dislike the introduction of additional business at the end of the agenda unless it is of extreme urgency.

The practice tends to the making of hurried decisions by tired committee members, without adequate time for proper consideration, and it has been frequently used to get approval to something that is fairly contentious, without adequate debate. It is also unnecessary since a committee chairman usually has authority to make decisions within certain financial limits on his own authority between meetings or with the consent of the leader of the minority party on the committee, where a matter of urgency arises.

The committee meeting will be opened by the chairman who will ask for confirmation from the members that the minutes of the last meeting, as circulated, were correct and for authority to sign them. Item 2 deals with matters arising from the minutes. The secretary of the committee has itemised the one matter that needs further consideration, but questions could be raised on any other item if a member wishes. As the meeting proceeds from item to item on the agenda, any member of the committee is given the opportunity to speak, usually after the chairman has first given a brief explanation. If the officers have to be asked questions this will be done by committee members through the chairman who will then call upon the officer. At other times the chairman will ask the officer in question to speak, and where the officer wants to speak of his own accord he will gently indicate this to the chairman. Many items on an agenda never reach the stage where voting is required. Library matters are not very contentious and, unless there is a distinct difference in policy on some matter between the opposing political parties, a decision will most likely be reached by general accord. If there *is* a vote then this is normally by show of hands and the secretary to the committee counts them and announces the result to the chairman. Nowadays the press is allowed into committee meetings and seats are reserved for reporters. The public is usually admitted too. However, certain items on an agenda may be confidential and, when they come up for discussion, the press and public will have to leave. This is usually arranged by having the agenda in two parts: the first for general business and the second, often printed on separate and different coloured sheets of paper, for confidential business. Few items come into the latter category but there are times when a committee has to consider something at a stage when it would be detrimental to the interests of the council for that information to become public knowledge at that time, (eg a proposal to purchase a particular site for a new library. If information about this leaked out in advance it might result in the price being much higher than it would have been.) Again the suggestion that a certain area be developed as a civic centre in which there was to be a new library along with offices and shops might also result in financial speculation.

The record of the meeting along with any decisions taken or recommendations to be made to the council will be written down by the secretary to the committee who will within days draw them up as official minutes. These have to be brief, unambiguous, and clear statements of the transactions. It is likely that they will have to be approved by the chairman before they are duplicated for distribution. From the minutes the secretary also prepares a report which goes to the council meeting. This will include any recommendation needing council approval, and for information only, the more important matters which have been decided upon by the committee in accordance with its terms of reference. Where some matters need to go to another committee for further consideration, the secretary arranges this. The two committees most likely in this connection are the establishment committee when staff matters are involved, (see pp 45–6) and the finance committee.

SUB-COMMITTEES

The intention of the Maud Committee was that the committee meetings of a local authority should be shortened by confining deliberations to policy, rather than administration which the staff could deal with. The librarian was to be allowed to manage without unnecessary interference. At the same time both Maud and Bains recommended fewer committees. To achieve this they had to be multi-disciplinary in some instances. It would be interesting to know how this has worked in practice. Although the number of committees has been reduced by most authorities, the necessity of having to group two or more functions under one committee has, one suspects, defeated the original objective of shorter meetings, for in spite of the removal of minor matters from agendas the remaining items, ranging over a number of different fields, require a considerable time for discussion. Some authorities have sought to surmount the difficulty by setting up sub-committees to deal with the separate aspects of the work but there seems little advantage in this as compared with separate committees so far as the time factor is concerned. With such a system and an overall leisure committee, libraries might be referred to a standing sub-committee. Where both finance and staffing were the remit of a policy and resources committee, then two separate sub-committees might be established to deal with the separate aspects before confirmation by the main committee. Although such an arrangement still keeps the overall control in the hands of one committee it could take more rather than less of the members' time.

Another device is to establish 'ad hoc' sub-committees to consider specific matters of a transitory nature. It allows them to be discussed and explored in detail, whereas it would not be possible to do them so much justice in full committee. Examples are numerous but they could include sub-committees concerned with any of the following: ways and means of reducing the library estimates for the coming year by a certain percentage; the requirements of a new central library before preparing a brief for the architect; how best to use a bequest; or the establishment of a community arts centre.

Separate standing sub-committees for specific divisions of library work are no longer justified for public libraries, but advisory committees or sub-committees for book selection are still to be found in some academic libraries.

University Libraries

POWERS AND DUTIES

The responsibilities and functions of a university library committee will vary from place to place but the following is an example of the terms of reference which might appear in the ordinances.

1   Subject to the authority of the senate and council, the administration of the library shall be the function of the library committee.
2   Appointment to the office of librarian shall in the first instance be subject to selection of a candidate by a joint committee of senate and council and approved by the library committee who shall forward the recommendation to the senate who shall report thereon to the council.
3   The library committee shall make recommendations to the council relating to the appointment of administrative staff of the library.
4   The library committee shall review from time to time the conditions of service of the academic staff of the library and their functions and shall make recommendations thereon to the senate which if it thinks fit shall make recommendations to the council.
5   The library committee shall have power to allocate and spend at its

discretion all funds entrusted to it by the council. The library committee shall prepare a report on the work of the library each year and present it to the senate.

6 The library committee shall be responsible for submitting to the council such statements of financial income and expenditure, and estimates thereof as may be required.

7 The library committee may make recommendations to the council in any matter concerning the maintenance of the library building. It shall be the duty of the senate to report to the council on any matter concerning the administration of the library which in its opinion needs the consideration of the council.

MEMBERSHIP

The library committee is usually kept reasonably small and probably meets once a term. A dozen members would be adequate, although in some universities the desire to give all interests representation seems to take precedence over the practical aspects. The aim is to have a committee which includes some of the most important officers of the university such as the vice-chancellor or pro vice-chancellor, and the senior member of each faculty (providing this is not too many). Apart from the librarian, the deputy librarian is often a member, and may act as secretary to the committee instead of the librarian. Most universities also include one or two student representatives on the committee, and in some the library staff may also elect a further member from among themselves, though the need for a third representative of staff seems debateable. The chairman of the committee will probably be appointed by senate and may have a fixed period of office of three or five years.

THE UNIVERSITY LIBRARIAN

It is inevitable that distinctions will be drawn between the responsibilities and status of the university librarian and that of the librarian of a public library, usually to the disadvantage of the latter, but by and large such criticisms are out of place. Perhaps the major differences lie in the social position of the librarian, and the atmosphere in which committee meetings take place. One might be tempted to add 'in the absence of politics and political parties' for in their own way, academics can be just as political and devious in their own particular sphere as the members of a local authority. In the university the librarian has the same professional status as the heads of other departments and he is continually working alongside them as an equal. He is looked upon as the expert in his field, and it is not the normal practice for an expert in one field to tell an expert in another his business. The members of university library committees are all library users to a greater or lesser degree; the academics also represent the research workers and students in their departments as well as the academic staff, and the student union nominees represent the great mass of students. Basically too, they all have the same primary interest. They are all user-conscious, though, admittedly, rivalry between departments might create some prejudice on occasion. Between them they should have an excellent idea of what the users expect from their library. They should be well acquainted with the library and know its strengths and weaknesses, especially in their own fields; they do not need to be convinced by the librarian of the value of the library. The value is taken for granted. The public librarian sometimes has to fight, not to convince his own committee of the library's worth but the other members of the local authority. As the Association of University Teachers stated:[5] 'It must be recognised, once and for all, that university libraries provide an absolutely fundamental service which affects the whole of the university and without which it would cease to function as a centre for teaching and research.'

While it is not true to say that the public librarian has a lesser status than the university librarian as so many librarianship students seem to assume (in fact the opposite could equally well be argued) he is acting in a different setting and operating under a different set of rules in a different social context. He is acting as professional adviser to a committee of men and women who, whatever else they may be, are not experts in librarianship. In fact they may have no real knowledge of libraries, and unfortunately in some cases, no real interest either. Primarily they are on the local council as members of a political party, and some of them may consider libraries have a very low priority for public funds as compared with social services and housing. While a committee will usually listen to the librarian with due respect, it will not hesitate to question his advice and may well decide to act otherwise. It may sound stupid to employ a professional, pay him a good salary and then ignore his advice, but it must be appreciated that councillors have a duty to their electorate in terms of *all* the local authority services, not merely libraries. However much they might be devoted to the library service they have to weigh up the claims of spending on libraries as against other services. Another point to be remembered is that they know the residents of their own particular wards very well and have a shrewd idea of priorities as 'the people' would see them. Other local circumstances, maybe unknown to the librarian may also influence their decision.

Many librarianship students describe the university library committee as being *advisory* by which they mean 'advising the librarian'. This is not so. As with the public library committee, there are many matters which the committee can decide upon and execute. Others may have to be reported to the senate, and, in turn some financial and staffing matters, as well as those of general administration, have to be reported by the senate to council before any decision can be made. It should go without saying too, that the university librarian, like the public librarian, is expected to manage the library efficiently and not to take minor matters to his committee. A glance at the agendas of some university library committees or the annual reports of university libraries will readily reveal that such committees are not just the rubber stamps that they are frequently assumed to be. Library estimates; cost effectiveness; staffing during week-ends and evenings; opening hours; reductions in staff; salary structures; inter-library loan charges; loan periods; action to secure return of long overdue books; review of library charges; rules and regulations; purchase of expensive equipment such as a mini-computer; the annual report; review of periodical expenditure; responsibility of the main library for halls libraries; regulations for new department libraries; binding policies; faculty requests for book funds; research collections; library instruction; book selection procedures; overcrowding of accommodation; applications for special funds; and subject specialisation: this list is culled from but a handful of reports and suggests that the committees discuss more aspects of the library service than would the average public library committee. This apart, however, it must also be appreciated that the public relations aspect of the committee is all important to the librarian. It serves as a means of obtaining informed opinion about certain aspects of the library service and decision as to possible courses of action; it is a means of testing opinion and gaining support; and it helps the librarian clarify his own thoughts. Naturally the administration of the library and the methods used are the librarian's own responsibility and to a large extent he can decide what to take to committee. In exercising his authority too, he will always have at hand the advice of the vice-chancellor, the secretary, the accountant, and other officers.

One other similarity between the public and university committee structure is that other committees have a very important rôle to play. For instance in the university, the council and the finance and general purposes committee have a rôle equivalent to that of the local authority's resources committee, or separate finance and establishment committees where these exist, and to which recommendations about major expenditure or major matters of staff policy must be referred. The university's development committee (or a committee with the same purpose but a different title) will be responsible for new building plans, minor works, upkeep of paths and buildings, public services, car parks, playing fields and so on in much the same way as the works committee of a local authority.

What has been said in this section about university library control is the general pattern. In practice there are many divergencies due largely to historical and local factors eg the Bodleian Library at Oxford and the University Library at Cambridge are basically 'national', and receive *on demand* a copy of every item published in Britain. The London University Library has a stock of over a million books, and meets the further needs of a host of scholars from all the university institutes and associated colleges, which all have their own libraries.

Polytechnics and Colleges

Library committees are also to be found in polytechnics and colleges but these are normally sub-committees of the academic board of which the librarian will be a member. Except for the voluntary and privately controlled colleges, these institutions will be the responsibility of the local authority and subject to a considerable amount of influence by the DES. The function of the sub-committee will depend largely on the size of the college, indeed in smaller ones the librarian can advise the academic board quite adequately by himself. Where there is a sub-committee, however, it has the advantage of being able to act as a sounding board for the librarian, particularly in matters of bookstock, periodicals, special problems, new courses, facilities and rules, and general user reactions. The academic board, when it decides to appoint a library committee or sub-committee will draw up its constitution. This is likely to include the principal or his deputy, the librarian, representatives of the teaching staff and a few students. The librarian is likely to serve as Secretary. In larger colleges and poly-technics the sub-committee will function more like the university committee. While acting in an advisory capacity in some matters and as a means of communication between librarian and library users, in more important matters of policy it will refer any recommendations to the academic board.

Societies and Associations

The libraries of some societies and associations are too small to warrant any committee, indeed many of them have insufficient funds to maintain even a modest flow of new books and a great number cannot afford a professional librarian but are looked after by an honorary librarian or in the spare time of a clerical assistant. On the other hand there are a number of libraries of this kind which have very valuable and extensive stocks together with reasonable financial backing.

All such libraries depend upon members' subscriptions for their maintenance, and where it is justified the practice is to elect a library committee from among the members. Like the public library com-mittee it relies on the controlling body of the organisation for its finance and its librarian is a technical or professional adviser to the committee rather than a member. It is unlikely that the library of a society or association will have a great deal of work for its committee because it is not in a position to launch out into new fields of develop-ment. Even large libraries of this kind such as those of the Royal Institute of British Architects, and the Fawcett Society have had very considerable financial problems in recent years. The committee's main value is in the public relations link with the membership at large. The librarian is quite capable of executing the day-to-day adminis-tration without a committee, but where there are substantial diffi-culties such as the need for more accommodation; financial problems, or a need for an additional member of staff then a committee may well prove its worth in acting as a catalyst for support from the mem-bership for increased subscriptions, appeals, or offers of help. There would be little formality at most meetings of such a committee, which might only be held two or three times a year. One would expect some brief agenda and a record of the meetings.

References

1 Ministry of Housing and Local Government. *Management of local government*, HMSO, 1967.
2 Department of the Environment. *The new local authorities, management and structure*, HMSO, 1972.
3 Royal Commission on Local Government in Scotland. *Scotland: Local government reform*, HMSO, 1969
4 Scottish Development Department. *The new Scottish local authorities: organisation and management structures*, HMSO, 1973.
5 Association of University Teachers. *The university library*, September 1964.

4

Goals, Objectives, Functions and Standards

Library goals, objectives, standards and functions have been of some interest and concern to librarians for the last twenty or thirty years, but it is only relatively recently that these considerations have been consciously recognised as essential to library management. This can be attributed to the accelerated growth of library services at national, state, local, university and industrial levels and also to the very sweeping changes that have taken place through large-scale reorganisations or amalgamations. In turn this has meant that while library budgets were not unduly noticeable when the libraries were comparatively small organisations, when they had been increased in size though reduced in numbers, their expenditure, being considerable, could scarcely hope to avoid close scrutiny. Such scrutiny is likely to be all the closer when library spending forms part of the much bigger expenditure of an omnibus leisure department. Thus library expenditure, whatever the type of library, is now prey to the authority's financial officer, who will want to know the constituent parts of the estimates together with reasons for the necessity for the different expenditures. He will not be inclined to accept subjective judgment or emotive arguments, but will look for some indication of the returns expected from the expenditure, and comparative figures between sections of the service, and, between one library and others of similar standing elsewhere in the country, and so on.

It becomes essential, therefore, for a librarian to be able to defend his service and its claims for spending with a carefully reasoned statement of its rôle and objectives and, so far as is possible, to have facts and figures available which evaluate the services provided. In times of economic stringency it becomes even more important to be able to convince financial officers, other members of the management team, councillors, governing bodies of universities and colleges, and directors of industry, and there is always conflict between the claims of one department and another when proposals for capital developments are being advanced. Reference to library literature will readily show how great is the interest in library objectives nowadays and the search for acceptable methods of evaluation, though little real success can yet be claimed. A method of correlating quantitative assessment with qualitative assessment still eludes us. Statistics measuring volume—number of borrowers, number of books in stock, or number of issues, are quite inadequate as a means of evaluation. They tell us nothing about the people who borrow the books, the standard of the books and the value of each loan to the borrower—they therefore fail to reflect the overall worth of the library.

Public Libraries

Much of the literature on objectives has been concerned with public libraries, yet the complete lack of interest in the subject in 1850 was such that the first Public Libraries Act in that year did not even envisage the necessity of buying books. The reasons (which we would now call 'objectives') of even those who did support the Act were mixed and contradictory. Although some genuinely saw the rôle of the public library as bringing the joys of reading to the masses, and as a means of education, information and recreation, these same people also supported the library as a means of weaning some individuals from the public house and others from petty crime.

After the First World War the library service, thanks to the Act of 1919, grew firmer roots and began to command public recognition; greater use was made of it by the student and the middle classes as more money permitted better book provision and higher standards of service. However, improved as it was, it scarcely deserved the effusive statement contained in the Kenyon Report[1] of 1927 which read: 'The public interest in libraries has greatly increased and we believe that there is now a far healthier belief in the value of knowledge and in the importance of intellectual life in all the busy centres of national activity than in any previous period of history. In such centres the public library is no longer regarded as a means of providing casual recreation of an innocent but somewhat unimportant character; it is recognised as an engine of great potentialities for national welfare and as the essential foundation for the progress in education and welfare without which no people can hold its own in the struggle for existence.' This was a very noble sentiment but as a statement of the public library rôle its superficiality makes it of little practical value. One cannot imagine it having much discernible effect upon a stony-hearted financial officer.

In 1959 the Roberts Committee[2] produced a far better statement when it adopted a more specific approach and spoke of the library function in tangible terms thus: 'the essential function of a public library is to supply any reader, or group of readers, the books and related material for which they may ask. *This provision should take precedence of all ancillary services* and should, of course, include a reference library where the reader may consult not only the standard encyclopaedias, bibliographies and other works of reference, but specialised books and journals relating to his own industry or profession or subject of research. . . . It is the function of the public library not only to satisfy but to promote the desire for books. Consequently the provision of a children's library with adequate stocks and expert guidance in the choice of books should be regarded as an integral part of the library service. . . . Finally, public libraries should be free libraries and freedom of borrowing should extend to music, gramophone records, photostats and other related material'. Thus, without once using the word 'objectives', the Roberts Committee produced the most satisfactory statement of what it conceived to be the rôle and functions of the public library. Considered in management terms, this statement in itself, like so many others, lacked any reference to finance (some minor reference to expenditure on books appears later). It must be emphasised, therefore, that no matter how well the objectives of an organisation may be framed, if the money is not there only an inferior standard of service can be provided, alternatively some of the objectives must be jettisoned. Thus when authors of text books on management, such as Flippo,[3] say: 'The determination of objectives or goals is of prime importance and a prerequisite to the solution of most management problems' it must be appreciated that the management of a library is not the same as the management of a firm which aims to produce enough of its products to sell at such a price as will bring in a reasonable profit. Within the laws of supply and demand the firm is free to fix its own volume of production and rate of profit. The library on the other hand, is dependent solely on the agency which provides the finances; the most laudable programme of objectives is only as good as the resources provided to augment it.

Following on the Roberts Committee report, it was not surprising that the Public Libraries and Museums Act, 1964 took its advice to heart. It made the service a statutory responsibility and listed the general objectives that the library authorities were to pursue and the specific services to be provided. To that extent therefore, all public libraries in England and Wales have objectives prescribed by the government. The weakness lies in the vagueness of the phraseology and the lack of any *prescribed* degree of financial support to turn objectives into reality as we shall see presently. S.7(1) of the Act gives the main objective as the provision of 'a comprehensive and efficient library service for all persons desiring to make use thereof, and for that purpose to employ such officers, to provide and maintain such buildings and equipment and such books and other materials, and to do such other things, as may be requisite'. Had the Act been no more specific than this, as a statement of objectives such a vague definition would not have withstood serious questioning but in the succeeding sub-section S.7(2) it went on to elaborate and listed the facilities considered to be desirable, including adequate stocks of books and other printed matter for lending and reference, of pictures, gramophone records, films and other materials 'sufficient in number, range and quality to meet the general requirements and any special requirements of both adults and children'. It also drew attention to the desirability of encouraging library use through advice and publicity and participation in co-operation with other institutions and libraries.

Thus by 1964 the library authorities did have official guidance from Parliament as to the objectives to be pursued. However, subsequent events have confirmed the fears expressed[4] in 1970 about the lack of definition in S.7 and the employment of such terms as 'comprehensive', 'efficient', 'requisite', 'desirability', 'special requirements', and other similar words and have demonstrated that the *government had no intention of prescribing in mandatory form any clear cut and inescapable objectives*. It is true that the minister did publish in 1962 the standards[5] drawn up by his working party but these were minimum standards, and moreover were only presented as guidelines. Their coverage was slight: the only quantitative standards were those applicable to books and periodicals and to staff; in addition there were some general observations on existing standards for library buildings. The standards were modestly updated in some respects in 1971 in a joint report[6] of the two Library Advisory Councils which had been given the task of keeping them under review. This report dealt with the provision of library service points of different kinds and factors to be considered in library planning, together with a very general survey of staffing standards. Further research into the latter was recommended and this was carried out in 1973/4 by the Local Authorities Management Services Advisory Council (LAMSAC) whose report[7] was published in 1976 without any recommendations thereon from the Secretary of State. There is a strange ambivalence in central government's relationship with local government. It restricts the policy of the latter to a very large extent by virtue of the Rate Support Grant and other measures, but at the same time it likes to pretend that it does not interfere with local government's freedom of action. Thus any standards presented are offered in the spirit of 'the advice is there, it is for you to decide whether you want to use it.' The LAMSAC report is strictly advisory and a large amount of subjective judgment is still involved with regard to the establishment of specialist posts. The decision to provide some or all of them depends upon the objectives and the priorities of individual local authorities.

The Public Library Research Group of the London and Home Counties Branch of The Library Association has published a suggested basis for national standards of the aims and objectives of the public library. The preamble to the brief report[8] in The *Library Association Record* makes clear the belief of the group that a set of defined objectives is the first essential to management by objectives and to the formulation of output measurements which library management theorists regard as essential if the library is to justify itself. The group discards any suggestion that it should prescribe an order of priorities among the objectives proposed. This is common-sense for the priorities of one library may be different from those of another, as indeed may those of one branch library from another in the same system, or one section of work from another.

A system of objectives also needs flexibility to meet changing circumstances such as external pressures and external developments, the changed economic circumstances of an authority, the falling birth-rate, exodus from the town to the country and developments at national library level. Indeed on this latter note Phillip Sewell[9] makes a very sound case for *drawing up national library objectives, based on a study of national communal aims and objectives, as the point of departure for considering what should be the aims of objectives of the different types of library*. This makes good sense for no library to-day can afford to act in isolation and its own objectives must be decided after a national plan has been agreed and the contribution of each type of library to this plan. The Sheffield Report on library co-operation[10] points in this direction.

Reverting to the L & HC objectives these have been divided primarily into four main divisions—Education, Information, Culture and Leisure. In turn each has been sub-divided into sub-objectives against which have been listed the principal activities or facilities provided to realise these sub-objectives, the elements or materials required (books, periodicals, etc) and a second category of elements labelled 'methods' which apply to staff and the use of catalogues, bibliographies, co-operation, assistance to readers, AVA, etc. The whole is set out in a single chart with a numerical notation making it very simple to see at a glance and to understand. Frank Gardner[11] has raised the question whether a statement of objectives such as these would be helpful or even possible for developing countries where the public library may still only be in its infancy or even non-existent. At the same time he has underlined a very important point, namely that a library service in itself cannot have objectives but that they are framed by the library authority, the officers, the tax payers and the users either individually or collectively.

Unfortunately, not enough is known about library users but it now begins to be appreciated that user opinion should be paramount. A serious attempt to research the user point of view was made in the Hillingdon project. Work began in 1971 and a report was issued in 1976. The project was financed by The Library Association, its London and Home Counties Branch and the Polytechnic of North London. Once more the Public Library Research Group of the Branch was to the fore and acted as a steering committee. The published report[12] contains an excellent summary of library goals, objectives and functions. It defines the broadest level of goals as the library role or purpose which is defined as the transmission of culture, and at the next level of goals comes the objectives or the satisfaction of all relevant needs, and at third level comes the library's functions or the actions it must take in order to fulfil its objectives. Though the report cannot be said to have arrived at any specific measure of effectiveness other than methods already known, it is important as the first systematic study in depth in this country to try to measure effectiveness and to discover what factors we need to understand and measure if we are to provide an effective library service. What does materialise quite clearly from the survey is a gulf between the librarian's concept of the efficiency of his service and that of the users concerned. It is a significant piece of work but still a long way from being a clear-cut guide to user satisfaction and cost effectiveness. Whether any overall assessment can ever be produced seems doubtful, as effectiveness must be seen differently by one class of user and another. How does one measure for instance the effectiveness of the loan of one book as compared with another, or of the supply of one piece of information with another, the loan of a gramophone record with a book, a library lecture with an exhibition, and so on? Some services can be judged quantitatively, eg 3 million books issued from a library which costs £1 million to run as compared with another which issues only 2 million books for the same money. How does one, however, measure the cost effectiveness from the community point of view of issuing 3 million novels at a cost of £1 million as compared with only 1 million non-fiction books for the same overall expenditure? F. A. Sharr[13] has also stressed the need for librarians to consider user requirements and to shape their library provision to meet the changing needs of society where new technologies are transforming the whole world of communication. He makes the point that the continual preoccupation with books and other allied materials rather than with the total media of communication will lead to the death-knell of the public library unless librarians wake up to the challenge of the times.

In the United States the formulation of collective standards and objectives (voluntary not mandatory) has been the work of the American Library Association. Apart from their interest in public libraries they have published *Standards for School Library Programs* and *Standards for Library Functions at State Level*. The last edition of their *Minimum Standards for Public Library Systems*[14] which was published in 1966, contains an introductory chapter by Gerald W. Johnson which is basically a statement of public library objectives. The second chapter defines functions in terms of materials and services and then goes on to list with explanations, some 66 standards. The term 'standard' is defined as 'a specific criterion against which adequacy and quality can be tested or measured'. The majority of these standards are in fact general objectives rather than quantitative standards, as were the Bourdillon recommendations in Britain. It is interesting to note that Standard 16 reads: 'The program of each library system and its member libraries should be focused upon clear and specific objectives.' This probably explains why, when a survey was carried out of large public library systems in the United States and in Britain in 1970,[15] 19 out of 25 libraries in America replied in the affirmative to a question asking whether the authority had any written statement of objectives, yet only 2 British libraries out of 26 could do so. However, perhaps the position is now different since local government re-organisation in Britain occasioned the new authorities to draw up a statement of existing library services and from these to develop proposals for the future. Of public libraries in the United States L. E. Bone[16] has suggested that many of their statements of goals and objectives leave much to be desired.

The standards for public library systems, issued by the ALA did however contain a warning to the effect that limitations of both time and money had prevented extensive research into the development of the standards and early in the 1970s the Public Library Association Division of the ALA, concerned at the inadequacy of the 1966 standards, *were pressing for more research and particularly for the production of quantitative measures, correlated with quality*, with which to assess library performance. They pointed out the need for standards based on the assumption of co-operation between libraries of all types and based also on user assessment. They also stated that the public library to-day must stand on the premise of social utility and that all activities must be planned with that goal in mind. Thus, like the Public Libraries Research Group of the London and Home Counties Branch of The Library Association the American equivalent body stressed the need for establishing empirical methods of assessing objectives in view of the fact that the loosely worded objectives and standards which were good enough for the 1950s and 1960s would no longer suffice in the 1970s, when librarians were constantly being challenged from many quarters about the need for some of their services, and to justify their expenditure in terms of results. When funds were received from the US Office of Education a project on the *Measurement of Effectiveness of Public Library Service* was put in hand by the Public Library Association Division in 1971; the report was published in 1973.[17] The project was conducted by the Bureau of Library and Information Science Research at Rutgers University and, as originally envisaged contained five phases. Only Phases 1 and 3 were funded and the report, therefore, was only to be regarded as a preliminary. The two phases dealt with (a) reviewing previous attempts to assess the effectiveness of the library service as reported in the literature, and analysing existing statistical reporting systems; and (b) testing the criteria and methodology thus obtained in a sample of public libraries on a nationwide basis and preparing a profile for each library. Thus as its preface made clear, the report was far from being the ultimate in measurement tests, a common yardstick or a series of yardsticks which could be applied to any library. What it does do is to elaborate the kind of statistics that most libraries keep and add others to them. It shows how a computer print-out can be produced for such statistics in respect of a single library and how they compare on average with other libraries of similar size. Basically, the statistics collected cover three areas: stock; users; and activity level. The print-out really amounts to an example of the use of statistics for special purposes, eg: the chart of hourly use of the reference library could be used as evidence in presenting a case for increasing staff; if figures of users had been collected instead of the number of questions received it could have been used as a basis for reducing opening hours or amending them otherwise. All librarians are aware of the value of this type of information collected for special purposes but this is a far cry from an assessment of the *worth* of a public library's service. Ultimately, as so many other surveys have asserted, worth can only be assessed from the user's point of view, and somehow a method has to be found of measuring this; similarly we need to know what services the non-users would like to see introduced so that they too would be induced to use the library. In these connections the Hillingdon Project seems to have gone farthest. However, one of the best examples of library objectives of a single library is to be found in the survey of the Chicago Public Library carried out by Professor Lowell Martin in 1970.[18]

Lowell Martin's survey is far more than a mere statement of objectives, it is a classic example of the study of objectives of a single library system. It is a study in depth of all the constituent features of the service and of its failings. What is most important is that objectives are framed against the financial situation of the library and the limitations of the library rating system, together with an assessment of the additional finances required. Having carried out all this research Lowell Martin and his team set out a system of priorities for three periods which together covered the years 1969–80. The first year, 1969/70 was a period of preparation and contained 30 items in the programme—it is significant that the first two of these were concerned with the methods of collecting taxes for library revenue. This underlines the point already made that to theorise about objectives without reference to library finance is an irrelevant exercise. The second phase called 'the Big Push' was to cover 1970–5 and again listed 30 items, while the third phase, 1975–80 was called 'the Holding Process' and was limited to 16 items, the emphasis being on the quality of the service and the need to review and change the system to keep pace with changes in American life. Again this demonstrates a further vital need of all library services: a built-in system for review and the ability to change with the times. The preface also underlined the need to base library objectives on the user.

Chicago, like so many other American cities at that time had more than its fair share of civil disturbances and crime; the flight from the cities was a constant source of press comment but in Chicago the population had remained constant over twenty years and was expected to remain fairly stable until 1980. On the other hand, outside the city the growth of population in the suburbs was very considerable and was expected to rise very rapidly by 1980 so that by that year the population of the city area would be a distinct minority of the total metropolitan area. The ethnic make-up of the population, the age groups, the occupations and the educational levels, all posed very significant problems so that it is not surprising that Lowell Martin says: 'A program of service is presented that calls for the Chicago Public Library to adjust to the people of the city in all their diversity, rather than expecting the people to conform to a standardised institution'—a phrase that should find its way into every text-book and article on library objectives. Obviously Lowell Martin has no great belief in the discovery of the ultimate in performance tests for although his research team have used all types of data and methods of assessment as indicated in the Appendix, he asserts without any equivocation whatsoever that *in an enterprise of this nature and scope one comes down, at last, to human judgment*.

Another American attempt to define needs and objectives of libraries generally, not only public libraries, resulted from *Executive Order No. 11301*[19] of President Lyndon B. Johnson in 1966 which established the President's Committee on Libraries and the National Commission on Libraries.[20] The duties of the Commission as set out in Section 4 of the Order, included: 'the appraisal of the role of libraries, library policies and programs and effective utilisation of libraries and the appraisal of library funding, including federal support of libraries; and to determine how funds available for the construction and support of libraries and library services can be more effectively and efficiently utilised'.

At international level the Unesco Public Library Manifesto, as revised in 1972, defines the overall objective of the public library as being 'a living force for education, culture and information and as an essential agent for the fostering of peace and understanding between people and between nations. . . . The public library is a practical demonstration of democracy's faith in universal education as a continuing and lifelong process, in the appreciation of the achievement of humanity in knowledge and culture.

The public library is the means whereby the records of man's thoughts and ideas and the expression of his creative imagination are made fully available to all.

The public library is concerned with the refreshment of man's spirit by the provision of books for relaxation and pleasure, with assistance to the student and with provision of up-to-date technical, scientific and sociological information.

The public library should be established under the clear mandate of law, so framed as to ensure nationwide provision of public library service. Organised co-operation between libraries is essential so that total national resources should be fully used and be at the service of any reader.

It should be maintained wholly from public funds, and no direct charge should be made to anyone for its services.

To fulfil its purposes the public library must be readily accessible and its doors open for free and equal use by all members of the community, regardless of race, colour, nationality, age, sex, religion, language, status or educational attainment.'

As a statement of objectives in an international setting and as a world-wide philosophy of librarianship the foregoing are difficult to fault. Proceeding from the general to the specific, the manifesto then goes on to list objectives with regard to resources and services; use by children; use by students; the handicapped reader; and the public library in the community. The manifesto is however limited to an overall statement of the rôles of the public library and this type of statement of objectives is very different from the programme of objectives which are regarded as a necessary prerequisite to library management, and further still from objectives one seeks to measure ultimately against performance tests.

In 1973 the Public Libraries Section of the International Federation of Library Associations published its *Standards for Public Libraries*.[21] In the main these are based on the experience of librarians in countries with developed library services. They cover 119 different aspects, including standards for administrative units; service points; materials; special groups of the community; staff and buildings. The emphasis is on quantitative standards. An introduction on 'The need for standards' stresses an important fact about objectives, namely that the emphasis placed on the various objectives of the service and the means of achieving these objectives will be different in different communities and will change with the passage of time.

Other Libraries

What has been said of goals, objectives and functions of public libraries is largely applicable to academic libraries and to special libraries. In the latter category a relatively small and select band of persons is using the libraries; basically the libraries are all user-orientated to a known degree; unlike the public library, the special library is provided for employees or subscribing members of an organisation. These are persons with a special interest or interests, and the library does not have to cover the whole spectrum of human knowledge as in the case of the public library. Where the library or information service is being provided by an industrial firm the obvious and immediate objective is to supply whatever material will add to the output of the research workers or others, and to supply it in the minimum of time. The assessment of its value may be subjective to some extent but with the users on the spot, able and ready to make complaints or alternatively commendations, and having the facility of being able to make practical suggestions for improvement, both the librarian and the management should be well aware of the staff's assessment of the library's services. Should the management consider the library to be inadequately used and its ratio of effectiveness to cost too small, it will not hesitate to prune it or even to close it down altogether. The most important factor is that the librarian should be aware of the objectives of the firm, be up-to-date with developments, and know what is afoot and planned for the future. Referring to objectives and assessment in special libraries Don Mason[22] has rightly said that all librarians have objectives, they know what they are trying to achieve although they have not committed their thoughts to paper. While paying due respect to management by objectives (MbO) he has also pointed out its fallacies and that the *important factor in an information service is its quality which can only be assessed by subjective judgment.* Elizabeth M. Moys[23] has dealt briefly with the professional library. She lists the number one priority of a law librarian as having a firm grasp of the reasons for the existence of his library, and of the policy he should endeavour to follow. Then she also makes the point that in a long-established library things have quite possibly been allowed to drift for years so that no very clear policy can be defined and the governing body has done nothing about it, nor has it kept up with the times. It would therefore behove the librarian to prepare a policy statement and lead the governing body to accept it.

In the university library too, there is a limited and specialist clientele, namely under-graduates, graduates, readers at post-doctoral level and staff. Scholarship is the basic aim of all, the difference lies in the level of studies and their depth, but the immense variety of users who patronise the public library is not found in the university and the need for written objectives is perhaps less necessary. Basically the goals and objectives of the library are the same as those of the university itself. Evidence of how recent is the current preoccupation with objectives is to be seen by the fact that the Report of the Parry Committee,[24] published in 1967, contained no mention of the word. However, the first part of that committee's terms of reference, dated 1963, did basically involve consideration of goals and objectives for it read as follows: 'To consider the most effective and economical arrangements for meeting the needs of the Universities and the Colleges of Advanced Technology and Central Institutions for books and periodicals, taking into account expanding staff and student populations, the possible needs of other users, the growth of research, the rising costs of books and periodicals and the increasing capital cost of accommodation . . .' The UGC's statement of 1921 to the effect that: 'We regard the fullest provision for library maintenance as the primary and most vital need in the equipment of a university', is also a basic assertion of the rôle of the library in the university. The Parry Committee also went to some lengths to describe the functions of the university library in paragraphs 17–35 of their report (though as part of an overall statement of goals, objectives and functions it is far too wordy).

From American sources there comes one of the best expositions of goals and objectives of academic and research libraries.[25] It was published in 1974 by the Office of University Library Management Studies which is administered by the Association of Research Libraries and financed by the Council on Library Resources. Like so many other reports on the subject the introduction tells us that: 'A future of change and uncertainty, limited resources, increased costs, technological developments and changing staff expectations' among other factors are challenges confronting the library manager so that greater emphasis is being placed on performance-based management techniques. 'One example has been the development of formal goals and objectives programs in many academic libraries.' It sets out in succinct terms the benefits which should accrue to libraries which have goals and objectives programmes and particularly pertinent, are the four broad principles which it enunciates for the formulation and development of such programmes, namely:

'Objectives should direct library programs and activities towards achievement of university purposes.
Broad statements of library intent should lead to the preparation of more specific statements at all levels of the library organisation.
To be successful the goals and objectives must have broad staff acceptance and support.
Objectives and goals should be used to improve the library services to users.'

The authors of this small book then go on to put their precepts into practice and develop the objectives for the different departments and services of the library. Quite rightly they maintain that goals and objectives become nothing more than written statements of intent unless supplemented by specific performance goals and they give examples of what might be required of certain units of the library system. They state that as each programme of objectives is achieved then fresh targets must be established and agreed with the staff. While this is fully in accord with general management principles, librarianship is not a profession which is particularly amenable to the realisation of set targets nor are professional librarians generally the type of people who like to work to productivity targets. Such schemes lend themselves best to manual work. This particular publication includes a chart as an appendix which is an exceptionally clear and straightforward explanation of management's goals and objectives, in striking contrast to the involved and turgid style so often found in text-books. In essence, however, it is concerned not so much with evaluation of the library service from the user point of view but more with work review and programming and allocation of staff to specific duties to ensure that work targets are achieved; in other words the approach is basically MbO.

J. R. Haak[26] has dealt with the subject of goals for undergraduate libraries in a rather similar vein. What is interesting about his article is the distinction he draws between 'intangible' goals, a term he uses to describe abstract purposes of libraries and 'tangible' goals or specific goals which lead to the realisation of the abstract purposes and which should be a guide or programme to achieve the desired results and include measures to evaluate their effectiveness.

Written standards and objectives have also been produced for college libraries in the UK, for example the ATCDE/LA standards for college of education libraries, in 1967 (under revision) which list nine basic functions: (1) to supply books, periodicals and other materials needed by students in all the subjects of study which they pursue, to the necessary level; (2) to provide support for the teaching and research of members of the staff . . .; (3) to provide for a wide range of background reading . . .; (4) to meet specialised needs of a college which arise naturally out of its specialities and interests by building up appropriate collections . . . and to provide bibliographical guidance by library staff; (5) to help students to become familiar with modern children's books, a representative collection of textbooks and audiovisual materials, and to suggest to them the potentialities of school libraries; (6) to help with the day-to-day needs of users by supplying them with ready reference information . . .; (7) to act as a link between the world of books and libraries outside . . .; (8) to provide the bibliographical training in the use of books and libraries necessary to help students . . .; (9) to produce guides, lists of additions, reading lists, and other publications and to hold displays and exhibitions of library materials.

The Library Association has also published other standards for colleges, including *College Libraries: recommended standards of library provision in colleges of technology and other establishments of further education*, 1971; *School library resource centres*, 1973 and 1977; and *Libraries in the new polytechnics*, 1968.

Conclusions

From this very short commentary on some of the professional writings on the subject of goals and objectives for libraries it will be seen that it is a matter of great interest on both sides of the Atlantic.

Unfortunately this very interest has created something of a mystical approach to the subject—an involved approach, and some confusion of terminology. One of the most straightforward accounts yet published is the work of two American library school staff[27] who have long practical experience in the university and public library fields. Their approach has been deliberately to eliminate this confusion and perhaps even more important, they distinguish between management in the business world and management in libraries. Their book, therefore, emphasises the rôles played by the community served, the governing body of the library and staff attitudes. It is written in the context of all types of library.

As Sewell and others have shown, library objectives should first originate at national level and should be based on the needs of the communities for which they are designed: the industrial library for the research staff; the academic library for research workers and undergraduates; and the public library for the community at large. Nationally set objectives and nationally-established standards should go hand in hand. The national starting point also enables planners to decide what services can best be provided collectively by all kinds of library through co-operation before proceeding to the next step at which each individual library decides its own objectives and standards. So long as they are left to find much of the money to finance their libraries, and while their staff work to different conditions of service, there must inevitably be differences in their ability to achieve national objectives and standards.

In the simplest interpretation of goals and objectives we have firstly a broad statement of purpose such as 'to provide a comprehensive and efficient library service', then the premise that it is the users' needs which should prevail, ie 'for all persons desiring to make use thereof'. Then this broad statement of policy is converted into a plan of action by sub-dividing into the various services and facilities required, eg books for loan, reference services, children's libraries, music and record libraries, bibliographical aids, study facilities, staff assistance, and other means. In turn each individual library authority will decide where these services are to be provided and their estimated cost. At this stage it may well be found that the cost of providing all of them to the required standard is beyond the authority's means so that the objectives will have to be more carefully defined and if necessary, a scale of priorities introduced. Priorities, ideally, should be based on evaluation of the merits and costs of one facility as compared with another, hence the pronounced current interest in trying to establish an evaluation based on both quality and quantity rather than the latter merely backed up by subjective judgment. Finally there is the separate aspect of management by objectives with which some library managers are concerned and which involve not only listing objectives to be pursued in annual programmes for instance, but also objectives geared to specific targets usually expressed quantitatively: clear off the arrears of 30,000 uncatalogued items at the rate of 300 a week in 2 years; computerise routines in 20 libraries in a system at the rate of 4 libraries a year over 5 years; increase the number of books per head of population from 1 to 2 over a period of 5 years. Examples of MbO as quoted are quite realistic and beyond reproach but if a librarian were to follow industrial methods and plan to increase output and sales by fifty per cent in a year with the same work-force this would be unlikely to be achieved as 'sales' or library use could only be increased to this extent at the expense of standards of service or impossible pressures upon staff.

Much library literature also tends to support the suggestion that librarians must be *continually* engaged in this process of setting and revising targets, and that the staff of each section of a library will meet at very regular intervals to search their conscience and set themselves even more ambitious targets. If this were so, one could visualise staff just walking out, for stopwatch control is alien to librarianship and librarians. What happens in practice is that every librarian is engaged in reconsidering his objectives year after year when he prepares his estimates, and when new plans are considered from time to time during the year (by a committee in the case of the majority of libraries) with a view to inclusion in a programme of development over the next year or thereafter. In terms of capital expenditure very long-term planning of objectives and frequent review is inescapable. (See Chapter 6.)

At the same time in most libraries the *basic* services have been established so long and are so much in demand that there is no question of having to review them annually, but from time to time, perhaps every three or five years, the service should be critically examined (see p 81). This type of survey is sometimes carried out by a local authority in all its departments under the title 'performance review'. Where demand seems to be permanently on the decrease or costs rising excessively it may lead to some curtailment, or to the consideration of new methods. New techniques and new media must also be considered with regard to any possible contribution they might make, changing social circumstances too may make necessary the revision of long-established objectives. The assessment of the individual library's objectives and finances may also becomes necessary in times of economic stress when a cut in the overall budget is announced and a decision is required as to where the cuts are to be made. Reorganisation such as has occurred in educational and public libraries, as has been pointed out, is an ideal opportunity for a reconsideration of objectives and in respect of the individual public library Lowell Martin's survey of objectives for the Chicago public libraries, and the finances required to meet them in a programme spread over a number of years was a perfect example of framing objectives and applying them. The Hillingdon project, too, was an extremely good example of considering objectives from the very starting-point—the user. All these favourable factors apart however we should not lose sight of the fact that little real progress has been made in the evaluation of library services and as a summary prepared by Evans,[28] et al, shows, our present methods leave much to be desired. On the positive side, however, we have the researches into this problem being carried out at Lancaster University by a permanent Library Research Unit. Graham MacKenzie, the former librarian, seems confident that a new methodology for the evaluation of library services is gradually evolving though it may take ten years to mature.[29]

References

1 Board of Education. *Report on public libraries in England and Wales*, Cmd 2868, HMSO, 1927.

2 Ministry of Education. *The structure of the public library service in England and Wales*, HMSO, 1959.

3 Flippo, E. B. *Principles of personnel management*, 2nd ed, N. York, McGraw-Hill, 1966, pp 39–40.

4 Corbett, E. V. *A comparative study of major personnel policies and their background in English and United States large municipal libraries*, University of London, MA thesis, 1970, p 25.

5 Ministry of Education. *Standards of public library service in England and Wales*, HMSO, 1962.

6 Department of Education and Science. *Public Library service points*, HMSO, 1971.

7 Department of Education and Science. *The staffing of public libraries*, 3 vols, HMSO, 1976.

8 Library Association, London and Home Counties Branch. 'Public library aims and objectives', *Lib Ass Rec* 1971, pp 233–4.

9 Sewell, P. H. 'The development of library services: the basis of their planning and assessment, *Journal of Librarianship*, Jan 1970.

10 University of Sheffield. Graduate School of Librarianship, *Library co-operation*, 1975.

11 Gardner, F. M. 'Public library aims and objectives,' *Unesco Bulletin*, July/Aug 1973.

12 Totterdell, B. *The effective library: report of the Hillingdon project*, LA, 1976.

13 Sharr, F. A. 'The public library: Dodo or Phoenix', *Libri*, Vol 24:2, pp 89–101.

14 American Library Assoc. *Minimum standards for public library systems*, 1966.

15 Corbett, E. V. *Op cit*, p 27.

16 Bone, L. E. 'The public library goals and objectives movement', *Library Journal*, 1975, pp 1283–6.

17 De Prospo, E. R. *Performance measures for public libraries*, PLA/ALA, 1973.

18 Martin, L. *Library response to urban change: a study of the Chicago Public Library*, ALA, 1969.

19 *ALA Bulletin*, January 1969, pp 91–2.

20 For details see: Knight, D. M. and Nourse, E. S. *Libraries at large*, New York and London, R. R. Bowker, 1969.

21 IFLA. *Standards for public libraries*, Verlag Dokumentation, Munich, 1973.

22 Mason, D. 'Management techniques applied to the operation of information services', *Aslib Proceedings*, November 1973.

23 Moys, E. M., ed. *Manual of law librarianship*, Deutsch, 1976, p 419.

24 University Grants Committee. *Op cit*, p 1.

25 Assocn of Research Libraries. Office of University Library Management Studies, Washington DC *Goals and objectives*, Occasional Papers No 3, August 1974.

26 Haak, J. R. 'Goal determination', *Library Journal*, 1st May 1971.

27 Stueart, R. D. and Eastlick, J. T. *Library management*, Littleton, Libraries Unlimited Inc, 1977, pp 32–8.

28 Evans, E., *et al*. Review of criteria used to measure library effectiveness, *Bulletin of the Medical Library Association*, 60 (1), January 1972.

29 Mackenzie, A. G. 'Bibliotheconomics; or library science revisited', *In* Shimmon, R., *ed. A reader in library management*, Bingley, 1976.

5

Organisation of the Library System

Objectives and Structure

In theory and in sound management terms, every individual library service, whether it consists of merely one small library, or a comprehensive system of a central library, with a number of branch or departmental libraries radiating from it, should have been planned on basic objectives thoroughly thought out. These objectives, expanded into divisions and sub-divisions, provide a blue-print of the totality of the services required, and the service points through which they are to be provided. Sound management would have then ensured adequate finances for establishing these service points, and the men and materials needed for day-to-day operations. The staff, of course, would be large enough, with the right mix of the professionally qualified and non-professionals, all endowed with maximum intelligence and enthusiasm for their work, and *the perfect library would have resulted.*

Unfortunately, perfect situations seldom occur. One could only reasonably hope for them in circumstances where a completely new library service is being established, let us say a total national library service for one of the developing countries, or, nearer at home, the British Library (but there is no need to pitch the example at national level). Even in these circumstances however the ideal is somewhat illusory: there will probably be a restriction on finance; political objections; and opposing viewpoints requiring compromise. More likely still, physical factors will have to be taken into account such as the impossibility of being able to provide new purpose-planned buildings immediately and, therefore, having to make do with old and unsuitable buildings. Pursuing the example of the British Library, although the concept was new and although the organisation has made remarkably swift and impressive progress in just a few years, no one could say that the setting in which it has to operate even approaches the ideal which the Board would prescribe if it had a perfectly free hand. In the first place its two chief functions are separated by nearly two hundred miles: the Lending Division is at Boston Spa in York-shire and the Reference Division and the central administration are in London. Physical provision at Boston Spa is good as the building there was purpose-planned for the former National Lending Library for Science and Technology and soon after the advent of the former National Central Library to Boston Spa it was able to double its accommodation with the addition of a huge extension which was almost a replica of the original. In London, however, the position is very different. Part of the administration, including the Board's offices and the Copyright Office and the Bibliographic Division, are in the old National Central Library building in Store Street; the Central Administrative Unit is in Sheraton House, Great Chapel Street, and the Reference Division itself still occupies the building of the former British Museum Library and that of the Patents Office Library, indeed the work of this Division is scattered over no less than fourteen buildings.[1] The problems of administering a national reference service from such a scattering of buildings are enormous and cannot be solved until the new building is erected at Euston to house all units of the British Library other than the Lending Division. The ideal administrative pattern cannot be established until the end of the 1980s or later.

The truth is that only a minority of librarians ever enjoy the experience of planning a new library service and seeing it in operation, or for that matter a really large building with all the attention to objectives that this necessitates. Instead the majority inherit a system which has evolved piecemeal over the years and which is handicapped by history to such an extent that even in a working lifetime the opportunity to rectify matters never occurs. All one can do is to persuade the governing body to extend here, improve there, provide a new facility or an additional service point, but one is never able to start all over again. The librarian will try to provide as efficient a service as possible within the limitations imposed upon him, but he will never be able to organise the ideal library service that he was taught about in his student days. It should at the same time be appreciated that the librarian who manages to provide a reasonably good library service under these conditions, and to inspire his staff with a sense of pride and service to the public, whatever the type of library, may be doing a better job, relatively, than the one who is fortunate enough to enjoy a modern and capacious building. It must be clearly understood that while various bodies such as the professional associations, and the Department of Education and Science, continue to prescribe standards for library service and systems, including the spread of service points and the planning of buildings, relatively few organisations can hope to achieve them in their entirety in the foreseeable future, however dedicated they may be to the library concept, or however well-versed in management theory their directors may be; the majority will still have to operate under most unsatisfactory conditions for many years. Indeed, of all the qualities that a librarian needs, perhaps patience is the foremost. The current showpiece of library building, the Birmingham Central Library, which cost over £4·5 million and was opened in 1973, replaced a building which was obsolete even in the 1920s. Plans for a new library were talked about then (and possibly earlier) but the prospects of one being built were remote. By some miracle of improvisation, by re-arrangement here, putting in an extra floor there, converting the old newsroom, and so on, the service was kept going and enjoyed a very high reputation indeed, even though this was at the expense of daily frustration and excessive physical effort on the part of the staff. Ultimately external pressures—the completion of the civic centre and the circulatory traffic system, were primarily responsible for the demolition of the old building and its replacement. However, once it had been agreed that a new library was to be built then management by objectives came into play, and a complete survey of the objectives of a Central Library in the largest provincial city in the country, and how best they could be achieved, became a lengthy business. Regular meetings between the staff and the consultants went on from the end of 1964 until the building was completed.

When we consider library organisation and planning it must be appreciated that this relates not only to new services and new buildings but, in most cases, to a review from time to time of the organisation of library services which have been operating for many years. It should be a general requirement of the governing body of any library for the librarian to review the existing library service every few years and report back. Even if no radical changes are necessary a survey creates general awareness. It can prompt a committee to formulate a proper development programme, which can be revised from year to year, and expressed in terms of capital provision. One of the best examples of a comprehensive review which had outstanding results was that made necessary in each of the new London boroughs as a result of local government reorganisation in 1965. Each of the newly appointed librarians had to review the services of those libraries being amalgamated in his own particular borough. They had to note the types of service points, their location, general distribution, and populations served; staff establishments and their basis and grading standards; the quality and standards of book provision; reference departments; music and records libraries; picture collections; technical services; extension activities; children's libraries; services to the disadvantaged; hours of opening; charges; issue methods; rules and regulations; cataloguing and classification methods; comparable standards of expenditure and of accommodation; local co-operative schemes, and other factors. Some of this work had to be done in the year preceding 1 April 1965, but that which could be safely left till later was done in the early years of the new library service when the library managers were in a position to learn from experience. Without going into any more detail it can be said that within two or three years practically every facet of each of the constituent library services was thoroughly investigated; the different procedures were made uniform where this was advantageous, and plans for the future were conceived. At the end of this period the library staff knew far more about their libraries' strengths and weaknesses than they would ever have known under normal circumstances. What is more, library authorities in London were at that time generally imbued with a desire to carry out the reorganisation in a thoroughly effective manner and to provide the best possible services they could within the finance available. In fact only a few of them were not prepared to spend more if a case for improvement could be justified. As a result the best features of the individual amalgamated library services became, more often than not, the standard for the whole and London's libraries gained enormously from the reorganisation, with much improvement in bookstocks, staffing, special services, the arts, extra-mural services and in additional buildings too, in due course.

When local government reorganisation became effective in the remainder of England and Wales as from 1 April 1974, similar reviews went on all over the country. The problems were generally greater than in London as more often than not urban areas and rural areas had to be combined. The number of authorities amalgamated into each new unit was generally greater than in London, and, there was more disparity in standards. In non-metropolitan counties there was the problem of servicing rural areas. Here again the library staff had to carry out very detailed studies of the services as they were, and decide how best they could be organised to provide a uniformly comprehensive and efficient service. Such surveys inevitably revealed the need for new purpose-planned buildings, more service points at adequate intervals, and levelling up of standards throughout the system. In some cases it also revealed a duplication of services, such as two branch libraries in close proximity, or a superfluity of small or medium reference collections but no large reference library. There were even examples of over-abundance: the new non-metropolitan county of Bedford inherited two large new buildings within a few yards of each other, the Bedfordshire County Library HQ and the Bedford Central Library! No doubt each of the newly appointed librarians drew up his blueprint for the future, but soon after re-organisation the country's economy was depressed, so that although some progress was made in the early stages, far from improving their library service many librarians have been faced with very severe cuts. The lucky ones have been able to maintain the 'status quo', but only exceptionally has real progress been possible.

In the polytechnics too, ideal library provision faces immense physical obstacles, which make it unlikely that many of these colleges will enjoy a perfect library in the foreseeable future. They were created, for the most part, by an amalgamation of a number of different colleges, small in size, catering for different disciplines and each with a limited subject range. In the majority of the polytechnics the teaching still continues through these separate colleges though they have been translated into 'departments'. The individual college library, therefore, still continues to serve the specific needs of each department though usually backed up by central administration and co-ordination.

The terrific demands made on the new polytechnic libraries placed them under immense pressure in building up stocks. In only too many instances the authorities failed to realise just how great this problem was. The funds voted for new books were inadequate and the need for a large increase in staff establishments to process the increased intake of books was underestimated. Rapidly rising book prices also exacerbated the problem, and even today the stocks of many a polytechnic fall far short of the numbers required.

Another important point is that the several college buildings are often scattered over quite a wide area of the local authority so that there is a distinct problem of inter-communication. As David

Bagley has reported 'communication between staff can be a particular problem'.[2] He quotes examples of the North East London Polytechnic which has to operate twelve site libraries, and the constituent colleges of Lanchester and North Staffordshire Polytechnics which are up to twenty miles apart. Ideally the polytechnics need a central campus and some of them have been fortunate enough to get it even, by moving out of the city centre to the suburbs. Many submitted plans for new buildings, and some of them such as Newcastle, Oxford, Sheffield, Hatfield, and Ulster actually moved into their new buildings by the early 1970s. Many more have been caught up in the economic situation and the likelihood of any improved accommodation is remote. Librarians in these circumstances therefore have to operate on a compromise plan with one of the libraries in the group acting as the headquarters housing the central processing section, the librarian and his administrative staff.

In the polytechnics, therefore, there is little scope for the consideration of library objectives divorced from the polytechnic itself. The library is there to serve the staff and students as a whole, the ultimate decision on centralisation will be dependent on the decision of the governors and the local authority as to whether the polytechnic should ultimately be replanned as a single campus (assuming the availability of land and the necessary capital) or whether it should continue to operate from several sites. As library provision is central to the whole purpose of the polytechnic however, the librarian should have a very important rôle to play in future planning. This being so, he must keep himself fully informed of all developments and hints of developments within the whole range of the curricula.

Standards, Norms and Users

Sufficient has been said to illustrate that a library service cannot be established and organised on theoretical management principles alone and that objectives have to be realistic and take into account the organisation of the parent-body, the competing claims of its other departments, the existing library pattern and its past history. However, these qualifications apart, in deciding upon the structure of the library's organisation the librarian and his governing body are almost certain to be largely influenced by official standards and norms.

It is again emphasised that there is a distinct difference between standards offered for guidance with no mandate to enforce them (as

84

most are) and over-riding standards of a different kind which impose financial limits more often than not, such as yardsticks or norms employed by the UGC for university buildings and the DES for buildings of voluntary colleges, as well as the overall cash limits which govern a local authority's endeavours in the field of non-essential capital development.

Most standards are based on those of libraries offering a good standard of service and are therefore, generally agreeable to experienced qualified members of the profession. However, standards must not be set higher than will be accepted by those who have to fund the projects. The librarian should always aim to lead, but never to get too far in advance of what is publicly acceptable. Of the many guidelines issued by official bodies, those of the International Federation of Library Associations in particular, contain a great deal of common-sense in terms of the universal acceptability of standards. For example they say: 'it is unrealistic to seek standards which will have universal validity. The most that can be offered are guidelines based on past experience in communities where circumstances are bound to be different from those in the communities where guidance is needed. . . . It must be expected that the emphasis placed on the various objectives of the service—and the means of achieving these objectives—will be different in different communities, and will change with the passage of time. . . . Levels of provision must be related to *the needs of individual users* because a public library does its work with individuals. The efficiency of a library service will be assessed in terms of what an individual can obtain whether from a mobile library, a branch library or a large city library.'

It is frequently stated nowadays that library administrators know very little about the needs of users; as most users are slow to voice criticisms of the service. They have meekly accepted whatever governing bodies and librarians have decided they should have, and in turn, the providers have decided that as there is little or no criticism, the user must be getting what he wants.

While it is reasonable to accept the censure that little *research* has been carried out into users' needs, nevertheless the user is central to all library provision. For example, in the public library the main objective is to provide for the needs of society as a whole (including both informative and recreational reading). This requirement is further refined by a precise definition of 'society' in the context of each individual library, ie 'persons of all ages who live, or study in the area or work there full-time'. The library has to provide material suitable to the needs of most trades and professions, to all kinds of academic and vocational courses, and to all standards of literacy and intelligence, as it is catering for 30 to 40 per cent of the population, if all its facilities are taken into consideration.

In contrast the librarian of a special library has a captive clientele with a restricted interest. Though the special library has to offer a service in greater depth than does the public library and anticipate rather than wait for demand to materialise, its subject fields are restricted generally to the areas relevant to the firm's or association's purpose. The librarian has only a relatively small number of users for whom to cater, but these few have demanding requirements. The university librarian too has well-defined groups to serve (see p 72). With under-graduates the area of demand is clear-cut, the most pressing problem being how many copies of a book shall be supplied rather than which books. The greatest difficulty is in catering for research workers, though the guidance of academic staff is always available. The variety of subjects researched seems limitless so that not only is a thorough service essential, but also the ability to supply the required resource material from the library's own stock, or via inter-lending, within a reasonably short space of time. No matter how good the library's stock no one library can provide everything. The librarian of the polytechnic has a more difficult rôle to play for although the demands upon his library are limited to students at various levels studying through the many courses provided by the polytechnic, *it is the very number of courses, their various levels, and the numbers of full and part-time students for whom he has to provide that constitute his major problem.* Polytechnics may not have as many research workers to cater for as the university, but they do provide courses for higher degrees and the academic staff will expect to find that the library meets most of their needs. Nationally too, users' needs come first. Both the Lending and Reference Divisions of the British Library have last resort functions and both have to provide a wealth of foreign as well as British material; the Reference Division also has a responsibility for the conservation of the nation's literary heritage. Each Division has to cater for a multitude of specialist and research workers from within the UK and overseas, and the needs of the user dominate the planning of the libraries' organisation.

PUBLIC LIBRARIES

A glance at any one large library system will readily demonstrate how the user in his geographical setting determines the actual structure of the organisation of the system as a whole. Take a London borough with a population of 300,000 for example. We first note that it is made up of anything between two and five formerly independent authorities which were amalgamated under London government reorganisation. The new authority may have a distinct centre which is the chief shopping and communication centre, and it may have a Town Hall in this centre which previously belonged to one of the amalgamated authorities and which has now been established as *the* Town Hall for the new London borough. The former Central Library in the near vicinity may have been large enough to have been designated to act in a similar capacity in the new library system. On the other hand, it could be that the new borough has no natural centre as it has been artificially created and therefore the former central libraries will have continued to give a service similar to that given previously though facilities and regulations will have been made uniform, geared to the standards of the best of those found in any of the constituent libraries of the new borough. They will probably have been reclassified as district libraries. It may be that it has not been thought appropriate to designate any one of them as a central library, instead the librarian and his administrative support staff, including the bibliographical services section and other specialists, may have been sited in offices in one of the district libraries, or in accommodation in the town hall or elsewhere.

Between them, the central library or the central administration, and the district libraries will provide a full range of library services to satisfy users with a need for advanced material as well as the recreational, popular and fairly elementary. They will include reference and lending stock up to graduate level and beyond, music and records, technical literature, children's services, the borough pool stock, audio visual aids, cultural activities and other special facilities. Each district library will serve the more demanding requirements of a large spread of population within a radius of two or more miles of the library, as well as the general needs of the immediate locality. Then within each district catchment area there will be three, four, or more branch libraries with a more popular stock adequate to the every day needs of those living within a mile radius. The children's library will be a very important feature of the branch and so will facilities for community functions. In other words the branch library will be designed to meet the recreational needs and more general requirements for information, rather than those for specialist literature, comprehensive reference work and prolonged study and research. While the branch library might be serving populations ranging from about 10,000 to 15,000 or perhaps more, the District Library might be meeting the more demanding requirements of from 50,000 to 100,000 people. Good transport services to the district libraries are to be expected as these would be situated in focal centres of the borough. It is possible in some boroughs there may be smaller branches in isolated pockets of the borough which may operate perhaps for no more than 30 hours a week.

From the administrative point of view the branches look to the district library for staff relief, perhaps the entire staffing; supplementation of bookstock; reference enquiry work other than the relatively simple; major matters of discipline; the arrangement of staff management and book selection meetings; inspection; control of wages sheets for manual and weekly paid staff; and any other aspect of the work which is decentralised. The borough probably operates a mobile library service with two or three mobiles serving the more remote parts of the borough where a small branch would not be justified, and possibly some schools. In addition there may be a service to Housebound Readers and to Old People's Homes operated by a small van delivery service, each van being in the charge of a qualified librarian. Mobile services may all operate from the central library or alternatively be based on district libraries.

Thus whatever criticism might be made of lack of consumer research in the public library area, it can be readily seen that the whole pattern of its organisation is to place a library within reach of all able-bodied residents, and to ensure that those who are unable to visit the library are not overlooked. This principle applies whatever the status of the local library authority and in non-metropolitan county areas the county is also divided up into districts or regions, though these will cover a much larger area than in urban authorities. Here again the local services are supported from the central administration provided by the headquarters. Each region or district has its full-time and part-time series of branch libraries looking to the regional library in the first instance for the specialist services and beyond that to headquarters. Mobile libraries are used extensively to take a service to outlying communities and schools. The interlending system is available to all either through enquiry at a service point or by telephone, and information can always be obtained in similar fashion. The public library, in its concern for the user, even remembers to cater for the inmates of prisons and detention centres with the support of a *per capita* grant from the Home Office strongly reinforced by library funds. It can be very few people indeed who *cannot* make use of the public library.

Apart from user needs, library standards on basic organisation also relate to the provision of different kinds of service points within a local authority area, such as we have just demonstrated. In 1960 The Library Association issued guidelines[3] on the structure of public library services, as did the Bourdillon Report of 1962, paras. 98–106.[4] Both of these have been out-dated by events. The IFLA standards[5] published in 1973 are more up-to-date but they were drawn up to cover all countries and all types of unit. INTAMEL (International Association of Metropolitan Libraries) has published standards for library services in cities with populations of 400,000 or more, and the ALA has issued its own standards[6] for public library systems. All of these provide useful background reading but in the UK the most up-to-date guide to the organisational structure is to be found in the report issued by the two Advisory Councils in 1971.[7] Among other recommendations this advises that:

> service points should not be more than 1 mile radius from any reader;
> populations of 4,000 plus, in communities with a natural centre should have a library open not less than 30 hours per week;
> between 1,000 and 4,000 there should be a library open between 10 and 30 hours per week;
> below this level a mobile should serve communities at least once a fortnight;
> the central library or HQ should be the administrative centre but some decentralisation might be advisable in larger authorities;
> district libraries should be provided for focal shopping areas with populations of about 25,000 and they should offer a full range of facilities and be open 60 hours per week;
> branch libraries in urban areas should be located near to shops;
> housing estates may need libraries and special consideration should be given to the need of part-time branches in rural areas.

It will be noted that the basic organisation follows that already illustrated for a London borough, the major difference being the population figures quoted for District and Branch Libraries. This is due to the dense concentration of population in London. It is also uneconomical to provide small branch libraries, and they can only be justified where the public would otherwise have a long journey to a library, as in rural areas and some suburbs of larger towns.

ACADEMIC LIBRARIES

In universities, with the notable exceptions of Oxford, Cambridge, and London, *the principle of one main library* is the norm. However, in some universities a degree of decentralisation has taken place if there is need for a library in a department or faculty which has moved away from the main campus. A departmental library may have originated through a gift of books or money given on condition that it is employed for library collections within the department to which it was given. Another cause, advanced by the Parry Committee is a department which has moved into a new building, and where a library has been established with the assistance of the UGC. Institutes of Education have also grown up with their own libraries. It is also a regular practice for academics to build up their own small collections of books specifically related to their courses, on the grounds that they are working tools for their students and must therefore be in close proximity. So long as the collections remain small and are under the librarian's control this practice is condoned. However, quite naturally, university librarians are zealous in conserving their book-funds and anxious to ensure that the provision of even small departmental collections does not materially affect the library's own buying power. The Parry Committee[8] went to great lengths to study this problem from both points of view. It supported the case for departmental libraries so long as they were under the control of the university librarian and were entered in the union catalogue. It maintained that departmental collections should contain no unique material, and that expenditure on them should in no way affect university acquisition policy. (In London University the depository at Egham for reserve collections, available to all the constituent institutions, is another kind of decentralisation.)

In April 1976, to the alarm of many university librarians, the Atkinson Report of a working party set up by the UGC was published.[9] This working party was established early in 1975 under the chairmanship of Professor R. Atkinson when it became apparent to the UGC that there would not be enough money available, either in the short or the long-term, for new university library buildings and extensions of existing buildings on a scale sufficient to house the ever-increasing numbers of books. In fact there was grave doubt as to the advisability of even attempting to do so. As an alternative the report advocated the principle of the 'self-renewing library of limited growth', by which additions to stock would be counter-balanced to a large extent by withdrawals and the deposit of little used material in local book-stores and at the British Library Lending Division. This policy was accepted by the UGC on a provisional basis, to be reviewed after two or three years' experience.[10]

The report is particularly important in the light of this chapter for *it illustrates the effects of standards imposed from without*, standards which, right or wrong in themselves, commit librarians to a principle of organisation opposed to their own professionally conceived views. Basically, the working party had a function to decide on new norms on which the UGC could determine the needs of universities for library space provision. (The norms then in operation are printed in Annexe C of the report.) The working party proceeded in accordance with the following guidelines:

(a) What was a reasonable minimum provision of shelving (excluding special collections) for the self-renewing library of a university of given size, assuming no major change in current library techniques?

(b) What provision should be made for future growth?

(c) Having regard to other factors which might affect space requirements, in particular: possible increase in the use of compact storage, of microfilm, and of unconventional methods of publication; possible development of inter-library lending; possible further development of local library co-operation; and, provision for special responsibilities.

(d) The position with regard to special collections.

(e) Methods of selecting books for withdrawal.

(f) The advantages and disadvantages of different types of reserve storage, in particular: closed-access compact storage within the library; a local store used by one institution; a local store used by several institutions; a regional store; and a central national store.

(g) The appropriate scale on which provision for stores should be made.

(h) The requirements for reader places.

As a result of their deliberations the working party arrived at new norms for library space per student, for net growth of accessions, and for reserve storage accommodation, which would entail a very severe re-appraisal of university library acquisition, withdrawal, and storage policies. The preface to the report disclaims any intention to use the norm as 'a blunt instrument in assessing particular library projects which a university may put forward for inclusion in a building programme'. It states that it would be used as a starting point in assessment from which special circumstances would then come into play, subject to their being substantiated. The very existence of such a plan, however, once more demonstrates the fallacy of the theory that librarians are *free* to draw up their own objectives and plans for development.

The organisation of the polytechnic library and libraries of colleges, as already demonstrated, is dependent in the first instance on the physical lay-out of the parent organisation but in addition the DES has established recommended norms for library space in polytechnics and advisory guidance for local authority college libraries. Cost limits are likely to make it impossible to depart from them to any great extent in any event.

The recent policy of merging some colleges of education with others to form institutes of higher education with a wider range of degree courses in particular, will ultimately affect the organisation and physical structure of these library systems, so that once more it is apparent that the librarians are not masters of their own objectives.

SPECIAL LIBRARIES

The vast majority of special libraries will have no problem of structural organisation and pre-conceived standards because most are small and operate within the confines of a single department which can be divided if necessary to provide separate space for the main stock, the periodicals, staff employed on bibliographic work, technical processes, translations, and administration. A central accessible position is, however, very desirable. Only in the major industries will the provision of branch libraries arise, and here there is no problem for the libraries must be attached to the branch works in different parts of the country. In the case of international organisations the branch libraries will be abroad, and run by nationals, so arrangement must be made for liaison and co-operation between all of them and the main one in the UK.

Subject Department Organisation

Apart from the basic organisation of the library service into different kinds of service points further decisions have to be made by the management about the divisions which might be necessary within the library buildings. This may well be unnecessary in many small libraries such as one-room college libraries, society and professional association libraries, and branches of public libraries. In very large district libraries and central and headquarters' libraries, and large academic libraries, the problem arises as to whether to divide the library into separate functional departments, eg lending; reference; periodicals; audio-visual aids; etc; or whether to bring together all types of material and arrange it on a subject department basis. As many new university libraries have been built in the last ten years or so (and a number of new polytechnics, too), it is in these libraries that the purpose-built subject department library is mainly to be found. Arrangement by subject departments is common in public libraries of the large cities of the United States, (eg: Queensborough, New York; Rochester; Washington, DC) it is rare in British public libraries, and for years the only example was the Liverpool Central Library where re-building after war damage made this possible (though not, perhaps, to the same specification as would have been possible in a completely new building). In fact it was not until 1967, with the opening of the new Bradford Central Library building, that the UK could boast a public library building deliberately planned on a subject department basis. Then, in 1973, when the new Birmingham Central Library was opened, its Reference Library was planned on this principle. Two years later, in 1975, there followed another in the London Borough of Sutton which integrated all types of adult library material into its subject departmentalised new central library.

The principle of subject department arrangement is one that has aroused considerable discussion and diversity of opinion in this country. There is also a certain looseness in the way in which the term 'subject department principle' is defined. The most precise definition is given by S. G. Berriman in *Library Buildings, 1967–1968*,[11] where in describing the Bradford Central Library, he says: 'The library is unique in that it is the first public library in this country to be specifically designed on the subject department principle whereby *all* books, periodicals and other material on a particular subject, whether for home-reading or for reference use, are housed in the same department, with its own specialist staff and with full study facilities.' In other words it is a complete break away from the traditional functional arrangement of adult libraries.

The underlying advantage of the subject department principle is that users can find in one place everything relating to the subject in which they are interested, and that they see the total resources of the library in their subject in this one place. Some of this would most likely be overlooked if kept in functional departments such as reference, periodicals, etc. The theory is excellent if it can be assumed that most library users are students and specialists (hence the case for the academic library) and that their speciality is, as it were, contained in a watertight compartment and does not overflow into some other field which is catered for in one of the other subject departments. To use 'Librarianship' as a simple example, is it possible to study librarianship without recourse at times to books on management in general, local and central government, finance, architecture, social science, psychology and many other subjects? If not, is the reader to be compelled to go to one subject department after another or is the difficulty to be surmounted by extensive duplication of stock? In the latter event how much extra money will the library need to pursue such a policy? Obviously everything cannot be duplicated so where is the line to be drawn? Where reference and lending copies of books are shelved together, although this certainly has the advantage of showing the user the total book resources, it can be very frustrating to find that having laid one's hands on a much desired book it cannot be taken out of the library because it happens to be the reference copy. Does this lead to bad feeling, or worse still, to illegal borrowing? Again, is it really convenient to divide *all* non-book material by subject and is this the way most people would want to use it? For example, how many periodicals confine themselves to a single subject; and how many have a wide-ranging content; and do back numbers involve other considerations such as consultations of microtexts? Do photocopying facilities have to be provided on every floor? Is it more logical to keep together all audio-visual material, and more important, what are the user requirements for equipment? Microtexts are purchased mainly for back files of newspapers and periodicals and need readers and reader-printers. If the material is distributed over several departments is the equipment to be duplicated and sited in every such department? Failing this is there to be one room housing the viewing equipment to which the user has to proceed after he has selected his microtext in the relevant subject department? Similarly with films, tapes, cassettes, records, etc, how are these to be related to projectors, tape recorders, listening apparatus, and so on? It can be a costly business if provision, wiring and sound insulation have to be incorporated into several departments; is it a problem best solved by confining all audio-visual material to one department?

Access to, and control of, the subject department library also has its difficulties. Although it is possible to have independent control on each floor, or for each department too for that matter, it is very expensive in terms of staffing, so that the generally adopted principle is for a single control area at ground floor level. This certainly makes for economy in staffing and facilitates the employment of electronic devices or uniformed patrols as is common practice in the United States, but it also means that all books are returned at this one point where they have to be sorted and returned in due course to the right department, which is time consuming, and involves the employment of additional staff.

Then again there is the problem of bibliographies, abstracts, indexes, catalogues, and general quick-reference information. Where are these services to be provided? Are they to be at entrance level along with the control desk where registration and simple information services would operate; or are they to be separated on a subject basis? A third option of course is duplication. In the case of general bibliographies this would be necessary, abstracts would presumably go alongside the appropriate periodicals so far as they could, but again some duplication would be necessary. Library catalogues present a more formidable problem for one can scarcely duplicate card catalogues for each and every department on a complete author and subject basis. The complete union catalogue would only be found at entrance level with a separate author catalogue in each department covering its own stock. The answer lies with computerised cataloguing and microfilm or microfiche catalogues (COM), together with the necessary readers in each department.

Shelf accommodation might also create something of a problem for it is not possible to forecast the rate of additions in given subject fields over a period of years with any great accuracy. Thus the shelving in one department might be completely filled while there was considerable spare space in others. If a stack provides reserve accommodation parallel to each subject department then the problem would be further accentuated.

One of the major advantages of the subject department principle is that it promotes the employment of staff, with the necessary subject background, to act as subject specialists. It is argued that it is impossible for staff in large libraries to find the answer to a multiplicity of questions on a multiplicity of subjects or to be well-versed in the literature of all subjects. This argument is a sound one and it is very true regardless of whether the library is arranged on a subject department basis or not. In research libraries in particular it is desirable that the staff collectively should have a wide range of subject interests, hence the policy in so many academic libraries of appointing graduates for the advantage of their training in specific fields and their acquaintance with part of its literature at least. A similar practice is to be found in many special libraries so that it is logical to extend the practice to any subject department library. Such staff would be expected to take over a much wider rôle than merely answering enquiries, they would have to liaise regularly with their public, keep themselves fully informed of the literature of the subject and new publications, deal with all suggestions for additions, and decide on purchase or borrowing where there is an alternative, possibly catalogue and classify the stock, prepare abstracts as necessary, maintain current awareness files, prepare book lists and other publicity, and generally supervise the department. In academic libraries they would be the link between the academic staff and the library, they would consult them with regard to book selection in particular, keep a record of the amount spent by the respective department and help avoid underspending or over-commitment. If they do the work thoroughly they should also be rendering the library a good service in the realm of public relations.

Apart from the value of the subject department principle to serious users of the library, the practice makes the librarian's work far more interesting and rewarding because of this relationship which he builds up with his clients; it encourages personal interests. The extent to which all the above duties are performed by the subject specialist in any one library will vary but it also helps in the division of staff into professional and non-professional with the advantage of being able to create a better career grade in the latter because much more of the purely administrative work is taken away from the subject specialist and made the responsibility of the non-professionals. The practice also has possible disadvantages: If the library is open from

9 am to 10 pm, how many subject specialists are going to be employed and will there always be one on duty? If so, then this will be very expensive, if not, what kind of service is going to be provided when the subject specialist is off duty; and what happens during periods of leave and sickness? There is also a danger of divided responsibility and delay through decision-making being invested in too many hands as distinct from a hierarchical establishment where each functional department has its prescribed responsibilities and acts without a great deal of prior consultation.

The subject department arrangement is most successful in university libraries and many new buildings of this category have been built with this purpose in mind though they probably do not go so far in integration as Berriman's definition presupposes. In these libraries, however, the division of stock into reference and lending has never been much of a problem as most of the printed material except for periodicals, special collections, rare material and definite quick-reference works, has always been available for lending. Reference collections have in the main been confined to quick-reference material and duplicate copies of books in great demand which latter are incorporated in the short-loan collection. Thus subject departments are the norm, though it is very likely that not all such departments will have periodicals displayed there. Where the periodicals have a specific subject field such as in science and technology they may be with the subject department but in the humanities they cover such a wide field that they are best displayed in a separate periodicals room together with the appropriate abstracts, and microtexts and sufficient reading equipment; sometimes current periodicals are housed in a separate room from back files. The remaining audio-visual aids would then be housed in a separate, relatively small room which has been purpose-built and has all the necessary equipment. The room may well be planned off the entrance area and within the supervision of the staff at the circulation desk. Again, while the subject specialists may have the responsibility for book selection and control of the book allocation within their subject field, the remainder of the acquisition and processing operations may be done by the acquisitions and cataloguing departments. James Thompson[12] has given a useful summary of the pros and cons of the subject department arrangement in university libraries and its varying applications.

The arrangement of public libraries on a subject department basis is far more debateable. In the case of a huge reference library such as that at Birmingham there can be little argument for it is even more of a research library than that of the average university—it is the research library for the whole of the Midlands. On the other hand, if we think of public libraries which amalgamate lending and reference stock, together with periodicals and all other types of material into a series of subject departments, ie libraries which conform to Berriman's definition, the case is less easy to support unless it can be said that the majority of the users are students. This would not be true of any public library. How satisfactory then is the subject department arrangement to the average user of such libraries? We have to remember that both Bradford and Sutton made some special concession to the general reader, the former with a 'popular library', the latter with a 'fiction and literature department'. Such a concession apart, the general reader—the one whose reading is not geared to one broad subject must have to proceed from floor to floor to indulge his general interests; some of his books may be on one floor and some on another. He first has to decide how they would be classified before he commences his search, or alternatively be constantly using the catalogue. He will find the whole process tiring and frustrating and the elderly will find it too much. If this kind of library is thought to be necessary then the authority must be prepared to provide a strong general lending library rather than just a collection of recreational reading. It would require duplication of stock to a large extent and would therefore be expensive. Staffing of subject department libraries in public libraries of this kind is also an expensive proposition. What W. Tynemouth[13] had to say in 1965 about the planning of the Newcastle upon Tyne Central Library still seems relevant: 'The possibility of subject departments was seriously considered and rejected because a city of Newcastle's size would be unable to produce a budget necessary to meet the additional duplicate stock and the additional staff required by separate departments.' Even thirteen years later the decision appears sound.

References

1   Richnell, D. 'The British Library Reference Division', Saunders, W. L., ed. *British librarianship today*, LA, 1976, p 49.
2   Bagley, D. 'Polytechnic libraries', Saunders, W. L. *British librarianship today*, LA, 1976.
3   LA. *Public library buildings: the way ahead*, 1960.

4 Ministry of Education. *Standards of public library service in England and Wales*, HMSO, 1962.
5 IFLA. *Standards for public libraries*, Verlag Dokumentation, Munich, 1973.
6 ALA. *Minimum standards for public library systems*, Chicago, 1967.
7 DES. *Public library service points*, HMSO, 1971.
8 UGC *Report of the committee on libraries*, HMSO, 1967, paras 358–396.
9 UGC. *Capital provision for university libraries*, HMSO, 1976.
10 The UGC set up a steering committee in connection with this and library research generally.
11 Berriman, S. G., ed. *Library buildings, 1967–1968*, LA, 1969.
12 Thompson, J. *Introduction to university library administration*, 2nd ed, Bingley, 1974.
13 Tynemouth, W. A. *Library buildings*, 1965, LA, 1966, p 17.

6

Finance—Estimates

Adequate finance is vital for the satisfactory running of any kind of library. No matter how perfect the system of organisation and its management, and no matter how efficient and well-qualified the staff, the fundamental requirement of a really satisfactory service is an income sufficient to operate and maintain the service to an approved standard. To this end, therefore, to varying degrees, all librarians and their governing bodies are involved in estimating the running costs of the library (normally for one year ahead), and then deciding on the extent to which these requirements can be met. Failing the ability to match estimates of expenditure with the desired income, the governing body has to take decisions, sometimes quite drastic and unpleasant, on economies which must be effected and the extent to which library services may have to be reduced. Merely to dictate cuts without taking responsibility for the curtailment of services and for informing the library's public of the reasons is an abrogation of management responsibility. It is also distasteful for the library staff which is thereby left to answer all the criticisms.

The estimating process also includes in many cases not only estimates for regular expenditure on the day to day operations of a library (called 'regular' or 'recurrent' expenditure) but also those for large expenditure for capital purposes, ie for the purchase of land for building purposes, for building new libraries or extensions, for the purchase of expensive equipment such as a mini-computer, for furniture and fittings for new libraries, and in some cases for the purchase of the initial bookstock of the latter. This type of estimate is usually referred to as 'capital' or 'non-reccurrent'.

The majority of libraries function on public money supplied either from central or local government funds. In the former category we have national and university libraries, and in the latter, public, polytechnic, college and school libraries though these are all heavily subsidised from the Rate Support Grant. Even the voluntary colleges receive very large sums from the central government. Where public funds are being spent it is axiomatic that the utmost regard must be paid to the *need* for expenditure before providing the funds, that there is no waste, that prices paid are highly competitive, and that there is a system of scrupulous accountancy (see also Chapter 7).

Outside the range of libraries supported by public funds there are those in the fields of industry and commerce, and of societies and professional associations. In the former it is the firm's money which is at stake, which will be reluctant to spend any money which cannot be seen to be to the ultimate benefit of the firm and its shareholders. The library and information service will therefore be judged strictly on its results, and estimates will be geared to them. At the level of society and association libraries where available funds will depend almost entirely on members' subscriptions, then the submission of estimates and a tight rein on expenditure will be even more necessary though the size of the problem is relatively slight.

Thus, although there are obvious differences in the methods of authorising and allocating funds for different types of library they have very much in common. To deal with them all in detail requires a book in itself but the main principles will be explained. The public library, being part of local government, is the one which is most closely controlled by law and precedent, so it is inevitably the primary example throughout this chapter, and in the next which deals with accountancy, but the major differences in other types of library will be noted.

In national, public, polytechnic, and university libraries estimating is a very long-drawn-out procedure which involves considerable discussion between the librarian and his administrative staff and the finance officers of the parent organisation as well as various committee stages. The estimates of local authorities and government-controlled libraries cover the period April to March, but in the university the financial year runs from 1 August to 31 July. Firms and societies are more likely to operate on a calendar year basis.

REVENUE ESTIMATES—PUBLIC LIBRARIES[1]

There is a considerable degree of formality in the preparation of local authority annual revenue estimates (and in those of the central government, too). They are presented in a manner which has been evolved by finance officers over the years and which is approved by the Chartered Institute of Public Finance and Accountancy. Thus, the revenue estimates are prepared under certain headings of expenditure such as 'books and allied materials'; 'salaries and wages'; and 'upkeep of buildings'; each of which is further sub-divided. Initial work on the estimates usually begins in November but in recent years the finance officers have done an immense amount of preparatory work on the local authority's estimates as a whole so that when the rate support grant is announced they have a very shrewd idea of just how much each individual committee can spend. Thus, by the time November comes the staff of the finance department will be able to tell the librarian what the council's policy is likely to be. It is no use setting targets high if the money will not be available. Against the headings of expenditure the estimates are drawn up in four columns, of these the first is for the estimates of the coming year, the second for the original estimates of the current year, the third for current estimates revised in the light of spending to-date, and the fourth for the actual expenditure of the year before. These four columns provide a comparative year by year guide, but they are not so meaningful to-day when inflation automatically increases each year; the finance officer will have to equate the figures in his accompanying report to a common standard. Income is estimated as well as expenditure but this a very simple matter.

Revenue estimates are prepared in conjunction with a senior member of the finance department but the advice of other council officers may also be required for certain items eg the architect for repairs and maintenance, the central purchasing officer for furniture and equipment, and the public relations officer for publicity material, exhibitions, etc. The librarian must also keep himself fully informed on prices, and anticipated increases in prices of items which he buys directly such as books, periodicals, microtexts and binding. In preparing estimates nowadays it is most important to include an element for inflation. This is not usually left just to the librarian's discretion. The finance department, which is engaged in preparing the estimates for all the other council departments will most likely have decided its own figures for inflation; in some cases there may be a little guesswork involved eg for furniture and fittings, uniforms, printing and stationery, but for the most part they have a fairly accurate assessment to guide them: salaries and wages will already have been dictated by talks between the government, the TUC and the CBI; public service charges will also probably have been announced well in advance, as will changes in National Insurance and fuel. It is in the field of books and periodicals, and binding, that the most uncertainty arises. Binding prices depend on materials and labour, and increases may not be definite before April; but most bookbinders will have a good idea of increases in the pipeline and can give the librarian a fairly accurate assessment. On the other hand increases in books depend upon the type of books published, the policies of dozens of publishers, the price of paper, printers' and bookbinders' wages, and other factors. Librarians rely to a great extent on figures published by The Library Association or *The Bookseller* but they are retrospective and cover prices generally, rather than what a library actually purchases. Perhaps the best way is for the library to keep its own record, year by year, of the numbers of books bought in various categories and the prices, eg new reference, new adult lending non-fiction, and similarly for fiction, new children's books, new picture books, and again all these categories in respect of replacements. If the costs for each category are totalled up and divided by the respective total numbers of copies bought then an average price per volume can be arrived at each year from which can be seen the average price increases year by year. Better still if these figures can be totalled and worked out every three months, then it can be arranged that the library estimates be increased each quarter in line with inflation over the corresponding quarter of the previous year. This method presumes agreement with the finance department and that the director of finance has a system of allocating inflationary charges of this type of material to an overall contingencies fund which he controls. From personal experience it works well, though of course it is not perfect as it assumes that the number of books bought in each category remains much the same each year. Periodicals are perhaps still harder to forecast as they often seem to increase in price almost unannounced, and if the library takes many foreign periodicals; fluctuations in exchange rates complicate the situation still further. The best steps are to keep a close watch all the year round for any announcements of price increases, make allowances for postal increases and exchange rate alterations, ask the advice of one's agent, and substantiate a case on as much information as is available. Above all it is important to carry out a survey of periodical use just prior to estimate time so that little used periodicals can be considered for deletion from the list.

The day has long since passed when a librarian used to adopt a principle of asking for something more than he needed so that he could do a modest amount of empire-building during the year; it is expected that estimates should be reasonably reliable in view of the circumstances existing at the time. They should, theoretically, not result in overspending or underspending. This means that a librarian has virtually no scope for getting his authority to indulge in any expenditure over and above that contained in the estimate. Any new form of revenue expenditure, that is additional to that of the previous year, must be approved in the year preceding the estimate so that due consideration can be given to the amount required, not only by the library committee which proposes it but also by the policy and resources committee or its equivalent. Where approval is given then the item can be included in the following year's estimate. Alternatively minor new expenditures can be made by reduction on some item in the estimates. Agreement to these is usually reached at a meeting of the library committee and noted by the finance officer for alteration in the next year's estimate. Where *capital* expenditure has been agreed by the council for the next year's estimates then the revenue estimates must also provide for any resultant monetary requirement such as salaries and wages, upkeep of buildings, loan charges and materials, eg a new branch library being built and due to be opened during the ensuing year. So far as building maintenance is concerned it is usual for this to be the responsibility of the director of technical services who estimates each year for the requirements, in terms of maintenance, of all the local authority's buildings. This covers painting and decoration and repairs. It often covers minor works too, such as conversions and adaptations within a building, that might only cost three or four thousand pounds. However, the director's funds will not be elastic and he will have to decide an order of priorities so that once more it probably becomes necessary to get the library committee to approve such schemes well in advance of estimate time. If necessary, at a later date some order of priority may have to be established.

When the estimates are drawn up in their final form it is usual to give a vote number against each item such as V1, V2, V3. This is used for accountancy purposes and has to be quoted on all official orders and accounts so that the expenditure can be coded to the relevant vote and thus ensure that the estimate is not exceeded. Regular computer print-outs of expenditure from the finance department to the librarian are made quoting the vote number and title. If the librarian has a balance under one vote which he knows he will not be going to spend and is urgently in need of some other item not provided in the estimates this can often be bought nowadays by transfer from one vote to the other, with the necessary permission, though the amounts are not likely to be very large. This practice used to be frowned upon as being *ultra vires* but finance officers seem to be more tolerant now. If the amount were to run into a few thousand pounds they might want the committee's approval first and in any event they would expect some kind of link between the substance of the proposed new expenditure and the original, eg permission might be given to use money provided for gramophone records, on musical scores, or money for buying furniture being spent on a microfilm reader, but nothing so radically different as employing money saved on salaries to buy more books.

When the expenditure side of the estimates has been agreed with the finance department, the estimated income from fees, etc is deducted from the total to arrive at the amount required from the rate fund. The next step will be to process the estimates through committees and council but it is probable that before this the chairman of the library committee will first see them and be asked for any comment. He will know of his political party's general rate policy for the coming year. It may be to keep expenditure down to a minimum (especially if an election is in the offing) or to keep the rate static, or better still to permit a certain level of expansion. The director of finance will also have a good idea of the council's general policy as distinct from libraries in particular, and the member of his staff who has been advising the librarian on the estimates will already have made this clear to the librarian while the two of them have been working together. It would be useless to be trying to advance a case for more money if the council's general policy were to keep the rates static.

After the chairman has seen the estimates they go forward to the library committee in about January where they may be amended, either upwards or downwards. While on this point it is as well to demolish the line of thought so persistent among students that library committees invariably reduce estimates. Indeed, to judge by some examination scripts the committee takes a fiendish delight in making cuts and thereby frustrating the librarian's plans! This is far from being the case, left to themselves committee members are more likely to propose increases, but if the majority party as a whole has agreed that no committee's estimates are to increase beyond x per cent of the previous year's figure, they will naturally have to look for some savings should the estimates presented to them exceed this. Even so, if they consider that in the case of their particular committee it would be unwise (the word 'unwise' has been deliberately chosen rather than 'impossible') to reduce the budget figures then the committee members would fight to maintain it to the best of their ability. Having passed through the library committee the estimates will then proceed to the policy and resources, or finance committee (we shall use the latter title henceforth as a matter of convenience). This committee may set up a small sub-committee to examine the estimates of all spending committees; it may or may not suggest amendments. The finalised recommendations would not be made until the director of finance knew what the Rate Support Grant was to bring in and what the demands of the precepting authorities were, ie the county council, the water board, and possibly the police. He would also have to estimate a revised income from the penny rate and to know what the estimated balances were likely to be at the end of the current year. Other factors also enter into these final calculations such as allowances for rate rebates, the cost of collection, and anticipated losses. Armed with all this information the sub-committee will then be able to put a paper to the full finance committee giving the complete picture and showing what rate will have to be levied to produce a certain working balance for the coming year. (It will probably give two or three suggestions based on different working balances and the finance committee will then make its decision.) This committee could, of course, amend the estimates even at this late stage but is unlikely to do so after the financial situation has been so thoroughly investigated by the sub-committee. Finally, the estimates having been approved by the finance committee, and a recommended rate in the pound agreed, a proposal to this effect will go to the council in late February or March. Even at this stage amendments to the budget could be made and the minority party is likely to make some such proposition, but it is very unusual nowadays for a council to make alterations. A typical example of a library estimate is given on facing page.

Rates and Rateable Value. For a proper understanding of public library estimates it is necessary to have some concept of the way rates are raised, who pays them and which authorities collect them. *Rates are collected by district councils, The City of London, and the London borough councils. The district councils collect the amounts required in rates by the county councils also, and the London borough councils for the*

LIBRARIES COMMITTEE
Estimates for the year ending 31 March 1977

	Estimate 1976/7 £	Estimate 1975/6 £	Estimate 1975/6 Revised £	Actual 1974/5 £
EXPENDITURE				
Employees:				
Salaries	268,800	249,500	248,250	230,108
Wages	28,500	24,250	24,750	22,306
Premises:				
Maintenance	27,250	25,300	22,450	20,574
Heating, lighting, cleaning	17,500	16,200	17,050	15,215
Furniture and Fittings	4,500	3,500	3,050	2,518
Rents and Rates	17,900	15,275	15,025	13,200
Debt charges	55,275	40,575	40,575	27,250
Supplies and Services:				
Books, binding, jackets	135,250	120,500	118,500	110,000
Records	20,000	18,750	18,600	15,375
Periodicals	5,250	4,750	5,100	4,225
Printing, Stationery	12,250	10,500	11,250	9,567
Postage	2,500	2,000	2,250	1,875
Telephones	3,400	3,000	2,850	2,489
Miscellaneous:				
Travelling and Subsistence	500	450	425	419
Conferences	75	70	45	58
Insurance	750	675	675	650
Subscriptions	2,150	1,850	2,050	1,755
Cultural Activities	1,750	1,650	1,600	1,580
Central Establishment	10,450	9,450	9,755	8,650
Total Expenditure	614,050	548,245	544,250	487,814
INCOME				
Fees and Fines	18,750	15,300	16,800	14,256
Letting of Rooms	575	400	450	359
Sale of Publications	1,250	1,000	1,100	795
Total Income	20,575	16,700	18,350	15,410
Total Net Expenditure	593,475	531,545	525,900	472,404

Greater London Council. In addition the twelve inner London boroughs, which are not education authorities, collect the amounts required by the Inner London Education Authority. In some cases the rate collecting authority also has to levy the amount required by the police and water boards.* Where the rate collecting authorities raise these amounts on behalf of these other authorities the sums raised are called 'precepts' and the authority on whose behalf they are collected are called 'precepting authorities'.

Rates are levied on the owners of property within the relevant local government area, the charge being based on an assessment or 'rateable value' placed on all property by the valuation officers of the Board of Inland Revenue, except for agricultural land and buildings and churches. Some non-profit making organisations may also obtain partial exemption. A local authority also has the power to charge rates on empty domestic property up to 100 per cent of the full amount. The sum total of the rateable values of the individual properties assessed is called the 'rateable value of the authority'.

The actual rate to be levied in a given year is calculated from the net amount the local authority has to raise to meet its own requirements and the precepts, after taking into consideration all grants to be received. This amount then has to be divided by the product of a penny (1p) rate and the resultant figure represents the number of pennies which every ratepayer must pay in respect of every pound at which his property is valued. Thus, if the total rateable value of an authority were £41,250,000 the product of a penny rate would be that number divided by 100: £412,500. If the total amount to be raised were £30,750,000, then the rate to be levied expressed in pennies in the pound would be 30,750,000 ÷ 412,500 or 74·5p in the £. In actual fact not all ratepayers would pay at this rate for the General Rate Act, 1967 requires rating authorities to charge a lower rate in the pound on dwellings than on other property, the difference being made up by government subsidy.

REVENUE OR RECURRENT ESTIMATES—UNIVERSITIES

While local authorities talk of annual estimates in respect of normal day to day running as 'revenue estimates' the term used in university financing is 'recurrent estimates'. Basically they both mean the same thing, but there are different procedures in estimating practice. Until recently university estimates, including those for the library, were based primarily on a quinquennial submission to the University

* Water authorities are to collect their own charges from April 1978.

Grants Committee in respect of the whole university so that the librarian had to draw up his appraisal of requirements in a year-by-year programme consolidated into a five-year period. Once the university estimates had been agreed by the UGC, which draws its funds from government sources via the Department of Education and Science, the university had to review whatever amount was finally agreed and then in the light of reductions made revise its own five-year plan and the annual allotments to the various departments, including the library. The Parry Committee[2] advanced the view that the university library should receive 6 per cent of the university's total, and university librarians have used this ploy consistently in bargaining for their share of the resources but have not been able to secure acceptance of this as a principle. In general, their funds are about one or two per cent below this figure. With rampant inflation it has become impossible both for the UGC and the universities themselves to budget on a quinquennial basis, consequently estimating is now on an annual basis and the process has thereby become much simpler. It no longer depends on making a submission to the UGC and then waiting, but instead depends upon the ability of the university to meet the combined expenditure represented by the total of the estimates of all departments from the amount that the UGC has previously notified in general terms will be forthcoming, eg the guideline for 1977/8 was a 4 per cent reduction on the previous year. (Guidelines for a triennial period are to be used in future.)

As compared with public library estimating there are certain differences in the responsibility of the librarian and the channels through which the estimates are submitted and approved. Salaries, for instance, are mainly the concern of the secretary's or accountant's department. There will be a fixed establishment for the library of both professional and non-professional staff, and this officer will be in the best position to calculate the total salary bill taking into consideration any increments due, cost of living awards and any other factors, and then including the total into the salary estimates for the university as a whole (though the procedure may vary between one university and another). However, if the librarian wants to make a case for additional staff it will be his responsibility to make it with the appropriate committee(s) well in advance of the final submission of estimates. In the light of adverse economic circumstances this will be very difficult as the UGC makes no allowance for new courses, arrears of work, etc, unless new buildings are being provided when there would be a specific allowance for staffing. Equipment generally is also outside the province of the librarian, as it would most likely be purchased by the estates and buildings officer for the whole university. Nevertheless, the librarian should keep him informed of his requirements, so that the library's needs can be included in this officer's estimates.

Basically therefore, the librarian is mainly concerned with the material aspects of the library service—books, periodicals, and binding being the main items, but also including printing, stationery, audio-visual aids, special library equipment as distinct from standard university goods, subscriptions to associations, repairs to furniture and equipment, attendance at conferences and other travel, and a limited amount for the entertainment of guests. The librarian enjoys a large measure of discretion in spending from these funds. He could, for example, use book money for the purchase of periodicals or for binding or any of the other items which have been listed above, or alternatively he could use the monies allocated for the other purposes to supplement his book-fund. He could deny himself attendance at professional meetings and conferences and be very mean in carrying out his duties as a host and thereby save on these two funds to buy more books. On the other hand he could not use book money for extra staff or vice-versa. (In some universities the library estimates may be geared to a percentage of the total estimated expenditure for the whole university (eg 6 per cent) and in this event the librarian's estimates would embrace all forms of expenditure including salaries. A large measure of discretion would thus be given to him in spending money from one heading of the estimates for other purposes.) Apart from the normal annual allocation for books and allied material some of the newer universities may also be lucky enough to enjoy a supplementary book-fund from the university's own resources, eg from the appeal fund, or from balances. The addition would usually be spread over a given number of years. University library income will be small, and normally confined to receipts from photocopying, fines and possibly publications. In a few cases there might also be income from bequests.

The current *procedure* for the submission of university library estimates may be on the following lines, but again it must be emphasised that no single policy will be rigidly followed by all universities.

1 The librarian, having prepared his estimates in consultation with other senior members of the staff, including the subject specialists,

and having made out his case earlier for extra staff if required, will then put his proposals before the library committee in about November of the preceding year. He will be looking for advice and guidance, and committee approval will be a useful factor at subsequent negotiating stages; it would be unusual for the committee to suggest any reduction in estimates as might happen in a local authority.

2 After the library committee has considered the estimates they will proceed to the university's estimates sub-committee which will deal with all departments. It has a good knowledge of the university's total financial position, and with a fair indication of the global sum likely to be forthcoming from the UGC will be far more critical in the examination of the estimates, and will require explanation of any large proposed increases. (The librarian will have given an explanation in report form with the estimate papers, but he may be required to answer further questions.)

3 When the estimates sub-committee has completed its meetings with all the spending departments (in about March) and having also been notified of the approximate total the UGC will be allocating to the university, it will review the totality of requirements to decide whether the estimates can be met in full. If not, discussions will have to take place with the appropriate heads of departments to secure reductions. After this, the estimates are to all intents and purposes finalised but the total amount to be allocated to all departments goes through further stages: to the senate executive committee; the senate; the finance and general purposes committee; and the council. Although the detailed estimates are not submitted to these bodies they can question the total allocation to any one department and could ask for amendment in the same way as the full council of the local authority but in practice this would be rare.

4 The estimates will have gone through all these stages by June, and by the beginning of July the departments will be notified of the amounts approved for the next financial year beginning on 1 August.

REVENUE ESTIMATES—COLLEGE LIBRARIES

Estimates of college libraries have to be agreed both by the board of governors and the local authority. As with the university the library estimates represent only a relatively small percentage of the whole. Under the terms of the Local Government Act, 1966, the cost of colleges (excluding the voluntary colleges financed direct by the Department of Education and Science) is spread evenly throughout the country in accordance with the Rate Support Grants (Pooling Arrangements) Regulations, 1967 as amended by later Statutory Instruments 1267 and 1654. The purpose of this is to ensure that every local education authority bears a proportionate share of the cost of maintaining colleges and polytechnics, and that the whole cost does not fall upon those local education authorities which happen to accommodate the polytechnic and college buildings. At the same time it must be remembered that the central government pays a very substantial proportion of the costs of higher education.

Naturally, the estimates have to be geared to the local government year, and apart from agreement within the college they have to be approved by the local education committee and the full council of the authority.

Like the university librarian the college and polytechnic librarian will not be concerned with maintenance and upkeep of buildings. Similarly any increases in staff will have to be agreed long in advance of the following financial year for inclusion in the estimates. Staffing matters will also involve the local authority to a considerable extent, particularly in respect of non-academic staff, who may be paid either on local government or Burnham scales.

In the first instance the library estimates may go to the library sub-committee for their comment and then to the academic board but the procedure varies and in some cases they may go to the director of the polytechnic or the principal of the college who would then submit them along with the estimates of all other spending departments to the academic board, or if the latter is too large a body, as it probably is, to a sub-committee. If it so desires the Academic Board could call for some revision of the estimates but this is unlikely. It is probable that any alterations which might be advisable will have been dealt with in discussion between the librarian and the principal. Should the college have a finance committee, as is likely in a polytechnic, then this committee will also consider the total estimate of the college before it is passed to the governors for their approval. While the governors have a duty to question the estimates, and can ask for adjustments upwards or downwards the real test lies with the education committee of the local authority and its finance committee. Again it must be emphasised that they are looking at the estimate of the whole college or polytechnic, not at the library estimate in particular. If however any cuts are imposed on the institution then it is very likely that the library will have to bear its full share of the total reduction; the final distribution of the overall sum is however an internal matter for the college alone. Once the estimates are passed by the local authority's finance committee they will be incorporated in the total budget of the local authority requiring approval by the council.

When the estimates have been approved by the local authority the governors are entitled to incur expenditure without further reference to it and have a fair degree of flexibility so long as financial regulations are observed.

REVENUE ESTIMATES—SPECIAL LIBRARIES

In industrial and commercial libraries estimates may or may not be required depending largely on the size of the parent organisation. In some firms a block allocation of money may be made to cover the purchase of books, periodicals, microtexts, and allied materials. The overheads, including salaries and building maintenance, printing and stationery, equipment, and so forth, would be borne by the general funds of the firm's administration. In others the librarian will be expected to prepare estimates which will be limited to books, periodicals and allied material, and for salaries. The estimates are prepared in accordance with determined principles: eg with the utmost economy, or as in the previous year with an allowance for inflation, or with a certain allowance for growth. In most such libraries the second of these three policies is the most likely, unless the firm is expanding. The estimates for staffing will be based on the previous year plus any salary awards. No additional staffing can be provided for in the estimates without the case having previously been made with the management via the personnel officer and finance department, well in advance of the new financial year.

The library estimate will proceed most likely via the head of the overall department (research; information; sales; or administration) to the finance officer and then to the management along with all the other estimates. In due course the librarian will be informed of the amounts finally allotted.

REVENUE ESTIMATES—SOCIETY AND PROFESSIONAL LIBRARIES

In small societies it may be that the librarian (who may not be full-time) is allotted a basic sum representing what the organisation can afford rather than what the library really needs. Few libraries of this category have enough income nowadays to develop as the librarian would wish. Where the organisation is large and fairly affluent its governing body may require the librarian to submit estimates related to books and allied materials, equipment, printing and stationery, photocopying and other similar items. Salaries may also be included but any additions to staff will have needed prior approval by the council of the society. Upkeep of buildings and running costs would be included in general administrative expenses. If there is a separate committee responsible for the library then the estimates would proceed to that committee, otherwise to the finance committee and the council. The treasurer of the society will have given a clear indication in advance of the policy to be adopted in framing the estimates. It sometimes happens in organisations like this, and in local authorities too, that the governing body likes to have a *complete* view of the cost of each of the departments. Thus, although certain services are provided by the central establishment they are in turn costed out to the estimates of each individual service. Thus, salaries, upkeep of buildings, insurance, and other items, as well as part of the salaries of the staff of the central administration, are charged out to the individual services. In effect, therefore, the estimates for these individual services, or departments in the case of the local authority, represent the full cost as nearly as possible.

REVENUE ESTIMATES—NATIONAL AND GOVERNMENT LIBRARIES

The financial year for national and government libraries runs from 1 April to 31 March. (The procedure adopted by the British Library is taken here as an example, bearing in mind that this library receives its grant-in-aid from the Department of Education and Science in whose overall estimates it appears.) For instance in 1975/6 the grant-in-aid from the Department was more than £16·5 million. The total expenditure of the British Library in that year was more than £19 million; of this total £2·5 million was derived from its own services and sales, the Lending Service had an income of over £1·4 million, the Bibliographical Processing Service £520,000 and the Reference Service £300,000, with a further amount from Central Administration. On the expenditure side the Reference Division spent almost £10 million, the Lending Division about £4·75 million, Bibliographical Services Division about £1·5 million and Management and Administration cost £1·4 million. A sum of £737,000 was spent by way of grants to external research. Gross expenditure for 1976/7 was estimated at £21,601,000 and income (exclusive of grant-in-aid) at £2,462,000 (See Insert).

The British Library

1975–76		1976–77
£		£
1,459,000	**A Board of Management and Central Administration**	1,485,990
831,000	(1) Salaries &c	752,000
25,000	(2) General administrative expenses	32,990
324,000	(3) Equipment, supplies &c	336,000
379,000	(4) Rent, rates, maintenance, repairs &c	365,000
9,329,000	**B Reference Service**	9,892,000
4,630,000	(1) Salaries &c	4,701,000
76,000	(2) General administrative expenses	96,000
981,000	(3) Purchases of books, periodicals and manuscripts, agents' fees and commissions	1,300,000
1,425,000	(4) Book binding and printing	1,852,000
427,000	(5) Other equipment, supplies &c	486,000
1,730,000	(6) Rent, rates, maintenance, repairs &c	1,457,000
1,316,000	**C Bibliographical Processing Service**	1,708,000
599,000	(1) Salaries &c	680,000
69,000	(2) General administrative expenses	109,000
142,000	(3) Printing	192,000
219,000	(4) Other equipment, supplies &c	505,000
	(5) Rent, rates, maintenance, repairs &c	222,000
4,969,000	**D Lending Services**	5,559,000
1,625,000	(1) Salaries &c	1,863,000
505,000	(2) General administrative expenses	726,000
1,306,000	(3) Purchase of books, periodicals and manuscripts, agents' fees and commissions	1,361,000
142,000	(4) Book binding and printing	148,000
905,000	(5) Other equipment, supplies &c	957,000
467,000	(6) Rent, rates, maintenance, repairs &c	504,000

1975–76		1976–77
£		£
780,000	**E Grants for External Research**	1,320,000
60,000	**F Grants to Library and Information Services**	122,000
196,000	**G Minor Capital Works**	265,000
800,000	**H Patent Publications (included in (B3))**	1,049,000
44,000	**I Reserve Fund**	200,000
—	**J Indemnity for objects loaned to the British Library for exhibitions to the value of £7,500,000**	1●
18,953,000	GROSS TOTAL	21,601,000
	Deduct:	
2,277,000	**Y Receipts**	2,462,000
50,000	(1) Central Administration	20,000
298,000	(2) Reference Service	342,000
521,000	(3) Bibliographical Processing Service	581,000
1,408,000	(4) Lending Service	1,519,000
16,676,000	NET TOTAL	19,139,000

The estimating procedure is based on detailed costing of British Library and British Library divisional programmes. The case for the annual grant-in-aid is based on development plans already decided by the Board and on current and forward economic considerations discussed periodically inside the perimeters of the PESC[3] programme. The case when authorised by the British Library Board is put to the Department of Education and Science for detailed discussion before presentation to the Treasury. Further discussions may take place with the Treasury before the estimates are submitted to Parliament. The figures as finally put forward to the House of Commons are published by HM Treasury in the first quarter of each year.[4] They are printed as an appendix to the estimates for Libraries, England, Class X, 3 of the complete estimates for Education and Libraries, Science and Art. Estimates for the National Libraries of Scotland and of Wales are found under Class X, 4 and 5 respectively.

CAPITAL AND NON-RECURRENT ESTIMATES

Both 'capital' and 'non-recurrent' have the same meaning, the latter term being favoured in the university world. They mean estimates for projects to be paid for from capital, as distinct from revenue for day to day administration and operation. Capital expenditure is incurred to finance projects of a lasting nature which are normally expensive. The purposes for which this capital is employed are regarded as being of value and service to, not only the current generation, but also to generations to come. Therefore, in the local government sphere for instance, they are not paid for directly by the rate-payers as part of the rates levied in the year of the actual expenditure but they are normally financed on a loan basis, rather similar to that for house purchase (ie by borrowing a capital sum and repaying it in regular instalments over a number of years, including interest). Thus if a certain project were financed over thirty years then the library annual estimates for those thirty years would contain an amount for repayment of principal and interest. The arrangement could be one of equal sums each year or it may be on a reducing scale. The normal purposes for which such loans are raised is for new buildings or substantial extensions to existing buildings, the loans may also include for the land, furniture and fittings and initial bookstock. Naturally, it is likely that all departments of a local authority will from time to time have capital proposals which they want to put forward, and as the sums involved can run into millions of pounds the effects on the revenue estimates may be very pronounced, so it is important that the council should be kept fully aware of any such proposal and receive reasonably accurate estimates of the initial costs *and* the revenue costs, which will include not only repayments of loans and interest but the cost of running the new service.

CAPITAL ESTIMATES—PUBLIC LIBRARIES

When a library committee of a public library is contemplating a new capital project, let us say a new central library, once they have agreed that such a library is desirable they will want to know what it will cost. Presuming they already have a suitable site then the next step will be to engage an architect, either the council's own or an outside firm, and ask the librarian to prepare a brief in conjunction with the architect and submit particulars to the committee in due course together with an approximate estimate of the costs, both capital and revenue (the director of finance would obviously be involved in the latter). If the cost, which would include for all furniture and fittings, bookstock and any special equipment, as well as the building, together with the fees of architects, surveyors, and structural engineers, were too high when the report was subsequently placed before the committee, then they might either forget about the project for a while, or ask for economies to be made and for a further report in due course.

If the revised brief and estimate were acceptable to the library committee it would recommend that the matter be referred to the finance committee. This latter committee might then decide to include the project in its long-term capital or development programme. Mere inclusion in the programme does not authorise a start, it only slots the item in among all the other projects in the pipe-line, shows the estimated capital outlay and the effect on the revenue budget should it be sanctioned. Library capital expenditure falls within what is called 'the locally determined sector' or the 'quota', ie the non-essential schemes which have to be financed from an annual block loan consent which controls the amount of non-essential work which a local authority can carry out. The total allocated to any one authority in a year is relatively small and with so many schemes competing for it in normal circumstances, it may take years before some cherished schemes ever see the light of day, if at all. However, the finance committee has to establish priorities, from time to time the items in the development programme are looked at and priority given to those which it sees its way clear to starting within the next year or two. When definite start dates have been allotted in this way then the items in question become part of the programmed development, the remainder are unprogrammed and have to wait till the next review comes round. This may not be quite so hopeless as it sounds, so far as small projects are concerned in any event. The quota has to be spent within a very strict time-scale and, if for any reason the programme of building should fall behind, the finance committee will be looking for some other project, which is not going to take a very long time in planning, which might be slotted in so that part of the quota is not lost. Thus, a small branch library, for instance, might suddenly come from behind to the building start. When the development programme is considered each year the estimates are also revised in the light of current prices.

Capital projects which have been approved for start or are actually under way will be included in the *annual capital estimates* which will be prepared by the director of finance and submitted for information to the departmental committee and to the finance committee. They will show the capital outlay for each year and the amounts spent to-date (this is not necessarily the total cost as many buildings take some years, particularly a new central library, so that the capital might be spent over a period of a few years; the revenue effect is also shown.

A local authority will also have a small capital fund of its own built up from contributions from the general rate fund (councils are permitted to make a very small annual contribution to such a fund) from which minor new projects may be financed without the need to raise a loan. A very small branch library or a mobile might be financed in this way but would, all the same, have to be in the development programme and subsequently agreed for start. The library's revenue estimates would be debited with an annual repayment charge. Still smaller schemes of improvement such as new lighting throughout a library or new flooring might be financed from the revenue estimates for repairs and renewals. This might be a separate fund for the whole of the council's buildings.

NON-RECURRENT EXPENDITURE—UNIVERSITY LIBRARIES

As in the public library field, non-recurrent expenditure in the university sphere relates mainly to buildings. In the days of quinquennial estimates universities had to prepare details of new building projects well in advance of requirements and submit details to the UGC; the latter was allowed a certain sum for all university building, and would decide priorities and allocations within the whole university field. The total non-recurrent grant from the DES has now been reduced to such an extent that the UGC is able to contemplate very little building of any kind in universities for the immediate future.[5] So far as libraries are concerned the outlook is particularly bleak as the UGC has endorsed for a trial period the recommendations of the Atkinson Working Party.[6] However even supposing there had been no such report (see pp 90-1) the library would have found itself competing with other university departments for support from a completely inadequate fund: the librarian would have had to advance his claims through the estates and building officer and the development committee, or a committee of a different name but with similar functions. The other governing bodies of the university, including the finance and general purposes committee and the council would also have been involved prior to a case being presented to the UGC to whom a submission would be made together with any other capital schemes the university wished to put in hand.

CAPITAL EXPENDITURE—NATIONAL AND GOVERNMENT LIBRARIES

As all government buildings are the responsibility of the Department of the Environment, capital for library buildings and estimates of expenditure are a matter for that department; the new British Library building to be erected on the Euston site for example.

References

1 The example given of estimate procedure relates to a London borough or district council. In the case of a non-metropolitan county the procedure in the library is much the same; the county's overall requirements are raised as precepts (see p 106).
2 University Grants Committee. *Report of the Committee on Libraries*, HMSO, 1967.
3 *Public expenditure to* 1977–78, Cmnd 5519, HMSO, 1973.
4 *Supply Estimates*, HMSO.
5 The outlook for university buildings (not necessarily libraries) improved in the early months of 1978 when the government announced increased allocations for capital expenditure as part of their programme to stimulate building construction and employment.
6 UGC. *Capital provision for university libraries*, HMSO, 1976.

7

Finance—Control; Audit; Charges

While the librarian has very substantial responsibility for ensuring that his library is adequately financed through careful preparation of his estimates he has an equal responsibility for ensuring that the money is spent legitimately on the purposes for which it was voted. He must also see that all transactions are properly accounted for, and that all items (except those of a perishable nature or with a short life) are brought on charge.

FINANCIAL REGULATIONS

Though it cannot be claimed that all, or even the majority of institutions which provide a library service have necessarily drawn up a written code of financial regulations, it can virtually be taken for granted that they have such a code. In local authorities the director of finance will have drawn it up and distributed it, either in the form of memoranda or as a complete pamphlet, supplemented as occasion requires. The regulations will have the approval of the finance committee so far as is required. Some universities also have the regulations in printed form but, if not, the secretary and accounts department will have issued instructions to all concerned covering all the relevant points. One would expect to find similar typed instructions in industry and societies. In libraries financed by the government very precise rules of finance and accountancy are drawn up by the Treasury which supervises the finances of all departments on a continuous day to day basis.

Local authorities are specifically commanded by legislation to ensure that they have adequate accountancy methods. For instance in England and Wales the Local Government Act, 1972, demands proper financial arrangements and the appointment of an officer with this responsibility. S.151 reads: '... every local authority shall make arrangements for the proper administration of their financial affairs and shall secure that one of their officers has responsibility for the administration of those affairs.'

Polytechnics, too, will be governed by the local authorities' financial regulations and the relevant 'Scheme of Government' may have a clause to the effect that: 'The Governors of the polytechnic shall comply with the financial regulations which the council shall make from time to time.'

The statutes of a university will include some clause covering this same point such as: 'The council shall govern, manage and regulate the finances of the university.' In turn the council will set up a finance and general purposes committee 'to control the finances of the university' and the latter then makes the secretary 'responsible for ensuring that accounts of the university are kept and that he shall be responsible for the accounting records kept in all departments'.

The British Library operates under financial regulations agreed between the Board and the Department of Education and Science and approved by the Treasury.

Without quoting further examples it is obvious that a very high degree of importance is attached to uniformity of accounting procedures throughout an institution. The regulations drawn up by the responsible officer will include such matters as a common system of ordering by means of standardised order and invoice forms having a system of running numbers which can be quoted in all references to these orders; a system of authorising certain officers to sign orders and accounts; a limitation perhaps on the amount a chief officer may spend without further authority from his committee (perhaps £1,000 to £5,000 but it varies); similar limitations on chairmen of committees but to an increased amount, and also for committees; the circumstances under which it will be necessary to obtain competitive quotations or go out to tender and how this should be done; certification of accounts; travelling allowances; banking arrangements; petty cash; audit; inventories; insurances; and estimates; though this list is by no means complete. Additional regulations will have to be formulated as circumstances arise.

One of the prime purposes of such regulations is the need to establish uniformity throughout the whole administration of an individual organisation, but over and above this is the aim of ensuring regularity and the elimination of any possibility of malpractice—to systemise the accounting procedures and make any departure from them obvious. Thus, the use of standardised order and invoice forms with an identifying reference is to eliminate verbal orders which tend to get forgotten or not brought into the commitment account; it also facilitates reference from the invoice to the original order in case a query should arise. The limitation of a chief officer's spending powers is designed to keep the responsibility for large orders to a committee, and to eliminate the possibility of nepotism. The employment of quotations or tenders is to test the market and to show there is no collusion in the placing of large contracts. Regulations covering petty cash show that as much importance is given to small transactions as to large ones and, incidentally, are a safeguard against accusations of dishonesty. The maintenance of inventories and keeping accession records is to show that goods ordered have actually been received and taken on charge; as the records show the destination of the items in question they can be called for by the auditor if necessary. Insurance is necessary to protect the organisation's property, to provide against accidents to staff and users and to make sure that proper action is taken when circumstances demand; and finally, audit of the organisation's accounts is again designed to ensure proper administration and, in its own way, it is also a protection for the staff as are all the financial regulations.

One further point in this matter of financial control is that good management also requires that the spending officers keep within their budgets. When orders are made out, therefore, and invoices passed for payment they will both bear a code number which relates to the head of expenditure in the revenue estimates. The finance staff will supply the librarian at regular intervals with figures of expenditure under all these heads and it will therefore be possible to keep a regular check on the way expenditure is keeping in step with the budget and eliminate the possibility of overspending.

AUDIT

All organisations handling money on behalf of others, whether it be public money collected from taxes, rates, public subscriptions or charges for services, or, whether it be money collected from the subscriptions of corporate or individual membership, or from business transactions, ensure that their accounts are regularly audited. They do this both in the interests of sound management and efficiency and to render an account of themselves to the tax-payer, rate-payer, society member, and shareholder. The general procedure is for the accounts (using the term in the widest sense of accounting for all incomes and expenditures, both large and small) as well as the accounting methods employed, to be kept under constant review and subject to inspection of the organisation's own internal auditors at any time, including provision for spot checks. Then, normally at annual intervals, a systematic check is carried out by external auditors who will finally certify the correctness of the statement of accounts and the balance sheets. This latter audit in some circumstances may not be as detailed as the day to day internal audit but it is nevertheless very searching and being carried out by independent auditors brings a fresh approach to inspection. When the external audit is completed these auditors, in whatever field they may be operating, give their signature to the correctness of the accounts and are free to comment thereon to the management with any suggestions they may have for improvements in method.

INTERNAL AUDIT—PUBLIC LIBRARIES

A local authority has a small department with the sole responsibility of audit. In theory it should be completely divorced from any other department but due to mutual interests it is often found as operating as part of the finance department but the chief auditor and his staff should have a wide degree of independence and be able to enquire into any aspect of the council's financial affairs without fear of upsetting the director of finance or any other chief officer for that matter. In the ultimate of course, the director of finance is responsible for the safe custody of the council's funds and the control of its accounts and the chief auditor would report to him if anything were found to be wrong.

Financial procedures for dealing with all income and expenditure will be drawn up originally by the auditor or by the appropriate department with the auditor's advice. For example, if a library wished to change from a fines receipt system to a fines box system, the auditor would be consulted and he would have to be satisfied with the new method; similarly if a library were to be holding a book sale it would be wise to consult the auditor with regard to the methods to be used for accounting for the income and possibly with regard to fixing the selling prices. If it were proposed to abolish an accessions register, then the auditor would again be consulted because he may require some alternative method whereby his staff could check that books invoiced had actually been taken into stock. A more substantial example is where the council may be establishing an arts centre under the control of the librarian. Many forms of income would be involved, including charges for rooms, admission to concerts, payment for artists' materials used, sale of refreshments, and commission on paintings sold at exhibitions. The librarian would make sure that the arrangements he was making for accounting for these incomes were agreeable to the auditor. It is much wiser to have this assurance beforehand than to receive some complaint subsequently.

Among the regular checks carried out by internal auditors the following are fairly common to all local authority libraries:

1 They check from library invoices that the books thereon have been duly received and taken into stock. Thus, they may wish to see the appropriate entry in the accession record and very often ask for some of the books to be traced and presented to them in due course.

2 Similarly with gramophone records and tapes: in fact some auditors seem to be obsessed with these items, and are particularly concerned to assure themselves that withdrawn records have in fact been withdrawn and destroyed.

3 They check accounts for binding, and ask the librarian to produce some of the volumes on an invoice to prove that the books have actually been bound.

4 With periodicals now being so expensive, the auditors might like to satisfy themselves about the method of receipt and invoicing as well as subsequent distribution.

5 Equipment generally should be entered in an inventory and the entry should link up with the invoice and show the location of the equipment within the library: eg purchase of a tape-recorder; a record player; a television set; or a video camera. If by chance the equipment is transferred from one library to another the inventory of each library should be duly amended. Small items costing only a pound or two and consumable articles would be ignored. Furniture may also be included in this inventory or another separate one. If the auditors take the job seriously they will on occasion check the inventory against the furniture.

6 They check incomes from fines, reservations and miscellaneous receipts. This will also include income from sales of publications and the auditors may require a record of the numbers received of each item so that they can check the numbers left and hence deduce the numbers sold and the cash which should have been taken.

7 All petty cash expenditure will be checked against receipts, and,

the remaining cash in hand plus the total of the receipts should add up to the original float.

8 From time to time the auditors may interest themselves in receipts from the sale of waste paper especially if they seem to be on the decline but this will probably be found to be due to lack of outlet.

The foregoing is not intended to be a complete list by any means but is offered only as a guideline. It is reasonable to suppose that over the course of time every aspect of the department's accounting arrangements will be investigated, and this is only right and proper. It keeps the staff on the alert as well as protecting it. If the internal auditors should discover anything unsatisfactory in visiting any library in a system they would draw it to the attention of the librarian-in-charge. If it were something of importance he would report to the chief auditor who would report in turn to the librarian. So far as is possible the latter would rectify the situation, but if the matter had implications beyond his immediate control he would report to his committee. For example, large-scale losses of books or records, which could perhaps only be stopped by the employment of additional staff, the introduction of electronic detectors, or perhaps some physical re-arrangement within the library, all of which would cost money. Should any serious matter of a personal nature arise such as regular and unaccountable deficits in fines, unexplained disappearance of equipment, an outbreak of burglaries requiring the provision of burglar alarms, and so on, both the director of finance and the librarian would be informed so that they could discuss steps which might be taken to deal with the situation and the preparation of a joint report to committee.

INTERNAL AUDIT—NON-PUBLIC LIBRARIES

Without going into procedures in other kinds of library in any detail it must be added that internal audit is likely to be as strict in government, academic and industrial libraries as it is in public libraries. For instance S.5(3) of the British Library Act, 1972 reads: 'The Board shall keep proper accounts and other records and shall prepare in respect of each financial year statements of account in such form as the Secretary of State may, with the approval of the Treasury, direct; and those statements shall, on or before 30 November next following the expiration of the financial year in question be submitted to the Secretary of State.' Accordingly, within the Central Administrative

Unit there is a finance section one member of which is an internal auditor, employed on a regular day to day basis in checking accountancy procedures in all divisions of the library.

In the university world the financial regulations will include provision such as: 'The secretary shall, so far as he may deem reasonable, conduct or arrange for the examination and audit of the accounts of the university and of its staff. Any member of the staff who becomes aware of any irregularity should inform the head of his department who will in turn report without delay to the secretary.' While internal audit will be a regular process both with regard to accountancy methods and matters of detail it is for the individual university to decide whether or not to set up a separate internal audit section. Apart from matters of strict accountancy such a section would also investigate proposals for new library systems, ie the auditor would act as management/systems accountant.

Polytechnics being controlled by the local authority in matters of administration will be subject to the council's audit procedures as will be made clear in the scheme of government in words such as: 'The financial regulations should contain provisions dealing with the arrangements for the receipt and disbursement of money, contract procedure, internal audit and estimates procedure.'

In the industrial field libraries will be subject to repeated visits from internal auditors who are part of the staff of the finance department. While special libraries of this kind have little in the way of petty cash income and expenditure requiring checking, the auditors can be very searching with regard to what is purchased, the need for the purchase, and by whom the goods purchased are used, and for what purpose, ie they will be particularly concerned with the general legality (in terms of the firm's objectives) of the purchase. Internal auditors will also need to approve of the order methods adopted by the library for it is likely that the methods used for the firm's normal purchases are unsuitable for books and allied material as they are far too slow and time-consuming.

EXTERNAL AUDIT—PUBLIC LIBRARIES

Audit by external auditors, as distinct from internal audit, is again clearly defined in the relevant local government acts (this legislation relates to all services provided by a local authority and is therefore equally relevant to college and polytechnic libraries as to public libraries).

Taking England and Wales for example, again the Local Government Act, 1972, makes very precise regulations for the 'external' audit of local authority accounts in Sections 154–67. Librarians of local authorities should know the general substance of these closely worded paragraphs. The basic facts are: all accounts of a local authority or a parish meeting for a parish, not having a separate parish council, or any committee of any such authority (including a joint committee of two or more such authorities) and the accounts of the rate fund and superannuation of the City must be audited by a 'district' auditor or an 'approved' auditor. The Act also provides for change from district auditor to approved auditor and vice-versa as well as the method for opting for such a change. The main difference in the powers of the two types of auditor lies in the action they can take when they consider something to be wrong, of which more later. Apart from this, the difference lies in the responsibility and method of appointment of these auditors.

District auditors are appointed by the Secretary of State for the Environment subject to the consent of the Minister for the Civil Service. They will be on the staff of the Department of the Environment.

Approved auditors have to be qualified and their appointment has to be approved by the Secretary of State. By 'qualified' is meant membership of one of the general bodies of accountants established in the UK and approved by the Secretary of State.

The general duties of auditors are defined in the Act as follows: 'an auditor shall by examination of the accounts and otherwise satisfy himself that—(a) the accounts are prepared in accordance with regulations made under S.166 and comply with the requirements of all other enactments and instruments applicable to the accounts; (b) proper accounting practices have been observed in the compilation of the accounts, and the auditor shall be under a duty to consider whether, in the public interest, he should make a report on any matters arising out of or in connection with the accounts, in order that those matters may be considered by the body concerned or brought to the attention of the public.'

The Act gives the auditor right of access at all times to all accounts and documents relative thereto and to call before him any officer or other person he may require to submit documents and to question him as required—all subject to various legal compunctions. The local authority whose accounts are being audited must also give the auditors such facilities and information as they may reasonably require.

Any person interested is entitled to inspect the accounts to be audited and documents relating thereto and to make copies. Local government electors of the authority whose accounts are being audited may ask to see and question the auditor. If the audit is being conducted by the district auditor the elector may make objections to the accounts, or, if it is being conducted by an approved auditor may make an application to the Secretary of State asking for him to direct a district auditor to hold an extraordinary audit of the accounts.

Within fourteen days of the completion of the audit, the auditor must send any report to the authority concerned with a copy to the Secretary of State and the authority must consider the report as soon as possible thereafter.

We now come to the chief distinction between audit by the district auditor and that by an approved auditor. If a *district auditor* considers that any item of account is contrary to law he may apply to the court for a declaration to this effect except where the item has been approved by the Secretary of State. Should the court make such a declaration it may also order the person(s) responsible for incurring any unlawful expenditure to repay it in whole or in part, and, if it exceeds £2,000 and the person responsible is a member of a local authority, order him to be disqualified as a member for a specified period, and order rectification of the accounts.

Similarly, if an authority suffers loss through failure to bring into account any sum which should have been included and the failure to do so has not been approved by the Secretary of State, or a loss has been incurred through wilful misconduct of a person(s) the district auditor may certify that the amount in question is due from the person(s) concerned and the authority may recover the amount. Disqualification of a member from membership of the council follows if the amount in question exceeds £2,000.

Where the audit is carried out by an *approved auditor*, and he considers there are grounds for believing that the accounts are unsatisfactory for any of the reasons referred to in the Act in the context of the district auditor, he must report the matter to the Secretary of State so that the latter may consider whether he should direct a district auditor to hold an extraordinary audit of the accounts.

Finally, the Secretary of State, may on the application of a local government elector in an authority whose accounts are required to be audited by the Act, or on application of any such authority, or if it appears to him from an auditor's report that it is desirable to do so may direct a district auditor to hold an extraordinary audit of the accounts of that authority.

It will thus be seen that the external auditor has very wide-ranging responsibilities and has a right to demand any accounts or documents which might help him in his work. While much of what he does will be very similar to the work of the internal auditor he will be bringing a fresh expertise to bear and he will have a vast experience of local authority accounting to guide him. Not being conditioned by the regulations and procedures of any one authority, he will be able to look at the whole structure rather than its individual parts—though he will look at these as well. He will be particularly concerned with the financial regulations, the powers vested in chief officers, chairmen of committees, and committees; the procedures for tendering and placing of contracts; the council's estimates and expenditure therefrom; terms of reference; order procedures; discounts; methods of accounting for fines, reservations, sales, subscriptions, and other like matters. He is likely to look through the minutes of the library and other committees, and in doing so his attention might be drawn to losses of books reported after stocktaking; book sales; installation of new issue methods; revised charges for gramophone records; or, many other matters which might prompt a particular line of thought. Armed too with experience in a library just visited, he may also carry out investigations to see how the experience of one library tallies with another; eg number of reservations and fees charged; relative scales of fines for overdue books and records; subscriptions to record or picture libraries; charges made for publications and how they were decided; attention given to up-dating inventories; accounting for withdrawn cassettes, and discounts received on non-book material, to name but a few. The possibilities are many but the well-managed library will come out well from such a survey.

EXTERNAL AUDIT—NON-PUBLIC LIBRARIES

A rôle equivalent to that of the district auditor is carried out in university libraries by a firm of professional auditors both as a matter of public policy and because it is a requirement of the UGC that financial returns have to be signed by professional auditors. They act on an annual basis and investigate departmental spending and accountancy on what is mainly a spot-check basis and perhaps looking at different aspects of finance each year. They finally certify the accounts for the year which are presented to the Court and the UGC.

Always zealous of their independence, the universities for long resisted any suggestion that they should be publicly accountable for their expenditure but in January 1967 the Public Accounts Committee recommended that they should allow their books and records to be inspected by the Comptroller and Auditor General. This was agreed by the universities both to satisfy the demand for independent check of their expenditure and to reassure both Parliament and the public generally. Since 1968, therefore, the universities have made their books open to inspection and the Comptroller and Auditor General is 'invited' to carry out an audit. This happens about every four years. The process takes about twelve man weeks and a report is made to the university. The Comptroller and Auditor General cannot take any action with the university, this would be the function of the UGC should any comment arise from the audit.

At national level the Comptroller and Auditor General has the duty of examining on behalf of Parliament, the accounts of income and expenditure of all services supported from government funds and he is the auditor of many bodies supported by public monies; he reports to the House of Commons. His department is responsible therefore for external audit of the accounts of the British Library and this work is carried on throughout the year by periodical visits and through the audit of the annual Statement of Accounts which is submitted to the Secretary of State. Like the district auditor the Comptroller and Auditor General has the right of access to all relevant accounts and documents.

In the industrial field libraries will be subject to audit by the firm of professional auditors who carry out an independent check of the firm's accounts and certify the annual Statement of Accounts for presentation to the shareholders. They are not likely to be in much evidence in the library as expenditure is slight compared with other of the firm's activities but any aspect of the accountancy could be questioned if necessary. In society and professional association libraries a similar situation will obtain and accounts too will be subject to audit and certification by a firm of professional auditors.

INSURANCE

Adequate insurance is as necessary as sound accountancy, and library property is usually covered against certain more obvious risks including third-party claims for damages to property or to individuals. Normally the insurance policies would be taken out by the finance officer of the organisation but, nevertheless, the librarian will have a responsibility for assuring himself that reasonable risks are covered, or if not, this has been as a result of a deliberate decision by the finance officer, not because the risk had not been brought to his attention. For instance the librarian might acquire a collection of rare books which might need a separate insurance cover and he should therefore inform the finance officer. It may be that after negotiations with the insurance company, the finance officer finds it not worth the additional premium or that it is undesirable for other reasons—in any event however the librarian should not fail to inform him of the purchase. Similarly with regard to taking over a new building, the finance officer would rely on the architect or the estates and buildings officer to inform him of its value in terms of building, furniture and fixed equipment; the librarian would have to inform him of the value of books and allied material, movable equipment, records and pictures, so that adequate insurance cover could be taken out immediately the building becomes the authority's responsibility. Again whenever the library purchases equipment such as video cameras, tape-recorders, record-players, TV sets, film-projectors and the like the finance officer must be informed.

Library insurance will normally form just a part of the authority's overall provision and the decision as to the type of policy(ies) and the degree of cover required will rest with the finance officer. While he will wish to have adequate cover he will have due regard to the likelihood of the risk and the cost of insuring against it. Not every possibility will be guarded against and the extent of the cover in terms of compensation may be deliberately limited in some cases. Insurance is a highly competitive business and tenders will probably be obtained from a number of firms before contracts are signed for the individual types of cover. The eventualities most usually insured against are fire, burglary, house-breaking, theft of cash in transit, staff fidelity guarantee, motor vehicles, lifts, boiler explosions and third-party claims; some of these may be covered in an all-risks policy relating to buildings and contents. Staff are covered against industrial injury through the national insurance fund.

While the librarian's responsibilities in respect of insurance are relatively slight he should, nevertheless, find out from his finance officer exactly what cover is provided and the circumstances under which additional cover might be needed (eg in respect of a travelling exhibition borrowed from an outside source, for films borrowed from elsewhere, or in respect of library halls let out to the public). He should also ascertain whether any special conditions apply to any of the policies, eg that any monies must be kept in a safe overnight; that staff property is not insured against theft or damage and that if they require such cover it should be included in their own personal household policy (many an assistant has discovered that when a handbag has been stolen there is no compensation forthcoming from the authority's insurance, similarly with damage to clothing); or, that there are special provisions relating to keyholders and the safe custody of keys.

In the event of any claim arising on an insurance policy the librarian must inform the finance officer of the circumstances without delay and send a brief statement of the occurrence; fuller details can be sent later if necessary together with a valuation of the loss or damage.

LIBRARY CHARGES AS A MEANS OF INCOME

Apart from the national libraries and libraries of certain museums perhaps, the yield from charges made from sales, fees, fines, etc, is small, and not likely to cover completely the cost of the administration or the service provided. With regard to public libraries in particular, however, voices are frequently heard advocating all-round charges for the use of the services and it might, therefore, be useful to recapitulate the position, taking England and Wales for example, though the position is much the same in other parts of the UK.

The Public Libraries and Museums Act, 1964, specifically rules under S.8 that no charge shall be made for borrowing: (a) a book, journal or similar article, or (b) a reproduction made by photographic or other means of the whole or part of any such article. It also rules that a charge *may* be made not exceeding such amount as may be specified in that behalf by the Secretary of State: (a) for notifying a person that a book or other article reserved by him has become available for borrowing, or (b) in respect of failure to return a book or other article before the end of the period for which it was lent. Charges are also *permitted* under the Act for supplying book catalogues or indexes, or similar articles where they become the property of the person to whom they were supplied. Finally, where facilities are made available to any person beyond those ordinarily provided as part of the library service, a charge can then be made for them.

In practice it is only those who do not live, work in, or study full-time in the area of a local authority, who can be charged for borrowing books, periodicals, etc, or for reproductions of books or parts thereof. Such persons are normally made to pay a subscription failing production of the tickets of some other library authority which are usually acceptable. However, charges can be levied and often are, for the loan of gramophone records, tapes, pictures and films as well as similar articles. In this event the charge may be in the form of an annual subscription or per item borrowed. Charges for publications of any substance such as catalogues of special collections, albums of local prints, library magazines and postcards, are normal but brochures describing library facilities, booklists and lecture programmes are free. Admission to library lectures and film-shows is again normally, but not necessarily, free; when the library is responsible for an arts centre, a charge is often made for hire of rooms, purchase of materials, and especially for admission to concerts. It is also possible for a library to charge for the provision of a service to industry or services to other special groups.

In respect of charges for reservations although the Act authorises charges for *notification* many libraries fix a charge in excess of the cost of postage though perhaps no library charges an amount equal to the full administrative cost of tracing the book, plus postage. Practically every library charges fines for overdue books: pensioners and children are exempt. The tendency nowadays is to make fines quite heavy, theoretically to induce people to return the books quickly but in fact as a means of income. Although the Act refers to a maximum charge both for notification of reserved books and library fines, the Secretary of State has never fixed a maximum, and library authorities seem to be able to charge fines, which many people would regard as excessive, without any reprimand from the Secretary of State.

There has always been a temptation for authorities to look upon reservations and fees as a source of income, but until about 1975 the temptation was generally resisted, partly because it was thought that the Minister would object. With no objection forthcoming and with local authorities receiving a general recommendation from the government to increase all of their charges in an endeavour to keep the rates down, library fees seem to have been regarded in the same light as admission charges to swimming-baths or hire charges for sports facilities, and still there has been no sign of ministerial disapproval;

indeed the British Library too seems to be motivated by a policy of increasing its resources through charges. Fortunately, the principle of the library's being free for studying, and for borrowing books, has been preserved intact but there are now signs that some people would like to see the whole service placed on a fee-paying basis. Letters in the national press advocating such a policy are quite common and the campaign for Public Lending Right has not helped those who wish to see the public library service remain free.

A determined attack on this basic principle is always possible and The Library Association, anticipating such a move has prepared a case against it should the emergency ever arise. It is based on the firm statement contained in the Unesco Public Library Manifesto of 1973 that the public library should be maintained wholly from public funds and no direct charge should be made to anyone for its services; that charges would limit accessibility and the development of the individual; the historical freedom of the service would be engulfed; that the steady growth of public library services and their widespread use by all classes of the community would be undermined; that charges are in contradiction to the promotion of literacy and self-education; that charges would cause great difficulty in inter-lending and technical information services, and that after exemptions had been made to old people, children, and students, and allowances made for administrative costs, the fees charged to the remaining borrowers would have to be high and in consequence would result in a rapid decrease in the volume of use.

Though it might be thought that this defence is somewhat exaggerated in parts there seems little doubt that library charges would rapidly undo much of the good work done in building up libraries over a period of 125 years into a service which is basic to the cultural and educational needs of society.

8

Personnel

Presuming that a library is adequately financed and housed in reasonable accommodation, the most important factor in welding its stock into a comprehensive and efficient library service is its staff. The staff must be adequate to achieve the objectives of the organisation—it must be sufficient in numbers to meet the demands made upon it; it should have the right mixture of qualifications and experience and be selected with due regard to the functions to be performed and the required levels of performance. In turn members of the staff should be adequately rewarded in relation to the duties they are called upon to carry out, and placed within a grading structure offering reasonable prospects of promotion and career opportunities. They should be given the opportunity for further education and qualifications, together with training on and off the job. The management for its part, must be seen to be concerned with the welfare of all members of the staff, not only their physical welfare—perhaps even more important is their mental well-being. In particular, however, it should try to ensure that people with the right interests and mental characteristics are matched to posts with these same requirements, so that the workers are happy in their work, and derive positive satisfaction from it. Conditions of service also need to be such as to eliminate worry about such matters as sickness, special leave, injury at work, financial commitments for study, and widows' pensions, not to mention ultimate retirement. Finally, there must be an efficient system of communication between the work-force and the management so that even the most junior member of staff knows to whom to turn in an emergency, and that in the ultimate he has access to the librarian or director.

THE PERSONNEL MANAGER

Salaries and wages to-day represent anything from 50–65 per cent of a library's expenditure, and even given the best of human material to work on, staff training and continuous education is expensive. Additionally, the smooth working of a library is dependent upon a well-structured organisation in which each section is managed by thoroughly competent staff without friction, so that the whole functions like a well-oiled machine. Thus the personnel function has become increasingly important in libraries in recent years and all librarians with responsibilities for supervising staff need to be aware of the general principles of personnel management.

The larger the library, the more important it becomes that one person should be designated as having the ultimate responsibility for the personnel function, though much of the day-to-day work will have to be carried out by the line managers. In very small libraries, with only a handful of staff, the librarian may have to carry out these responsibilities himself, otherwise it will be some other member of the staff at second or third tier level, and in a few instances there will be a professional personnel manager, qualified both in management and personnel management, or perhaps in librarianship and personnel management. However, it must be emphasised that few such posts are found in Britain: that is to say there are few positions established for specially trained and qualified personnel managers, as distinct from senior librarians who combine the personnel function with other duties.

There is a great deal of professional literature which might lead the uninformed to suppose that we are well-endowed with personnel managers, and that the personnel management rôle is well-carried out in all libraries; but this is far from being the case. The bulk of this literature is of American origin where the establishment of a separate personnel department is a common practice. This is particularly so with large American public libraries but they operate against a different background from that in the United Kingdom. The libraries there have a greater independence, they are usually controlled by their own boards which have their own regulations with regard to staffing and conditions of service, subject very often to civil service or local government rules. This independence automatically requires a personnel department within the library under the control of a personnel manager with ancillary staff according to the size of the library. This department is responsible for salary scales and payment of salaries and wages; conditions of service; appointments; promotions; resignations; dismissals; staff assessments; training and workshops; welfare; disciplinary matters and everything relating to staff employment. In the United Kingdom, on the other hand, most matters of this nature are controlled by a committee such as Policy and Resources, or Establishment, and the salary scales themselves are formulated by national negotiating bodies representing the employer and the employed; similarly with conditions of service. The local authority has its own establishment or personnel department which includes senior staff trained in special functions such as recruitment, training, job evaluation, pay and conditions and welfare. They will provide these services for all departments of the local authority and thus, so far as is possible, ensure like treatment for all employees. With large departments such as this already in being, it would be difficult indeed for a librarian to persuade his authority that a separate library personnel section, with its overlord, were necessary. If such a proposal were accepted it would open the door to every other department making a like claim, thus increasing expense and perhaps causing divergence of practice between one department and another. There is also the natural opposition of the council's personnel officer who would prefer to see his own empire built up rather than share part of his functions with the other departments. Then again with a system of corporate management the idea of a centralised personnel department is strengthened. In spite of this there are a few large libraries[1] which are fortunate enough to have an established post for a professional personnel manager and possibly a training officer in addition. For the most part, however, both of these staffing functions in the library will have to be carried out as part of the duties of some other senior member(s) of the staff, probably the deputy librarian or someone at third tier level, though one or two middle-rank administrative posts might be established to deal with some of the more routine aspects of personnel management such as advertising, notification of candidates for interview, preparation of wages sheets for weekly paid staff, leave entitlements, appointment of temporary and part-time staff, appointment of manual staff, car allowances, and for general liaison with the personnel department at the town or county hall. Where the libraries are part of Education or Leisure, there is likely to be a small personnel section as outlined above responsible for these relatively routine matters for the whole of the department, under the immediate control of an administrative officer (non-librarian) with the major functions again being exercised from the town or county hall.

Not only public libraries but also those of polytechnics and colleges will be largely controlled in staffing principles by the local authority committee and its central personnel department though the academic board and the governors will have their own spheres of influence. In the university, staffing matters will also be vested to a considerable extent in the secretariat which will probably include a personnel manager and small staff. National schemes of salary grades and conditions of service will again apply and as with the local authority the basic principle will be to ensure uniformity of application in all departments of the university. Personnel functions which devolve on the library will usually be performed by the deputy librarian or a sub-librarian responsible for administration. In most special libraries, too, staffing matters will be dealt with by the seccretariat or the personnel department and the librarian.

At national and government department level the basic regulations and procedures are prescribed by the Civil Service Commission which arranges recruitment and selection procedures. Day to day personnel management will be that of the departmental administration with the director or the librarian being responsible for carrying out the required procedures in his own section.

ESTABLISHMENT

The first basic requirement of staffing is the 'establishment' or total complement of staff needed to operate the services decided upon by the governing body. The occasions when a completely new establishment is drawn up are rare, occurring only with the formation of entirely new libraries. Even when reorganisation has brought in its train so-called 'new library services' they are in fact largely amalgamations of existing libraries, and the establishment drawn up is based upon existing staff levels with adjustments. However, presuming a completely new establishment, the following are factors which ultimately determine its structure and numbers:

(i) *The objectives* of the library as formulated by the governing body.

(ii) *The organisational structure,* ie the complete plan of the whole organisation broken down into the component parts through which it operates, eg in an urban public library system:

Central Library; District Libraries; Branch Libraries; Mobile Services; Extra-mural services; Cultural Activities.
In turn each of these divisions would break down further, eg:

Central Library—Lending Dept.; Reference Dept.; Music and Records; Technical Dept.; Audio-visual aids; Children's Dept.; and Administration.

District Library—Lending Dept.; Reference Dept.; Music and Records; Children's Dept.; and small Administrative Section.

Branch Library—Lending Dept.; Children's Dept.; Library Hall.

Mobile Services—Mobile Libraries; Housebound Readers; Delivery.

Extra-mural Services—HM Prison; Hospitals; Old People's Homes.

Cultural Activities—Arts Centres; Theatre; Public Halls; Exhibitions throughout the whole area and Library lectures.

Some of these sub-divisions would break down still further but it will be sufficient to take Administration of the Central Library as an example. This could divide into:

Administration—Committee planning and correspondence; Personnel; Accounts; Orders (non-book); Stores; Bibliographical Services; and Public relations.

(iii) *Quality of service to be achieved.* This is all-important as standards can vary from a minimum providing for little other than having the library open with the least possible number of staff to operate the issue system and ensure minimal security, to a standard where there is a sufficiency of staff to guard against unexpected illness; to provide professional advice to readers; to prepare reading lists and other material; to give reasonable assistance to research workers; to encourage children to make good use of the library; to introduce new readers; to promote extension activities; to arrange displays; to provide an information service; to go out to schools and organisations to talk about books and libraries and generally to promote the service further. In all to aim at maximum potential use and overall efficiency.

(iv) *Hours during which the service is to operate.* This is a very important factor as a library which opens beyond normal office hours is going to be much more expensive in staff. If it opens another three or four hours after 5 pm, it will have to provide extra staff. Again if it does not close for a half-day or a day in the week, or if it keeps open at lunch-time, more staff will be needed. Similarly Sunday opening, as with universities, will affect staff numbers. Overtime rates may also come into operation.

(v) *Staff conditions of service.* ie the number of hours staff are contracted to work each week; annual leave allowance; whether, in emergency, staff are contracted to go out on relief to other service points.

(vi) *Sickness.* An allowance must be made for coverage in cases of absence of this kind.

(vii) *Study leave.* Where staff are allowed day-release and other study time, an addition to the establishment will probably be necessary. This should include for attendance at study courses, examination leave, leave prior to examinations, and attendance at conferences, if this is permitted. Where a quota of staff is given time off to attend library school, eg three a year, then provision must be made, temporarily at least, for replacements.

(viii) *The types of user; numbers of users and peak periods; depth of service.* Research workers are likely to be much more demanding on the time of professional staff and to need more personal service. The numbers of users and peak periods should be considered together. Staffing should be planned to meet maximum demand, but at the slack times of the day or year less staff will be necessary. This helps to plan days off, half-days and evenings off as well as annual leave. It may also help in the allocation of the lunch hour. Depth of service relates to facilities provided by way of information and reader assistance, reservation and inter-loan services, numbers of books that can be borrowed, provision of photocopying services, carrels, visual aids, listening booths, and so on. The greater the facilities, the more staff required but it may be that the level of service after hours for instance, or in vacations, and at week-ends, is deliberately reduced.

(ix) *The skill-mix.* In other words the relative representation required of qualified, part-qualified and unqualified librarians. Other professional skills may also be required: in personnel management and in the arts, for example. Manual staff is also needed for caretaking and cleaning duties and possibly technicians for visual aids, photographic services and theatre duties.

(x) *The buildings in which the library service operates.* For example, a library built on a subject department basis with a centralised control area will need a different system of staffing, and different numbers, from one divided on traditional patterns; multi-storey buildings are likely to need more staff than those on one floor. A new library designed with 'see-through' supervision may also need less staff than an old building with solid dividing walls between departments. Furthermore a new library may be built to ensure maximum in staff economy, certainly with regard to the issue system and other computer applications.

(xi) *The extent to which centralisation is practised and also the extent to which the parent-body provides certain services.* In a system for example, where all the book processing is decentralised, more staff would probably be needed; similarly in a system with computerised routines less staff should be required not only for circulation purposes but also for book processing and cataloguing. Centralised procedures for purchasing, book processing, repairs to buildings, publicity, personnel, and accounts among other items, should also reduce staff numbers at individual service points.

(xii) *Whether the establishment is to be drawn up on a pyramid basis,* with direct line of responsibility from the chief to deputy to chief assistant, and downwards to the most humble member of staff, or, *on a broader basis,* with a number of specialists immediately below the chief, all of whom are responsible for a broad-ranging service, or the service in a geographical area. Furthermore, in this connection some public libraries have dispensed with posts for professional librarians in branch libraries. Instead the day-to-day running is left in the hands of non-professionals (this has the advantage of providing career prospects for this category of staff) and arranging professional staff in teams which provide all the professional services to a group of branch libraries, both full and part-time, in a wide area. These librarians are made responsible for the full range of bibliographic and advisory services, as well as special services such as children's libraries and schools, information work, cultural activities, and community services generally. The latter involve taking the library to the public in all places where groups of people meet regularly, eg youth clubs, nursery schools, clinics, clubs and societies, hospitals, day centres, old people's homes, and the like. The idea originated in the former county libraries among which Leicestershire was to the fore and the activities of which have been described by J. Hinks.[2] This structure is particularly well-suited to rural areas for it facilitates the provision of professional staffing to many small service points which would not warrant a fixed establishment of professionals and it is also claimed to promote better job satisfaction. It owes much to the American innovation of their 'Outreach' programmes, designed to extend the influence of the libraries to groups who would never of their own accord venture into a library building, particularly the socially disadvantaged. It is not only the non-metropolitan counties that use this structure however but is also favoured in some heavily urbanised areas such as Lambeth in London and more recently by the Liverpool City Libraries.[3]

(xiii) *Standards.* There have been plenty of standards issued regarding the numbers and composition of staff required by different types of library. The Library Association has issued statements of this kind relating to university libraries, polytechnic libraries, college of education libraries, public libraries and schools. The American Library Association has also issued its standards as has the International Federation of Library Associations. The Minister of Education was responsible for issuing the Bourdillon Report which also contained staffing standards (1962) and more recently in 1976 the Department of Education and Science published the staffing report of the Local Authorities Management Services and Computer Committee which considered in great detail the staffing needs of public libraries. All of these standards are purely advisory and except for those of LAMSAC are based on a great deal of subjective judgment. The latter however, involved a great deal of research and although not above criticism they do show how staffing must be calculated largely on the basis of the standard of service to be provided; they illustrate the several points made in the preceding paragraphs (i) to (xii).

In addition to all these factors and maybe others which have not been mentioned, there is the over-riding one of finance. If the money is not there to provide for the number and mix of staff that is wanted under ideal circumstances, then something will have to be sacrificed, probably the hours of opening would be reduced, the number of service points reduced and less staff made available for reader assistance—there are numerous ways in which staff can be reduced at the expense of service.

It will thus be seen that if an establishment is to be drawn up in a systematic fashion it means that the whole of the library's organisation and its objectives will have to be closely scrutinised to establish the types of staff necessary and the numbers in various categories. Furthermore, the appropriate salary must be decided for each category of post. Consideration must also be given to the employment of more sophisticated equipment which might help to reduce the total number of the staff required. If the total cost for the establishment thus arrived at is too high then the objectives will have to be amended and standards reduced as suggested above.

Establishments are not likely to remain static; as new circumstances arise and as new developments are introduced then they will need revision: the addition of a new branch library, the introduction of computerisation, acquisition of a large special collection, provision of an information service to the whole of the parent organisation, or a large increase in student numbers. It is also good practice, to review the organisational structure from time to time in the light of changing circumstances. This will lead to a consideration whether all the services given by the library are still really necessary, whether some service points might be amalgamated, hours reduced or even extended, new equipment introduced, or some work put out to contract such as cleaning, punch card sorting, public relations, data processing or book processing. On the other hand, work which is already done by outside firms might be taken over by the library, eg bookbinding. A review of this nature might well pay handsome dividends but unfortunately it is rarely that there is anyone of sufficient seniority and experience available in a library to spare time for the most essential task of all—thinking! More often than not where the exercise *is* carried out it is performed by a firm of Organisation and Method consultants, or the organisation's central O&M section at quite considerable cost but without coming up with any ideas other than those the library staff could have produced far more quickly and more cheaply had they had the time.

In terms of pure management Thompson[4] calls the various processes which we have shown to be inherent in the framing of an establishment as 'the task-specialisation process'. French[5] has defined them as 'the complex flow of events (which) can be divided into segments that determine the nature of each individual's job'. In the ultimate, the personnel manager must have a very clear idea of the contribution each member of the staff will be called upon to make to the work of the library service and how each category of post fits in with the others; similarly each employee will need to know what is expected of him. It follows, therefore, that each job an individual is called upon to perform must be closely analysed, and in addition, it is necessary to know the kind of qualities the employee will need to perform this work satisfactorily. Thus the process of analysing staffing requirements involves job descriptions, job analysis, job specifications, and personnel specification.

JOB DESCRIPTIONS

These are the statements of the purpose of a particular job, its scope and responsibilities, together with details of to whom the post holder is responsible. Job descriptions are generally written for a group of posts with the same responsibilities, eg for branch librarians in a system, rather than for each individual branch librarian. (If there are any duties peculiar to any one of the branch libraries then these could be added to the general job description.) The job description is then said to have a *job-title* of 'Branch Librarian'. Job descriptions can be used for a number of purposes; for planning the overall establishment; for reviewing the organisational structure, including transfer of holders of posts made redundant to other positions; for job evaluation, ie rating a particular job with others on a relative basis for salary assessment; to give employees a list of their responsibilities; to send out to applicants who reply to advertised vacancies; and for staff appraisal. The method of compiling the job description and the precise content may vary in accordance with the purpose for which it is intended. An interesting article on the use and preparation of job descriptions to ascertain the kinds of people that are required for different categories of library and information work by Sergean and McKay[6] describes the different uses of job descriptions and various methods used to compile them, together with their advantages and disadvantages. It goes on to show how the Manpower Project funded by the former Office of Scientific and Technical Information (OSTI) devised a special questionnaire for the description and classification of jobs in the library and information field.

The job description is a fundamental feature of personnel management in industry and commerce, and is well-explained in most textbooks. One aspect that tends to be overlooked, however, is that if an employee is given a copy of his job description with his contract of employment he sometimes uses it as being a *complete* statement of every possible duty that he may be called upon to carry out. Consequently, if at any time he should be asked to do something not specifically mentioned he may, with his union's help most likely, seek to use it as a means of getting more money. While this may be considered, from the employee's point of view to be an advantage of having a job description, from the employer's angle it is very difficult indeed to draw up a job description which covers every duty an employee might be asked to undertake at some time, or, to list duties in language which might not, in the light of some future and unforeseen claim, appear to be ambiguous. This problem is most likely to occur with job descriptions which have been compiled for job evaluation. Where a major change in responsibilities occurs then of course a review is warranted but the special pleading referred to above is linked with unlisted duties that are really only of a minor nature.

JOB ANALYSIS

Where a job is minutely observed by personal observation, and the employee and his immediate supervisor interviewed, and then the job checked with a standard checklist and the circumstances under which it is performed are noted, this is known as 'job analysis'. It can be used for the preparation of job descriptions, for careers' guidance, personnel selection, training programmes, ergonomics, and work study. Pre-supposing that the library has long since been provided with a reasonably satisfactory establishment, then the remaining uses would be for a regular review of the organisational structure (perhaps once every three years); in the event of reorganisation; for job evaluation and for training.

Job specification. This term is applied to the description of the physical and mental abilities required for the job. It lists the skills required of the worker and the knowledge used in doing the job, together with the judgment required in decision making and the experience required to carry it out.

Personnel specification. A statement of the kind of person who would be suited to do the job as interpreted from the job specification.

PROFESSIONAL AND NON-PROFESSIONAL POSTS

Posts in libraries are usually classified into two or three categories—professional, non-professional, and in some cases sub-professional or trainee. As far as possible the groups should each be allocated duties which are mutually exclusive. This ensures that valuable professional staff time is not wasted on non-professional duties, and also affords the trainees the opportunity to get the right kind of training and experience. It also helps to promote job satisfaction for professionals and trainees. Unfortunately, the non-professionals are left with all the routine and repetitive duties, and they may find little job satisfaction unless they can be given some minor responsibility which is theirs alone. There is usually little or no career prospect for them. Only in a few libraries such as those using team staffing is there any kind of senior rank among non-professionals. (The Library Association's proposals for the future qualifications of librarians should assist in this direction.)

Fortunately, there does appear to be a large number of people who are only looking for short-term employment, such as those waiting to go to college, others waiting for a year or so to begin some vocational training, and girls only wanting a job for a year or two until they get married. Then there is no shortage of married women only too anxious to take up a part-time post so that instead of taking on one person full-time the library can take on two part-time. In any event, when non-professionals are first taken on the limited prospects must be made quite clear to them, otherwise the librarian will soon have a lot of disgruntled people on his staff.

The actual standards required for entry to each of the three categories of staff will vary between different types of library and even between libraries of the same type. In national and government libraries the primary requirement for professional library posts may be a first or second class (div 1) honours degree; librarianship qualifications may be an advantage but not necessarily compulsory; some posts at lower level may be open to professionally qualified non-graduates, and there will be large numbers of non-professionals recruited on clerical grades. In large libraries of this kind other professions may also be represented such as accountants, personnel managers, computer programmers, public relations officers and technologists, as well as a number of technical assistants of various kinds.

In the university world the top ranks are almost certain to be filled by graduates with a good honours degree and possibly a higher degree. Though a professional qualification may not be regarded as vital it is common to find that senior members of university library staff are graduate chartered librarians. In the middle ranks may be found some chartered non-graduate librarians who are in the main employed on administrative and technical aspects of librarianship and with little chance of reaching the higher ranks without a degree. Below them are the purely non-professionals who will have difficulty in improving themselves unless they have the initial qualification for admittance to library school. In the special library the top posts may be reserved for someone with a degree in an appropriate subject field, and preferably a librarianship or information science qualification. If there is more than one senior post it may be that the top post is for a graduate in the subject field covered by the library and the second person down is a chartered librarian. The everyday routine work will be carried out by non-professionals who may have no relevant educational qualifications for subsequent training as professional librarians. In local authorities, ie in polytechnic, college and public libraries, a mixture of professional graduate, and professional non-graduate libraries, is likely to be found at top level. Academic boards will favour graduates, but for the moment many of the college libraries are managed by non-graduate chartered librarians because they were appointed to one of the previous autonomous colleges which have now been amalgamated into a larger institution. Non-professional staff may not be required to have educational qualifications beyond 'O' levels.

In the public library there is less emphasis at present on degrees, and the basic requirement is the ALA or FLA for the professional posts. As yet there is no obvious preference on the part of the local authority for graduates in public libraries, and they have to take their chances for promotion alongside the non-graduates. As the younger ranks of senior assistant librarians now contain large numbers of graduate chartered librarians, and as a degree seems likely to be necessary for entry into the profession shortly, then in due course the top posts must inevitably be filled by them. An intermediate rank of trainee librarians is usually found in public libraries and may include some who have been guaranteed a year's training before going to library school on full salary and all expenses paid (a few such posts are also to be found in other types of library). The routine duties will be performed by non-professionals with perhaps three 'O' levels. Although career prospects will be generally lacking they may be able to be promoted to another department of the authority as it is usual for vacancies in all departments to be circulated, and for existing staff to have priority over outsiders, all other things being equal.

RECRUITMENT AND SELECTION FOR INTERVIEW

Apart from the relatively few trainees who may be recruited and whose posts will be advertised nationally, recruitment falls into two classes. The *non-professional* posts are usually advertised locally in the newspapers, or they may be filled from lists maintained from direct applicants. An official form of application will have to be completed and in due course some of the applicants will be interviewed: not more than six for each post, preferably less. Where there is a personnel section, it will probably be responsible for filling all such vacancies, with a librarian helping in the interviewing. If there is no personnel section then the interviewing may be done by one or more librarians. It is generally the custom to ask all applicants to declare on their application form whether they are related to a senior officer of the organisation or to any member of the governing body. References too are generally required and at least one of these should be from the current employer if the applicant is at work otherwise from the principal of the school or college. Appointments are also usually subject to passing a medical examination or the approval of past medical history as submitted on a special form by the applicant and signed as correct.

Professional positions and others of senior rank are almost invariably filled as a result of advertising. In the United States they have what seems to be an admirable practice of *inviting* likely people to fill a *top* position, or at least to be considered for it, but this would be very rare indeed in the UK and certainly never in government and local authority circles. In the first instance advertising may be directed to persons already on the staff, but if it is known that there is no suitable candidate then immediate resort would be made to public advertisement. Many employers nowadays, especially local authorities, are very anxious to ensure career opportunities for their staff; hence initial internal advertisement only. There may also be an agreement to this effect with the union. The advertisement (whatever the kind) will give details of the post including: title, location, salary and very brief outline of duties; it will ask for references and give a closing date and probably invite interested parties to write in for further particulars. These will be sent by post and will include the job description, and a description of the library and of the amenities of its location; perhaps a copy of the last annual report will also be enclosed.

When the completed applications have been returned they will be collected and registered by the assistant in charge of personnel and probably placed in alphabetical order. Those not having the necessary qualifications will be weeded out, and then a preliminary sifting out process will be made dividing the applications into those who might be interviewed and the others. The forms would then pass on to the librarian or his deputy for the selection of a small number. Sometimes the personnel officer of the parent organisation may have to approve this list, but when it has finally been agreed the candidates will be informed by letter and asked to attend for interview on a given date.

SELECTION METHODS

In spite of the well-known limitations of the interview as a means of selecting future employees, it is still more or less universally adopted for filling professional posts in libraries. Much depends on the thoroughness with which preparations are made for the interview, the selection of the interviewers and the conduct of the interview. These factors will be dealt with shortly, but the major factor is that no other method has been satisfactorily proved to be superior for appointments of this nature. Some of the other methods would need the presence of a trained psychologist. These alternative, or supplementary, methods include intelligence tests, aptitude tests, proficiency tests, and personality tests. At the interview level there is also the alternative of group interview.

Of the non-interview methods it has to be remembered that applicants for professional posts have already obtained professional qualifications and, what is more, had to have either a degree or 'A' levels to sit the appropriate examinations. Most will also have already been interviewed at one or two levels before being admitted into the profession, eg for initial employment in a library for twelve months before going to library school; for admittance to the authority's trainee grade; and, for admittance to library school. Candidates for the more senior posts will also have previously had actual experience in a subordinate professional post in one or more authorities. Thus, tests of intelligence, proficiency and aptitude seem to be quite unnecessary and psychological tests are suspect because it is relatively easy for candidates to prepare themselves for them, analysis of the results is open to question, and, they depend so very much on the training and background of those carrying out the analysis. If there were time, a series of simulation exercises such as those carried out in library schools[7] might be more reliable but even these are dubious in the realm of selection. They are more suitable as a teaching aid and to be satisfactory need to be employed over a fairly long period so as to train students in perception and reaction to circumstances. Thus the conclusion is that though some of the tests mentioned above might be useful for selection for certain non-professional posts they do little to assist at professional level. When employing a shorthand-typist it is quite useful to ask the candidates to take an informal test of their speeds; a punch-card machine operator to show familiarity with a high-speed sorter; and, an audio-visual aids technician to demonstrate acquaintance with different pieces of equipment, but in the field of the professional librarian it should be sufficient to select by past experience, qualifications, and impressions gleaned at interview.

Both at non-professional and professional levels, however, it is standard practice to ask for references. The reliability of references is notoriously unsound, and many a person with glowing references has subsequently proved unsatisfactory. Nevertheless, it cannot be said that references are useless. It is often a good practice, where a reference seems to be somewhat lacking in praise, or possibly ambiguous, to telephone the writer and ask a few discreet questions. Referees are often prepared to say in confidence over the telephone what they would not commit themselves to in writing.

THE INTERVIEW

The most popular method of interview is that carried out by a committee, a panel, or just one person (though the latter is not to be recommended even for non-professional junior posts). Usually candidates are interviewed for a period of about half an hour, sometimes a little less, but with very senior posts there may be a preliminary interview which cuts down the list of interviewees from about six to three.

Apart from this *individual interview* there is another method which has been used extensively by the civil service selection boards, the armed forces for commissioning, and industry for certain types of post. This is called *group selection*. There is no single pattern for conducting this type of interview and the employing body can devise its own programme, but the basic purpose is to see how people react in a group under varying circumstances. Depending on the time at the disposal of the employers, the testing period can occupy half a day, a day, or even two or three days. In the latter case the candidates are brought together in the surroundings of a staff college or, failing this, a suitable hotel where they mix together and with a small panel of assessors (perhaps four men and women in total). They will be under the observation of these assessors not only in formal sessions but at meal times, coffee breaks, in the bar, and on organised visits outside. Meanwhile, they will as a group be involved in programmed discussions of chosen topics, or as a committee, or perhaps in simulation exercises. It will be the aim to create an informal atmosphere throughout and to put candidates at their ease.

The panel will be observing the reactions and attitudes of the candidates in all these activities and will meet at the end of each part of the programme to analyse the qualities displayed by each candidate in his social skills, logic, leadership in discussion, initiative, grasp of problems, and certain personal characteristics, particularly the ability to get along with others. Finally, all the candidates might also be interviewed separately at the end of the group activities by each member of the panel. The latter will then meet for further discussions and ultimately will have to make a decision on which candidate is most suitable. Obviously this method of interview relies very largely upon the personalities and experience of the panel. Although one would expect that selection spread over a fairly long period of observation would be better than that resulting from only a half hour's interview, much of the assessing still depends upon subjective judgment.

The individual interview is, in many instances, still carried out by a committee of laymen with the librarian and the organisation's personnel officer in attendance. This practice is employed in local authorities in particular, though it is very much on the decline. The objections should be obvious enough, the committee is frequently far too large; few of the members may have any real knowledge of the requirements of the job, and they may be influenced by trivial rather than important factors; they may have had little managerial experience themselves and may ask completely irrelevant questions if left to their own devices. They can also inhibit and intimidate the candidates, and in brief fail to give the applicants the opportunity to show themselves to the best of advantage. If committees are employed in interviewing they should be restricted in size. Six would be ample, and they should be prepared to be guided by the senior officers in attendance. Between them the personnel officer and the librarian should have drawn up a list of questions to ask and the chairman should arrange it so that each member of the committee has his or her own question(s) from this list. It goes without saying that committee members should have been given copies of all the relevant application forms, references, and job descriptions, well in advance of the interview day, and that they should have read them.

The alternative to the committee, except in the case of very senior appointments where a small sub-committee may be chosen for the purpose, is to have a panel of senior officers from within the library department and the organisation's personnel officer, and the head of the section where the vacancy exists. Space does not permit detailed discussion of the qualifications required of interviewers but it is desirable that all members of the panel should be experienced in the work and if possible should have attended a course of training therein. The aim should be to put all candidates at ease and to give them a fair opportunity to talk and express their ideas in the context of the post in question. They should have been invited to look over the library some time before the interview and should have been given any information about it that they might require. All candidates should be made to feel that the panel is really interested in them, not merely going through the motions before they appoint someone decided upon in advance, and they should also be given the opportunity to ask questions of the panel if they so wish. The chairman should introduce its members to each candidate as he comes in for interview. As far as possible candidates should not be kept waiting around for their turn for interview; a time-table can be worked out in advance. Similarly at the end of each interview the candidates can be told that they will be notified of the decision by post or telephone, rather than keep them waiting in a state of nervous tension. Most appointments have to be confirmed after a medical examination or receipt of a satisfactory statement of health and no one should resign the post he is holding until all such formalities are over and the appointment finally approved. The letter of confirmation will also probably be accompanied by the contract of employment (Contracts of Employment Act, 1972).

CONDITIONS OF SERVICE

The Contracts of Employment Act, 1972, provides for certain contractual relationships between the employer and the employed which lay down obligations on both sides with regard to the notice the employer has to give the employee and vice-versa, and require the employer to give written details of the conditions of service applying to the appointment. In most libraries these conditions are already available in printed form and have been agreed by the employers and the unions in respect of the whole range of services operated by certain categories of employers, eg as in the civil service, local government, and the universities. They will include agreed salary scales but in some cases the employer may be given a fair degree of flexibility in their application. Thus, for example, in local government the salary grades used for librarians are those of the non-manual staff generally, namely those of the National Joint Council for Local Authorities, Administrative, Professional, Technical and Clerical Services but apart from laying down minimum scales for qualified librarians and trainees they leave the local authority free to choose for itself in what grade specific posts should be placed, thus some authorities will pay a higher salary than others for a comparable post. In the polytechnics and local authority colleges some of the library posts will be graded on these NJC scales but the top professional posts will be equated with the teaching staff and paid on Burnham scales or above. The university librarians for long pressed their claim to be equated with academic staff for salary purposes and this claim has always been an important reason why a degree has always been considered essential for a professional librarian in the university world. They have now realised this ambition with a national scale which places the librarian on the professorial grade and senior librarians on grades for senior lecturers/readers or lecturers. There are also grades for clerical and certain administrative staff on which professional non-graduates and non-professionals are placed.

Apart from salary scales, conditions of service include such matters as annual and special leave, sickness, maternity leave, hours of work, probation, promotion, post-entry training, travelling and subsistence allowances, official conduct, discipline and appeals procedure. According to the type of library in which they work, each member of staff should be fully conversant with the conditions which apply to them: they can be numerous and detailed. The contract of employment is most likely only to refer to the printed conditions of service so that it is essential to get a copy and digest the procedures and 'rights'. Nevertheless, it is surprising how many members of staff scarcely bother to do so and may, therefore, fail to get the benefits to which they are entitled.

JOB EVALUATION

From the foregoing reference to salary scales it will be seen that with the exception of industry, commerce, and the special library field, most library staff are paid according to recognised official scales which have been negotiated between employers as a body and trade unions. Thus we get negotiated scales, not only in local government but also in the civil service, in the universities, and in colleges. Just how the particular scales were originally framed is a matter of history and most have been amended beyond recognition with the passage of time. For example the National Joint Council scales, operating in local government, go back over thirty years to the formation of the NJC itself in 1944. More important than the salaries attached to the grades, is the application of a particular grade to any one job. Although there is a certain rough kind of relativity between the scale attached to one group of jobs and others within the same department and supposedly between one department and another (although the jobs may differ enormously) this has been established largely by subjective judgment. Thus, for example, librarians' salaries in local government have always been influenced by the judgment that the librarian's job is worth less than that of some of the other chief officers (in fact the librarian may not be classified as a chief officer). In turn the salary of the deputy will be related to that of the chief, and that of other members of the staff will be related. It has always been a problem to establish a true relativity between all the many different types of post which are to be found in a large organisation. University librarians have perhaps, been the most successful inasmuch as they have been able to get their salaries geared to those of the academic staff, with the university librarian on the professorial scale. Even so, of course, it could well be argued that the salaries of the academic staff are not adequately related to other high-ranking officials in other fields (eg in the civil service), however, a national evaluation scheme is something of a pipe-dream. On the other hand, relativity within the parent organisation and between like jobs in these organisations is more possible and certain steps in this direction have been taken which have partially improved things.

This process of methodically establishing scales of salaries and applying them so that they reflect the relative responsibilities of one job with another is called 'job evaluation'. In libraries in the United States, one finds that such a method has been applied for many years to the extent that it is common practice in public libraries to *classify posts* within broad categories and then to establish a 'relative' scale between different groups of posts. Such scales would need the approval of the library board, or where a civil service system, or its equivalent, operates, of the Civil Service Commission or the city's personnel officer. The classification of posts involves job analysis, job description and job classification, so that the duties expected of the post and the qualifications required of the holder are fully considered in deciding the classification, but something more precise is needed for equating the relative value in money terms of the requirements of specific groups of posts. Job evaluation schemes have attempted to do just this and in the United Kingdom the most popular method has been to attach a number of 'points' to the basic requirements of all posts and thereby produce a relativity as expressed by the sum total of points scored by each post or group of posts within a given department and between departments, which should be rewarded in a consistent and fair manner. *Such a scheme automatically accepts the grading scheme employed, such as that of the National Joint Council, and therefore cannot remedy any defects in the scheme itself.*

Not all job evaluation schemes work on this 'points' principle; there are others but this is one that the Prices and Incomes Board, in a survey published in 1969,[8] found to be the most popular in this country. They found that job evaluation schemes applied to six and a half million workers, of these 47 per cent favoured points rating; 28 per cent grading; and 5 per cent factor comparison. For further studies of these different methods the reader is referred to articles by J. L. Schofield,[9] Assistant Director of Research, University of Cambridge and by B. G. Dutton[10] of the Division Information Unit, ICI (Mond).

In the local government field, the first use of job evaluation was the Greater London Evaluation Scheme in 1971. This was the work of the London Boroughs Management Services Unit. Basically it involved each member of the staff of an authority completing a detailed questionnaire about his job. The officer was then asked to sign that this was correctly completed and it was then counter-signed by his immediate supervisor. With the use of the questionnaire, the job analyst then interviewed the officer to get an all-round impression of the job and its content. He then prepared a job description which the post holder was asked to read, agree, and sign as being a fair representation of the job. Once agreed, then the job had to be considered by a panel of evaluators, armed with the job description. Consideration was focused into a number of broad headings such as 'Education'; 'Experience'; 'Supervising responsibility'; 'Decisions made'; 'Work complexity'; 'Responsibility for assets'; 'Contacts'; 'Creative work and Reports'; a responsibility level factor had to be allocated for each of these headings. Advice from a senior officer in the appropriate department was available when necessary. The responsibility factors then had to be translated into points from fixed scales. The total points scored then represented the relativity of that person's post to all others in the organisation, and was in turn converted into a specific salary grade within the NJC's grading structure.

No job evaluation scheme is perfect but any scheme used consistently throughout London would theoretically produce a complete standardisation of grading. In the case of this particular scheme, although it went some way towards doing so, it could not be claimed that every authority which did use it did so in exactly the same way, and, as subjective judgment was inevitably involved to a large extent, it is not to be expected that every group of evaluators came up with exactly similar results. Apart from attempting to establish relative scales of salaries, this job evaluation exercise was important, however, inasmuch as it required a complete job analysis of the whole of a local authority's staff and the production of agreed job descriptions. It provided an opportunity to review the operational structure of each department and it also revealed any over or under employment of different categories of staff. Naturally arrangements had to be made for appeals, and, once carried out, it was essential to arrange for all new posts subsequently being added to an establishment to be evaluated before the salary was agreed and the position advertised. Regular revision is also a requirement of any such scheme and individual members of staff should be given the opportunity to ask for a further evaluation of their post if they consider the duties and responsibilities have been materially changed.

Following upon the job evaluation carried out in London boroughs, the national employers commissioned the Local Authorities' Management Services and Computer Committee (LAMSAC) to advise on the establishment of a similar scheme for local authorities outside London so that a uniform system could be put into operation. The scheme which was approved followed very closely the London pattern and is included as Appendix H to the National Joint Council Scheme of Conditions of Service, together with explanatory notes and a code of guiding principles governing the application of the scheme as well as guidance for the evaluation panels in dealing with the job factors.

If and when, this job evaluation is completed for all local government officers outside London then, in theory, there should be uniformity in grading of all posts in all public libraries and between posts in libraries and other departments of every local authority. In practice, however, the scheme is still far too subjective, and there is no possibility that this utopian state of affairs will materialise. The best that can be said is that where job evaluation has been carried out many injustices have been rectified, and a standard way has been provided for looking at hundreds of thousands of posts in local government. Although the scheme can be criticised on the grounds of fairness it is based on a principle that can be easily understood and on which the individual can build up a case for appeal should he think he has been unfairly treated and it should therefore assist in the promotion of better staff relationships.

PROBATION

Many authorities have a provision that all new appointments are subject to probation. The period may vary between three and six months, or in some cases even longer and is a safeguard against appointments which turn out to be unsatisfactory. In effect it means that at the end of a probationary period, providing a satisfactory report is received from the appropriate head of department, the member of staff concerned is appointed to the permanent staff. On the other hand, if the report is unsatisfactory, in theory, the assistant's services can be dispensed with, but a very good case has to be made out nowadays to avoid a charge of unfair dismissal. Consequently, a carefully laid down procedure has to be followed before resort can be made to dismissal. (Probation may be dispensed with where the person appointed has come from another library with transferable superannuation benefits.)

APPRAISAL

The probation system usually entails a regular continuing system of staff appraisal, sometimes called 'assessment' or 'evaluation'. With a six-month period of probation this may call for reports at the end of the fourth, fifth and six month. Just how detailed a report is made depends upon the authority. In some cases it may be on a printed form listing a whole range of qualities, both physical and mental, which an individual may be expected to exhibit in his work, with columns provided against each item for assessment as 'Excellent'; 'Good'; 'Fair'; 'Poor', etc. Some of these appraisal forms list dozens of characteristics which have to be assessed by the supervisor but others may be very brief just indicating overall assessment as being fit, or otherwise, to be taken on the permanent staff. Assessment forms are very common in America, they are not merely in use for probation but throughout the working life of the members of staff. They are used for many purposes but particularly for assessing eligibility for promotion at various levels. It must be remembered that promotion schemes are very formal in America where candidates have to get placed on an eligibility list before they can apply for promotion—a very different situation from that prevailing in Britain where anyone on the staff can apply for any vacancy on the establishment, no matter how exalted the position. Two recent articles show the use of staff assessments in Brooklyn, NY,[11] on one hand, and in Shropshire CL[12] on the other. Apart from use in probation, appraisal forms are *not commonly* employed in libraries in the UK with the exception of the civil service and to some extent in industry. They are generally considered to rely too much on subjective judgment and the difficulty of establishing common levels for interpreting standard assessments such as: excellent, good, average, below average, poor, makes it very hard for supervisors to complete the forms in a manner fair to all staff. The time-consuming nature of the exercise also makes these report forms unpopular; different supervisors are known to have marked differences in standards they expect; prejudice can often creep into assessing; and, sometimes there may be a wide variation between the comment of the immediate supervisor and the one above him—a variation which may be almost impossible to resolve.

It often is the practice in Britain to show regular appraisal forms to the individual concerned *only if considered to be unsatisfactory*. This is done to forewarn the person in case some disciplinary action may arise at a future date because of the poor standard of work, and as a precaution lest he should claim that he was never warned. At the same time it seems to be a waste of the opportunity provided by the assessment form not to use it to encourage someone to better effort whose work, though not exactly unsatisfactory, could be improved. Similarly, if a person's work warrants a high rating it seems common-sense to encourage him by showing him the assessment form. By far the largest employer of librarians in this country is local government but in a survey carried out in 1970[13] in large public libraries only a tiny minority reported the use of assessment forms and in fact many of the librarians expressed surprise at their mention. The survey reported as follows: 'The English attitude towards evaluation is well demonstrated by the reply to the questionnaire which indicates that 18 out of 26 libraries have no regular evaluation reports. Of the 8 that do, some of them seem in doubt as to their purpose and gave "references" as a reason. . . . There is without doubt in England a marked dislike of reports on staff and a very strong belief that they are often a vehicle of personal prejudice.' (On the other hand all 25 USA libraries used them.)

Thus the situation in Britain can be summed up by saying that while assessment reports are a normal feature of probationary service and are usually also employed with training schemes, they are otherwise little used outside the civil service. Although the N J C *Conditions of Service*, for instance, now require a report after one year's service in addition to probationary reports and give authorities the right to demand further reports if they so desire, these conditions are not binding and do not appear to command much respect for assessment reports from either the employers or the unions. As pointed out previously, an unsatisfactory report when shown to the individual concerned and signed by him as having been seen, is necessary evidence in any subsequent disciplinary action; in addition it could happen that where a panel is undecided between the merits of two applicants for promotion, the assessment report may be the deciding factor, but apart from this when indeed they *are* kept, they just tend to remain in the archives.

The fact that assessment forms are not used does not mean that staff is not under constant appraisal. The immediate supervisor will know only too well particular strengths and weaknesses, and will be able to use the former to advantage. When the possibility of promotion arises it is therefore essential that the view of the supervisor(s) is obtained and it is equally possible to ask for a report on any member of the staff should special circumstances so require. The only danger is, and this is a point in favour of annual assessment, that supervisors come and go and staff also move around from one department to another. The assessment form does provide for continuous assessment and for more opinions than one.

INDUCTION AND TRAINING

At whatever level an appointment may be made, it is a fundamental that all new members of staff should receive an adequate induction and, except for the top tier posts, further training. It is essential to encourage a sense of belonging and participation and to this end induction is a preliminary and also helps to promote job satisfaction. The induction process will be much the same whether it be for professional or non-professional staff and will be organised by the member of staff responsible for personnel through a senior officer who has been given the overall responsibility for co-ordinating training. Most of the actual teaching and demonstration will be done by selected members of the staff with a long experience of the work of the individual sections of the library service. It follows that the instructors should ideally have had training themselves in the art of instruction. Induction is aimed at familiarising the individual with his surroundings and with his colleagues, with the total organisation of the institution, and the place of the library within it, and with the basic regulations. Thus, the newcomer will be given an introduction to his immediate supervisor and the staff with whom he is to be in regular contact; he will be told briefly about the function of the department in which he is to work; given a tour of the building with a brief explanation of the functions of other sections and introduced to their supervisors; introduced to the library's union representatives; told about his conditions of service, including working hours, leave, staff facilities, etc; and perhaps shown a film of the library's work, or failing that, a film about some other library of the same type; alternatively, the deputy librarian might give a talk about the library service and illustrate it with coloured slides. The proceedings should at some juncture include the demonstration of a chart of the organisation and the staffing hierarchy so that the chain of communication will be understood. The attention of new members will be directed to the staff manual for information about the detailed working of the library and all should be given a booklet describing their conditions of service, methods of payment, deductions from salary, how to apply for leave, what to do in case of sickness or other emergency, study facilities, financial help with examinations, and any other useful information which an intelligent newcomer will want to know.

It is best if a number of new people can start work together so that an orderly programme of induction training can be followed as a group thus making less demand on the time of senior staff called upon to give talks. If this cannot be done, a standardised induction course can be followed without the formality of group time-tabling. The whole exercise must, however, be given priority and treated as an essential rather than as a nuisance factor disrupting the everyday work.

The initial induction course may be completed in one to three days, according to the size of the library and its parent organisation, and should have helped the newcomers to settle in but, this apart, all of them will require further training over a period of some weeks. The non-professionals are likely to receive this direct from their immediate supervisor and one or more of the most experienced of the junior staff who will be delegated to take the newcomer under their wing. A report booklet should be made out for each non-professional under training in which is a list of all the duties he will be required to perform with a space for the supervisor to initial as the necessary skill has been acquired. At the end of the booklet there should be space for a general assessment of the assistant's capabilities and personality. This will be of use later on when the probation report has to be completed. The training of non-professionals will be incorporated into their daily work which will involve practising the skills taught gradually until fully capable of being able to carry out all the duties of the post. By the end of this time it is likely that the end of the probationary period will be in sight.

Professional staff, although fully qualified by examination and in some cases by experience in other libraries, will all need some training in the practices of the individual library. For preference they should also first be allowed to spend a week or so in each of the main sections of the library under the eye of the supervisor. The purpose would be orientation and learning in very broad terms the place of that section in the overall organisation of the library. The two most important sections in this respect would be the administrative and bibliographic services. As the new professionals are likely to have frequent contacts with other senior officers of the parent organisation, they should be introduced to their opposite numbers in the other departments of the council, university, college, firm and so on. Each newcomer must be made aware of his own particular responsibilities, be given a copy of the organisational chart of the library and of the chain of command so that he knows to whom and for whom he is responsible. The Standing Orders and Financial Regulations must also be drawn to his notice. Any particular abilities should be noted and the opportunity given to attend appropriate courses as and when available and generally the staff should be encouraged to proceed to further education and professional qualifications. The newcomers should be encouraged to get to know the staff of neighbouring libraries and members of outside bodies with a rôle relevant to the work of the library.

Provision must also be made for members of staff at this level to participate in staff management meetings and working parties; in general they should be made to feel that they are important and that their ideas will be welcomed. The aim should be to encourage complete involvement in the library service and management must therefore be receptive to any ideas that they may care to put forward; in this way job satisfaction will be considerably enhanced. Training of professional staff should not be regarded as something which will be completed in a few weeks. Orientation should take no longer than this, but training and education should be regarded as a continuous process involving experience and courses, both within and without the library, and which keep up with the constant changes in librarianship. Librarians working for local authorities are very fortunate in their opportunities for further education and training as, thanks to the Industrial Training Board, the authorities are able to pay the whole expenses of attendance at courses related to the work of the individual officer. This sometimes provides an opportunity to acquire an additional skill and leads to improved chances of promotion. The Library Association has issued three excellent publications on this subject of training.[14]

STAFF RECORDS

An efficient system of personnel management presupposes that within any concern, a systematic record will be kept of every member of staff from appointment to resignation or retirement. It may well be that the parent organisation will insist that this is the function of its central personnel department and that there is no need for the library to keep parallel records. Nevertheless, experience tends to show that though *the library* need not retain or duplicate many of the records relating to each member of the staff (eg the original application form for appointment and its references, the medical report form, sickness certificates, applications for study leave or to attend specific courses, annual report forms, and others of a like nature) there is without doubt a need for the library management to have certain basic facts at its finger tips. Only too often when all such records are left to the organisation's central department, the vital information cannot be traced, records have not been brought up-to-date, or have been lost, or some similar misfortune has occurred.

Computerisation has led to more and more centralisation of records but unless the computer is on-line and can be accessed at will, it is not very useful for everyday needs. It is ideal for the preparation of statistical records of recruitment and resignations; analysis of staff by departments and by age, sex, education; and for many other purposes including manpower planning, but the librarian needs something very simple for ready reference. There is therefore a place for a basic card index giving simple facts about staff such as full names, address, next of kin, telephone number, date of birth, date appointed, previous posts, educational and professional qualifications, courses attended, present studies, salary and grade. In addition to the card index, records of staff sickness and leave of various kinds should be kept, either on the same or a separate card index. Any matters of disciplinary action would also be noted on the individual's record (eg 'Reprimanded 20 June 1977') but the details of the charge and inquiry would most probably be kept in a separate confidential file under lock and key. It is normal to expunge records of such a nature after a given period because offences should not be held against someone indefinitely. It goes without saying that probation reports and training records will be kept for some time in the library files but there seems little point in keeping these for more than a year or two. All staff records should be treated as highly confidential and staff in charge of personnel matters should ensure that no unentitled person has access to the files.

WELFARE

Personnel management is also concerned with the general welfare of staff at all levels. By 'general welfare' we mean both physical and mental well-being. Responsibilities of this nature need the co-operation of both the employers and the employed. Some of them arise from legislation such as 'The Offices, Shops and Railway Premises Act, 1963, which in effect brought workers in such premises within the requirements relating to factory workers under 'The Factories Act, 1961'. It specifies certain basic provisions such as sanitation, ventilation, heating, lighting, cloakroom facilities, rooms for eating meals, seating where appropriate to the job, workroom accommodation, fire precautions, safety of staircases, and provision of first-aid boxes. Compliance with the regulations is supervised by the factory inspector. The most recent legislation of this specific type is 'The Health and Safety at Work Act, 1974'. It is a very comprehensive piece of legislation which makes it vital for managers to be aware of all regulations and codes of practice relevant to the health and safety of all workers in their employment. This includes library managers who therefore have a duty to ensure that adequate attention is given to staff working conditions and that potential sources of danger are eliminated. Statutory powers are embodied in the Act to enforce its requirements and it covers all people at work. It also calls for a positive contribution from employees in discussing with employers any risks involved in working processes and conditions and for the encouragement of a positive attitude to health and safety at work. 'The Health and Safety at Work Act, 1974' is further amended and strengthened by 'The Employment Protection Act, 1975' which re-defined regulation-making powers so that the appointment of statutory safety representatives is vested solely in recognised trade unions and the initiative for requesting the appointment of statutory safety committees vested solely in those representatives. The Act also pro-vides for an Inspector of Health and Safety to supply to anyone likely to be a party to civil proceedings a factual statement of matters he has observed which are relevant to the proceedings.

In the light of the legislation, and particularly as a good employer, the librarian should ensure that no member of his staff has to work in unsatisfactory conditions; that fire regulations are posted throughout the building and that everyone knows what to do in the event of the alarm being sounded (the occasional trial exercise is a good practice); that fire extinguishers are adequate in number and are serviced regu-larly; that no obstacles are left obstructing emergency and other exits, that there is a secondary form of lighting in the event of failure of the primary system (this is also very important from the public's point of view, especially when lecture halls and other library rooms are used for extension activities); that any equipment such as electrically operated guillotines are properly guarded; that steps and ladders are in good condition; that boilers are regularly serviced and that the janitors are properly trained in their use; that lifts and hoists are regularly inspected; that floors are not polished to such a degree as to make them dangerous; that the staff is not called upon to lift extra-heavy loads; that handrails are provided as necessary and are in good condition; that the staff is not exposed to dangers from air pollution, chemicals and other similar hazards; that the staff is not required to work for long periods in basement areas without adequate ventilation; and many other similar factors. Above all the management must inculcate into the staff a general realisation of hazards and the need to take adequate precautions against creating potentially dangerous situations for others through sheer carelessness and ignorance.

With regard to the normal health of the staff, the line managers in each section of the library have a responsibility to ensure that anyone who seems not to be fit while at work should be persuaded to see a doctor; if the member is advised to stay off work the employer must insist on a certificate of fitness before he is allowed to return. Normally there is little difficulty in persuading people who are physically ill to take sensible precautions, but mental problems are much more difficult to deal with largely because the manager may not even be aware that a member of staff has a problem.

Most people, however, in the course of their career, have personal problems which cause them great worry and anxiety, and which affect their work. Being personal and private matters, people are reluctant to let their immediate senior officers know about them, so that their reduced output becomes a source of concern and friction between them, and this worries the unfortunate assistant even more. This state of affairs can only be remedied by sensitivity on the part of supervisors to anxiety states, and by their being prepared to extend a sympathetic hearing to anyone in trouble. Not every senior assistant possesses these qualities and they are not to be expected of everyone, but the librarian could choose one or two suitable persons on the staff to act as welfare advisers. In this event it should be made known that where personal problems exist, Miss X or Mr Y is available to offer help and guidance to anyone so requesting. Once such help has been given to one or two members of the staff and gratefully received, the news soon circulates and others then have less reluctance in availing themselves of a sympathetic ear. In all libraries it must also be made known that the personnel officer, the deputy librarian and the librarian are always readily available to help where necessary. It may not always be possible to remove the circumstances prompting the anxiety but more often than not it is possible to alleviate the anxiety by flexibility in the time-table, a few days' leave (with pay if possible), arranging for an interview with the Social Services Department, or the medical officer, consultation with the Finance Department for an advance of pay, transfer to a place of work nearer home, or in some cases just by being a good listener.

COMMUNICATION

The most important of the factors which determine a satisfactory staff relationship is *communication* yet somehow a completely foolproof system of communication seems unattainable. This can be due to faults on both sides, for instance managers may not always be aware of the need to disseminate information—what might seem to be quite familiar and straightforward to them, is not so clear to some members of the staff. On the other hand, there are members of staff who do not bother to listen properly, who are prejudiced and do not want to know, and others who are opposed to change of any kind. However, even when the management consciously strives to ensure adequate communication and the staff is receptive there is still a major difficulty to overcome in many libraries in that most staff work on some kind of shift principle, so that what one group may be told at 9 am another might have to be told at 1 pm. Many library employees also work on a four, or four and a half day week basis so that the difficulty then becomes greater with a delay of twenty-four hours or even a long week-end between telling one part of the staff and the other. Flexitime has made its own contribution to this already difficult situation. Whatever the difficulties, management should be aware of them and should appreciate the fact that the better-informed the work force is, then the less scope there is for ill-informed rumour and speculation which is certain to have a disruptive effect on production and minimise the chances of job satisfaction.

Communication in terms of personnel management means keeping all levels of staff informed (manual as well as non-manual) about matters which affect them, about the objectives of the library and its parent organisation; factors promoting change in the parent organisation, eg government plans, new legislation; elections affecting the membership of the organisation or new appointments at top level eg a vice-chancellor, managing director, or chief executive, and revised conditions of service or pay awards. Changes within the library or external factors directly affecting it should also be made known, eg a new type of committee; amalgamation with another college; appointment of a new chairman; additional services to be provided; proposed new working methods such as computerisation; reduced hours; the library budget; matters to be presented to library committee and decisions made by them; and proposed closing dates over a holiday period.

The means of communication can be oral or written, direct or indirect. *Oral communication* is not too difficult a problem where the numbers are relatively small. The branch librarian, for instance, can get all his staff of seven or eight together in the morning for half an hour before the library opens and impart the information. *The fact that it has been understood, and this is the crux of all communication, can be checked on the spot by asking and inviting questions.* When the information has to be conveyed to a wider gathering complications begin to obtrude. First there is the time factor in going to and from the meeting place from outlying districts. The service must be kept going so obviously not everyone will be able to attend. Then there is the difficulty of putting over the message in terms which *all levels* of staff will understand; time will not permit asking and answering everyone's questions. A decision has to be made how the information is to be relayed to the absentees and by whom. Finally, there is the difficulty of ascertaining whether the information or the instructions given have been acted upon; subsequent feed-back, or better still, inspection is required.

Oral communication is also time-consuming and should not be regarded as the normal method of communicating information which every member of staff must know. When it does have to be employed it should be followed up with a written memorandum. This should ensure that everyone gets the message (though even then one cannot be sure that all will read it) and they can ask questions. Oral communication is ideal where the librarian wishes to put a problem before smaller groups of staff such as a meeting of subject librarians or branch librarians, to get their point of view and to observe their reactions to proposals. Small working parties established to investigate certain propositions also benefit by an initial explanation of the proposals. The major advantage of oral communication is that each person present is told exactly the same thing and if anything which is said is ambiguous then the doubt can be cleared up straightway, but to achieve the best results everyone concerned must be gathered together at the same time. If the content of a speech has to be relayed down the line, from representatives present to staff working in outlying posts, then the dangers of distortion multiply in proportion to the numbers who have to recount the speech. It is inevitable that no two persons will tell exactly the same story.

Written communications do have the advantage of disseminating one uniform message; they also provide a permanent record and can be referred to and quoted from again and again as required; they can be more precise than oral communications and can be conveyed at any time and over any distance. On the other hand it can always be claimed that a copy of a memorandum was never received; written communications cannot always convey the same emphasis as the spoken word; they provide no immediate means for cross-questioning; and, unless there is comprehensive feed-back it cannot be assumed that all the recipients have properly understood the message.

A written communication of a different kind is *the staff manual* which should contain a written statement of the library's organisation and its relationship with the parent body; the chain of command within the library; staff conditions in general terms; fire precautions; general safety precautions and security matters; and routine instructions on all the basic library procedures. This will be a large document and a copy should be kept in all sections of the library (though the specific routines it contains could be limited to the relevant section). It will form an admirable *vade-mecum* to library practice and should be an invaluable source of reference to staff, including newcomers, though to give the latter a copy of the manual to read should not be regarded as any substitute for practical training. Writing up these instructions for the manual means giving very careful consideration to every routine and can in turn lead to improvements and modification. Once a library has committed itself to a staff manual, however, this must be kept up-to-date. The more comprehensive the manual the more useful it becomes, but at the same time the more formidable becomes the task of constant revision. Written communication can also be conveyed through the media of house journals familiar to industry and commerce, or management information sheets, staff magazines and the use of staff notice-boards.

Finally, there is the consideration of *indirect communication*, ie communications with the staff, or from the staff, by means of an intermediary: either the trade's union or staff committee. In local government most of the non-manual staff belongs to the National and Local Government Officers Association (NALGO) and many of the manual staff to the National Union of Public Employees (NUPE) or to the General and Municipal Workers Union (GMWU). In academic libraries the professionals may be members of the Association of University Teachers (AUT) or of the National Association of Teachers in Further and Higher Education (NATFHE); their administrative staffs and non-professionals will probably join NALGO. Librarians in the civil service may be members of the Institute of Professional Civil Servants (IPCS), and in industry they may belong to the Association of Scientific, Technical and Managerial Staffs (ASTMS). While trade unionism is not very evident in library relationships generally, in the local authority area it has made large strides in recent years and a large proportion of public librarians belong. Some authorities require every employee to belong to a union. In each local authority there will be a local branch of NALGO which may or may not be very active. Where it is, then the branch will show an interest in most matters affecting the staff, including changes in organisational structure; staff holidays, especially bank holiday closures; grievances; disciplinary matters; flexitime; working conditions; and amendments to the establishment. In some cases the management will be required by agreement between the parent organisation and the union, to participate in joint discussions on staff matters before proposals are considered and decided upon at local authority committee level, and alternatively, to receive observations from the branch committee or the library department's union representatives. Even where the branch committee of the union may not be so very active the parent organisation may have a joint staff committee of members of the organisation and representatives of the staff. Thus, two-way discussion will be a feature of the management.

As time goes by it is inevitable that the unions will play a more and more important rôle in staff relationships as evidenced by *The Employment Protection Act 1975* which, among other things, actively encourages collective bargaining and gives trade's union members new rights, including time off to take part in union activities. The rights extended to employees and the provisions for job security inevitably place the unions in a strong position and relate to all full-time employees and a large number of part-time employees. Librarians and others with staffing responsibilities need to familiarise themselves with the rôles and rights of the unions. To some librarians the very suggestion of trade's union influence is unpalatable, particularly as it has not been felt yet in many libraries. There is no doubt, however, that the current government attitude is to give the unions greater influence even to the extent of participation in top level management and it should be no more difficult to work alongside the unions to get satisfactory staff relationships than it was for librarians to adjust themselves to the computer age.

References

1 Edwards, R. J. *In-service training in British Libraries*, LA, 1976, pp 61–64.
2 Hinks, J. Leicestershire libraries: a team based organisation structure. *In* Holroyd, G. *Studies in library management*, Vol. 4, Bingley, 1977, pp 67–84.
3 *Lib Ass Record*. July 1977, p 371.
4 Thompson, V. A. *Modern organisation*, NY, Knopf, 1961.
5 French, W. *The personnel management process*, 3rd ed, Boston, Houghton, Mifflin, 1974.
6 Sergean, R. and McKay, J. R. 'The description and classification of jobs in librarianship and information work', *Lib Ass Rec*, 1974, pp 112–15.
7 Williams, James G. and Pope, Elspeth. *Simulation activities in library, communication and information science*, NY, Dekker, 1976.
8 National Board for Prices and Incomes. NBPI Guide 3, Job evaluation, HMSO, 1969.
9 Schofield, J. L. 'Job evaluation, job analysis, job satisfaction and resistance to change', *Lib Ass Rec*, October 1975, pp 241–3.
10 Dutton, B. G. 'Job assessment and job evaluation', *Aslib Proceedings*, April 1976, pp 144–60.
11 Brandwein, L. 'Developing a service rating programme', *Library Journal*, 1 February 1975, pp 267–9.
12 Messenger, M. 'Professional staff assessment: the Shropshire pattern', *Lib Ass Rec*, January 1975, pp 2–4.
13 Corbett, E. V. *A comparative study of major personnel policies . . . in English and US large municipal libraries*, MA Thesis U of London, 1970, pp 56–66.
*14 LA. *Training in libraries*, report of the LA Working Party, 1977.
Edwards, R. J. *In-service training in British universities*, LA, 1976.
Anderson, Ursula *Management training for librarians*, LA, 1977.

9

Library Stock—Selection; Acquisition; Records

Librarians use the term 'library stock' in a very general sense to cover all material thought worth acquiring by purchase new or second-hand, or by gift or exchange. It includes books, newspapers, periodicals, abstracts, indexes and bibliographies, maps, illustrations, prints, drawings, photographs, postcards, deeds, archives, patents, standards, specifications, plans, reports, trade literature, conference proceedings, company annual reports, catalogues, laws, regulations, standards, statutory instruments, sheet music, records, tapes, films, video tapes, slides, microforms, and in fact anything which might be of use in providing information to the special categories of library users.

The make-up of the stock of an individual library will depend upon its size, purpose and clientele, and in particular on its resources and finance. For example, that of a small branch library in the public library field will be confined, except for a small collection of current newspapers and periodicals, to books, and these will be mainly works of fiction and popular non-fiction. On the other hand, the large city central library will have extensive collections embracing *every* type of material: material which must cover every standard of readership from the very young to the very old, from the semi-illiterate to the research worker, and which will include a large volume of recreational reading as well as material of an informative and instructional nature, and primary documents for research.

At university level the stock will have to meet the needs of undergraduates, research workers at various levels, and lecturers. Most of the categories of material already mentioned will be included, but the extent to which some of the commercial and industrial literature and ephemera will be collected for instance, will depend on whether relevant courses are provided within the university. Special collections are an important feature of some universities, and within the particular subject area of such collections every possible type of material might be sought. While having a very wide range of subjects on which to provide material in depth for the different faculties, the university unlike the public library, will not have to spend a large part of its funds on fiction and popular non-fiction. Although the concept of the university as a custodian of library resources for posterity is under challenge, so long as this policy persists the university will be engaged in purchasing second-hand a considerable amount of source and secondary material to strengthen its subject coverage. A large part of the expenditure will be spent on periodicals, English and foreign, to an extent which only one or two public reference libraries might aspire. Polytechnic and college libraries will also be geared to the syllabuses of the parent organisation and will also have different levels of scholarship for which to provide (particularly the polytechnics). They will be mainly concerned with current and recent literature, rather than in building up huge research collections even though the polytechnics will number a proportion of research workers in their ranks.

In industrial and commercial libraries the emphasis will be on current information: it is today's intelligence rather than yesterday's news that is important so that monographs will be less significant than periodicals, abstracts, report literature, conference proceedings, patents, specifications, trade intelligence, government department publications, statistics and other categories of material of a similar nature. Much of the required material is of a fugitive nature and needs tracking down, which can be very time-consuming.

Whatever the type of library there will be a certain limit beyond which it cannot expect its own stock to be sufficient to meet occasional demands. Therefore, even the largest and best-endowed library will have to resort at some stage to borrowing from elsewhere, transmitting its enquiries elsewhere, or getting the required information direct from some other source by telex, telephone or letter.

SELECTION POLICY AND PROCEDURE

It follows that in every library there should be a specific policy with regard to the selection of library material. This should firstly have regard to the types and ranges of items to be purchased and secondly to the administrative task of selecting the individual items to be bought in accordance with a regular timetable. So far as the first policy is concerned this will be geared to the objectives of the organisation, eg provision of a comprehensive and efficient service for all who reside, work or study in the area of a public library; or, in the case of a university, the provision of all types of material in all the subject fields and special collections relevant to the work of the university, for the needs of both staff and students at all levels; or in the case of a special library the basic objective could be described as, to further the interests of the firm or other organisation, by keeping abreast of its development plans and by liaising with its research workers to provide the information they require, at the time they need it, by ensuring that material which is likely to be wanted is available in the library itself and readily retrievable or is known to be available at short notice from other sources; in addition to keep the research worker actively informed of developments in his particular field as reported in current literature.

These broad objectives would then have to be translated into specific policies with regard to types of material and categories of user, obviously the amount of money available will also colour the policy to be adopted. This matter of the importance of an acquisitions policy received special attention in the report of the Parry Committee[1] which divided university library materials into certain categories—student texts, currently published books and series, currently published periodicals and a further category called 'other materials'. This latter category included items such as maps, sheet music, microforms, and audio-visual aids. The report then proceeded to give advice regarding the formulation of a purchasing policy for each category. College of education libraries received the same kind of attention in the ATCDE/LA document *Colleges of Education Libraries*,[2] 1967. In all libraries the effort should be made to write down an acquisition policy in the light of the likely commitments and financial and staffing resources. Far too many libraries still operate on vague and imprecise policies which have never been committed to paper.[3]

SELECTION PROCEDURES—PUBLIC LIBRARIES

Regardless of the type of library, the selection process cannot be satisfactorily carried out in isolation, by one person; even in the smallest library the assistance of the users, either directly or indirectly is fundamental. Undoubtedly there are still libraries where selection is still performed by the librarian alone; this used to be his time-honoured prerogative in many public libraries, the very large ones as well as the small. More than one much-esteemed chief has been heard in the past to say: 'I am prepared to delegate practically any responsibility but the one thing I will not delegate, which I will keep to myself, is book selection.' That was, of course, in the days when chief librarians were supermen! Incidentally, the volume of published literature was very much smaller than today, and now the selection of library stock, particularly current publications, is a team event. In a public library the team might consist of the librarian in charge bibliographical services and the librarians in charge reference services, and mobile services, together with the regional or district librarians. (Selection for the children would be done by the corresponding children's librarians and the librarian in charge schools.) The mechanics of selection will be affected by local circumstances and the size of the library system. It is usual, however, for a regular meeting to be held at weekly or fortnightly intervals at which the requirements of all departments are discussed. Discussion could centre round marked-up copies of the *British National Bibliography* or on lists prepared centrally from selection slips sent in by each department. As a supplementary method, it could be arranged for one or more booksellers to send in copies of all new books they have received that week, for approval inspection at the meeting. To be reasonably effective, these deliveries must include consignments from specialist booksellers, eg those who specialise in technical and scientific books, otherwise the procedure is likely to be devoted largely to books of a popular nature which virtually select themselves. Each book will be accompanied by a selection slip on which each librarian will indicate his requirements. It will be left to the meeting to decide ultimately whether all the copies so requested are really necessary or can be afforded. (The system must also include for the selection of replacement copies and older titles to fill gaps in the stock (see pp 176–7).)

There are many ways in which the book selection can be organised, but while one senior librarian must have the final responsibility for centralised co-ordination, the principle is that the librarian who is in contact with the readers is the one who knows best what is needed in his library. This should be patently true but the statement needs qualification. It means much more than merely knowing that two readers have asked for this book, and three for that, or that last week someone asked for a book on Staffordshire pottery but there was nothing on the shelves. And there is a lot more to book selection than just the consideration of new books as they are published. Much is heard about professional librarians being wasted on non-professional duties and it is true that in most libraries, particularly public libraries, too much of this still exists. On the other hand, too many professional librarians ignore their responsibilities for book selection to a greater or lesser degree and who can blame them in view of the profession's absorption with techniques and mechanisation, or the theory of management; how often does the subject of book selection ever make the headlines in our professional journals?[4] Too few librarians systematically edit the stock on the shelves; withdraw out-of-date and dirty books; deliberately check up how many books in the catalogues are not represented on the shelves, or which subjects are neither represented on the shelves nor in the catalogue; check the balance of elementary and more advanced works, or the availability on the shelves of the classic works of fiction and non-fiction; know how long it takes before some books ever appear on the shelves at all as they are permanently reserved or whether, on the other hand, some books on the shelves never go out; know how many times people come into the library looking for a particular book and never find it, or wait so long for books reserved for serious study that when they do arrive they are far too late to be of any use. How many librarians deliberately engage serious readers in conversation to try to find out how the library measures up to their needs? Perhaps even more important, how many of the staff regularly read book reviews and go out of their way to read several reviews of the same title? Even those who do so probably rely almost entirely on reviews of the more popular material. The fault is not necessarily that of the librarians in question for it also reflects the failure of management to emphasise the importance of book selection and maintenance of stock, failure to provide the necessary range of review literature and, above all, failure to allow sufficient time for this purpose in the assistant's normal working week. Pleasurable as it may be to read reviews, it ought not to be regarded by management as a luxury to be indulged in one's spare time. Provision of library stock is one of the most important duties any professional librarian is called upon to carry out but in spite of a great volume of lip service paid to it, the major attention in many public libraries is only too frequently geared to the purchase of *current* literature, most of it of a popular type which virtually selects itself in any event. It is reviewed in every newspaper and popular journal, and it is few librarians who could withstand the heavy volume of demand which results, particularly at the beginning of each week, after the perusal of the Sunday newspapers. The more important aspects of stock revision, replacement, withdrawal, and augmentation unfortunately often suffer and it is to these that management needs to pay more attention. The requirements of each individual library in these respects can scarcely be discussed adequately at any weekly book selection meeting. They should be debated at senior level within each branch or department, and the agreed requirements then discussed further with the stock editor or librarian in charge bibliographical services, and an agreed order drawn up as and when required. It might also be considered wise to allocate part of the overall bookfund to purchases of this nature and thus ensure that too much is not spent on purely current publications.

Other classes of material will have to be selected in a different way, eg government publications from lists and catalogues supplied by HMSO, and placing orders as required. In larger libraries it might be thought more expedient to place a standing order for *all* HMSO publications; even if it is more expensive than just ordering titles which are necessary, the saving of time in reading the lists and making out individual orders might justify it. Many other types of material will also be ordered by standing order (ie an authority placed with a bookseller or other supplier to deliver copies of some publications as produced). Annual publications, in particular, lend themselves to this treatment as do British Standards, series of maps from the Ordnance Survey, serial publications generally, and special library editions such as those frequently offered by bookbinding firms. Publications of specialist publishers, or of those in the non-print field, need to be selected from their catalogues or from specialist journals, eg gramophone records, tapes, films, prints, pictures, sheet music, and microforms. Other material will be obtained by establishing exchange arrangements or by writing to various organisations for free copies (usually material of a more ephemeral nature). The selection of some of this material will probably be best left to specialists on the staff rather than to a general book selection meeting, ie to the audio-visual aids librarian, the music librarian, the technical librarian, or the local history librarian, but even when the selection is left in the hands of the subject specialists they should do this in co-operation with their own subordinate staff. This tends to eradicate a certain amount of prejudice, gives a wider range of opinion, and helps to create better job satisfaction. Above all, the librarian should ensure that no matter to whom the selection responsibility is delegated he is given every support from above, equipped with all the necessary trade literature, catalogues and journals, and encouraged to visit bookshops and other sources of supply so as to keep himself fully informed.

There is a tremendous amount which could be done to encourage staff to improve selection techniques and to promote increased user participation. It is however very costly in staff time to carry out selection in a thoroughly competent and professional manner. Unfortunately most libraries do not have enough staff. Another factor in these days of mass production and processing is the cost-effective approach—it is so much quicker to order multiple copies of a popular work of biography or travel and to process them all together, than it is to trace and acquire an equivalent number of fugitive pamphlets or just one such pamphlet published overseas. The acquisition of difficult material and particularly the follow-up of orders not supplied, tends to get neglected in favour of that which is easily handled. Suppliers themselves are equally reluctant to spend too much time in following up orders for single copies of out-of-the-way material coming from an obscure publisher or agent. If the item has to be ordered from abroad they are even more reluctant for there is no profit in such transactions; on the contrary they can incur the supplier in a definite loss.

The allocation of funds to branches and departments needs to be considered. This practice is frequently adopted and appeals to departmental heads. As a result the librarian will inform each of them at the beginning of the financial year how much money is allocated to their department for the purchase of materials for the next twelve months. The figure may be a total for all kinds of material or on the other hand the allocation for records and cassettes may be distinct from books, and that for periodicals separate from both. There may be other divisions. Whether this is a good practice or not is debateable; it can encourage a librarian to spend his allocation whether or not there is a real need to use it all. It is impossible to estimate with any degree of precision what kind of material is going to be published in the next twelve months, how much of the stock is going to wear out and need replacement, whether any special new commitments may arise, whether the issues of some libraries may go up and others down due to movement or ageing of the population. The result is that there could be a certain amount of unwise spending. On the other hand if there is no allocation then the enthusiastic librarian may be getting more than a fair share for his library, while the one who is somewhat work-shy may not be over-zealous and his library thereby starved of material which it ought to be acquiring. One answer would be for the librarian in charge of bibliographical services to have charge of the funds and to spend them as orders are proposed by the departmental librarians; at the same time he must keep a record of expenditure, department by department, and by category of material (the computer would help), and investigate any apparent over or under spending. Obviously he will need to have worked out in advance an approximate estimate of the amounts he thinks each department might require for the year.

It is very easy to state categorically that a basis of allocation is essential to good stewardship but if one pauses to consider the different branch libraries in a system and their individual problems the difficulties of devising a fair basis of division become apparent (when the central or headquarters library and its several departments are considered they are even much more formidable). Here are just a few examples in the branch library context however:

i Library X was opened three years ago and with a completely new stock. Its requirements in these three years have therefore been relatively modest, being confined mainly to new publications. Now, however, a large part of the fiction stock and the popular non-fiction will need replacement, perhaps 30 per cent in all.

ii A new college has opened only 300 yards away from another branch, and there has been a resultant heavy demand for text-books and background reading.

iii In the area of three branches there is a large semi-illiterate population and a large concentration of immigrants for whom special provision should be made.

iv In another branch a new technical department has been provided by conversion of a former newsroom, but there has been no capital provision for books, these have to come from the revenue estimates.

v A cut-back in the local education authority's school libraries has resulted in a very heavy run on most of the children's libraries.

vi Stocktaking has revealed very heavy losses of books in library Y, and in consequence a large sum is required for replacement of essential material.

vii Persistent shortage of staff in some branches results in there having been no time to edit the stock over a long period. The staffing situation is rectified but the number of books needed to bring the stock into good condition is far more than was anticipated.

Many more examples could be given but enough have been listed to demonstrate that the needs of individual libraries differ enormously and that they can change almost imperceptibly. Taken into consideration, along with those already discussed, there seems to be a very good case for no hard and fast system of allocation.

SELECTION PROCEDURES—NON-PUBLIC LIBRARIES

The elaboration of the organisational and administrative problems to be found in the selection of material for public libraries can be translated in many respects to the academic world but other problems also arise there. The allocation of book-funds is a problem of long-standing, but this is not so much one of division between libraries as between departments of the university and the academic staff. In *universities* the academic staff has traditionally played a very important part in book selection, and in many of these libraries it has been customary to divide up the book-fund on a departmental basis with the librarian retaining a certain amount for general works, special collections and other non-departmental purchases. Needless to say, many of the objections raised with regard to a system of allocation within public libraries still apply in universities even though the fund is being divided among academic departments and not libraries. In fact the difficulty of controlling over-enthusiastic academics is one that would tax the capabilities of the most diplomatic librarian.

Today, however, the practice in many universities is for book selection to be a joint affair between subject specialist librarians and the academic staff in the related field, based upon regular liaison. This is in accord with the proposals of the Parry Committee[1] which endorsed the idea of training subject specialists to cover the subjects taught in the university and to whom should be given the fullest responsibility to carry out the book selection in co-operation with the academic staff. The committee also voiced non-approval of allocating book-funds to the departments by the library committee, and of giving the academic staff freedom to spend them without reference to the librarian. Nevertheless, there are still plenty of universities where the book-fund continues to be allocated in this fashion. Where the spending is controlled by the subject specialists, the university librarian will quite possibly still draw up a notional departmental division for his own private use and information to serve merely as a guide to what he anticipates departmental spending might be.

To a much greater extent than in the average public library, a large part of the university's acquisitions will consist of periodicals and a whole range of pamphlet literature. Long runs of periodicals will be maintained and many older volumes purchased second-hand as they become available. They will be reinforced with extensive holdings of English and foreign sets of periodicals in microfilm or microfiche and a special room with reading equipment will be provided. C. F. Scott[5] has written on the place of microforms in a provincial university library together with a review of associated problems. The proportion of money spent on periodicals varies from university to university in accordance with student numbers and the faculties but is particularly large in a technological university.

Whereas the public library may have a problem in deciding the extent to which funds should be allocated to providing for the needs of minorities such as the housebound, those with defective vision, or immigrant populations, the university's special problem is the provision of text-books for undergraduates. The polytechnics and colleges have a similar problem also, but none of these libraries appears to solve the difficulty completely as the public library is still faced with heavy demands from students who are unable to get all their reading material from their colleges. It would not seem to be too difficult for a lecturer to determine the number of copies of certain text-books his undergraduate students will be requiring, but apparently this happy state of affairs is elusive. Librarians claim that lecturers are overoptimistic about their students' eagerness to read and that heavy duplication in accordance with their forecasts tends to result in unwanted copies of books sitting idle on the shelves; students, on the other hand, complain that the books they have been told to read are never on the shelves. No doubt there are faults on both sides but from personal observation some lecturers' reading lists are in need of drastic revision and much more liaison with the subject specialist is desirable. Some appear not to have been revised for many a year, they are too long, and often not graded into essential and supplementary, alternative reading is not indicated and the lists contain too many titles out of print. Sometimes the reverse happens, books being included long before they are available because they have been selected from announcements long in advance of publication.

In practice, university libraries (and other academic libraries) try to surmount their text-book problem by the provision of a 'short-loan' collection of books most in demand. These are lent for very short periods—overnight, a day or two, or possibly a week-end, but those most in demand are limited to a period of no more than three hours. The short-loan collection may also incorporate further copies for reference only, and the whole collection may be housed in an 'undergraduate collection room' with facilities for study on the spot.

Perhaps the greatest problem affecting university libraries is that of trying to reconcile the research concept of the library, a concept which envisages the library as a permanent repository, with the physical provision of more and more shelving space. This is referred to in detail on pp 90–1.

The *special* library is in a class of its own, for in this kind of library the criterion is to purchase or otherwise obtain material for its informational value, regardless of format. Thus, in many the non-book material is often more important than books, which must, inevitably, be dated to some extent. The emphasis, therefore, is on reports, standards, specifications, abstracts, trade literature, intelligence reports, and periodicals in particular. Literature issued in connection with conferences, exhibitions and courses, is also useful and can sometimes be collected from employees of the firm who have attended. The librarian of an industrial firm will also be working alongside those for whom the information is being supplied, they are all employees of the same firm and on-the-spot communication should present no difficulties. Thus, the librarian is in an excellent position to get advice from these employees about their needs and to keep himself fully informed of developments. Although the emphasis will be on collecting all types of material, the collection will be limited to that which justifies its acquisition for he may well be called upon to demonstrate the cost effectiveness of the library, particularly at budget time. Therefore, allied to acquisition, must be adequate indexing of the contents and circulation of the information to those likely to need it, not merely on demand but in anticipation of its usefulness. Selection in this type of library will be related to a relatively narrow subject field but within this field stock provision will be in depth. It will be essential for the librarian to scan the appropriate literature in the search for all relevant items of information, both English and foreign, and where he has a staff of a sufficient size he should divide the scanning responsibilities among them. Being well-briefed in the firm's objectives and development plans is a top priority.

In all libraries a good collection of professional library literature, English and foreign, must be supplied to keep library staff well-informed and all appropriate bibliographies, abstracts, indexes, and trade publications made available. The librarian will maintain contact with specialist booksellers and agents, with trade institutions, governments, and other relevant organisations and will arrange to be supplied by them with copies of their own publications. He must ensure that all members of the staff who are engaged in the acquisition of library material have every opportunity to keep themselves thoroughly informed on new publications and developments in the world of communication.

ORDER PROCEDURES

It is unlikely that the order system of any two libraries will be exactly the same, but they all perform the same functions. The emphasis throughout should be on simplicity and the avoidance of creating any unnecessary record. It is in this latter direction that the computer scores so heavily for it has made possible the combination of the regular library routines such as ordering, accessioning, cataloguing and classification, and issue for home reading, into one computer programme. While more and more libraries are certain to turn to computer processing, many small and medium-sized libraries will remain in which this could not be justified. Computerisation or not, however, the methods employed are all geared to the same objectives and it is these which are our basic concern.

Order requirements—books. Whoever carries out the initial selection of books and other printed material will write out selection slips for items which might be required, or alternatively mark up the document from which the details were obtained. When the orders come to be placed on a supplier they will then have to be written up in uniform fashion and a record retained of the order at the library (occasionally the library has to use a supplier's own order forms but only rarely). One very simple method which can be used for both selection and ordering of new books published in the United Kingdom is for each selecting librarian to mark up a copy of the *British National Bibliography* with his own selections. At the regular book selection meeting, one more copy of the BNB is marked up by the librarian in charge bibliographical services to indicate the selections approved for each library. This is done by using a rubber stamp grid having a square representing each library or department in which a tick can be written to indicate copies approved for each. After the 'on order' files and the union catalogue have been checked as a safeguard against buying books already in stock, a further copy of the BNB would be marked with just the total number of copies required of each title. This would then go to the supplier as the order for the complete library system, the other copy used at the selection meeting would remain in the library as the order record and would be used to check off the books on arrival and for allocation. An official order form would have to accompany each order (see below).

Another method, which is that most commonly used and which is suitable for practically all printed material, not merely new publications, is for every selection to be made on a 5in × 3in slip on which is written author, title, publisher, date, price and International Standard Book Number (ISBN), with a space to indicate the name of the library or department and the number of copies wanted. When the selections have been sent in, the order department then lists the titles eventually decided upon at the selection meeting and indicates against each item the number of copies wanted for the system, with an identifying code to indicate each library's or department's requirements. If made out in duplicate one copy can go to the supplier and the other kept as the library record. Alternatively carbon-backed duplicate selection/order slips can be used in the first instance, with one copy eventually going to the supplier and the other being the record; the choice will probably be dictated by the number of libraries and departments within the library system.

In the case of large orders selected from special lists or catalogues supplied by booksellers the most convenient method might be to arrange for them to supply their list in duplicate. One of these can then constitute the order list and the other the record.

OFFICIAL ORDER FORMS

Apart from making some kind of list of the items being ordered, most libraries have to comply with the order system of their parent organisation. In some cases this system can be very frustrating and time-consuming but there might be little that the librarian can do about it. For example in a firm the order system might be based on ordering ball-bearings and tyres, but the librarian might not be able to persuade the accountant that books have an individuality and that different methods are needed, and that orders may have to be placed with a host of firms rather than just one; again the school librarian's complaints about having to wait three months for deliveries of his orders would get no support from his principal or the local education authority because the procedure is to order everything via a central purchasing department which is able to command larger discounts for purchases in bulk. Government department libraries have to indent on Her Majesty's Stationery Office, and public libraries have to use the official order forms employed by all departments of the authority. The principles involved in these latter forms are generally embodied in those of other organisations.

The order forms are printed in triplicate or possibly quadruplicate, and each set has the same running number. One copy goes to the supplier, one to the finance department, and possibly a third to the central purchasing department; the fourth remains in the library as the record of the order. Where only a few items are being ordered at one time there will be sufficient room on the order form to write them all out, but where there are many, as is usual with library books, then these must be listed separately and attached to the bookseller's copy of the official order form. The total cost of the order will be filled in on the order form and the finance department will input this amount into the computer as part of the 'commitment' accounting procedure. Ultimately when the order has been completed, or as much of it as can be supplied, and the amounts of each delivery have been debited to the library book-fund, the original 'commited' cost will be expunged. By this means the finance department keeps a check on amounts to which the authority is being committed as well as actual expenditure as represented by invoices for goods supplied. The official order form usually has to be employed for all orders placed. This includes non-book materials and services, eg for periodicals, microfilms, furniture, equipment, binding, window cleaning, lift maintenance, servicing electrical appliances, etc. One exception is where goods are ordered direct on the central purchasing department which orders from the supplier, pays the bill and raises a book-keeping charge against the library estimates, the invoice for which has to be certified by the librarian before it is actioned by the finance department.

Use of the authority's official order form is very advantageous.

i It ensures that each order form has to be signed by a responsible senior official of the library who has been designated as a certifying officer by the director of finance. Therefore there is a check; no orders can be placed without the sanction of a responsible officer.

ii As each order bears a consecutive order number which has to be quoted on all invoices relating to that order, there is a link between order and invoice.

iii If, as a principle, the amount for each invoice passed is written on the duplicate copy of the corresponding order form kept at the library and this copy is crossed through when the order has been completed, then it is a very simple matter to run through the file of duplicate order forms to see which orders are still outstanding, either in part or in whole.

iv It is very simple for the library staff to keep a manual record of expenditure in respect of invoices passed for payment and commitments, rather than have to bother the finance department. Experience shows that much more up-to-date figures can be obtained in this way as the finance department are nearly always a couple of weeks in arrears in feeding such information into the computer.

SUPPLIERS AND TERMS

The choice of the individual booksellers with whom a library deals may be a matter solely within the discretion of the librarian or they may have to be approved by the parent organisation. In the case of a university or college library if there is a bookshop on the campus and especially if it is run by the university or college, then a large part of book orders may have to be placed there though specialist suppliers and agents may have to be employed for some material and for periodicals. Special libraries will need to employ agents for periodicals; to order certain publications direct from publishers, institutions and societies; to organise exchanges through a national exchange centre (as will the university); and to employ specialist booksellers and agents for the most elusive types of material, especially that published abroad but much of the ephemeral material will have to be obtained by direct correspondence and by being placed on mailing lists.

Books are subject to price control and their sale is governed by the Net Book Agreement 1957 made by the Publishers' Association. This directs that net books shall always be sold to the public at net published price except in certain specified circumstances. These include books that have been held in stock by the bookseller for more than twelve months since the last purchase of any copy of that title and have been offered back to the publisher at cost or reduced price, and the offer has been refused, and also if books are second-hand and six months have elapsed since publication. Sale at a reduced (discount) price is also permitted to libraries, book agents, quantity buyers, and institutions as authorised from time to time by the Publishers' Association. This latter provision is very important to some libraries because under the Library Licence Agreement made between the Publishers' Association and The Library Association in 1957, booksellers are permitted to grant discounts regularly to certain libraries: these libraries must be named on the back of the licence and be authorised by the Publishers' Association. The discount is limited to 10 per cent of the published price and subject to certain conditions including, limitation to net books on which the bookseller receives a certain minimum discount from the publisher; the library must purchase not less than £100 worth of books from the bookseller; servicing of books by the bookseller shall be at not less than cost price; and, the books must be for use by the library and not for resale. (This has not affected recent sales of surplus and obsolete library books.)

The Publishers' Association has made the licence discounts available to libraries which grant access to the public and this automatically entitles all public libraries to the 10 per cent discount when registered with the bookseller. Many special libraries would be ruled out especially those belonging to firms but academic libraries have usually been granted the privilege as long as they admit the public for reference purposes. This has caused some friction on occasion because the Publishers' Association has suspected that some academic libraries have done little more than pay lip service to their responsibility for public access. While the association considers that these libraries should *actively* publicise their general accessibility it is certainly true that only a very small part of the population know of this facility.

Where a library is entitled to benefit from the discount its name must be added to the bookseller's licence by the Publishers' Association; in the public library field it would be a normal procedure for the librarian to ask his committee's approval for dealing with any additional firm of booksellers. (This is to satisfy Standing Orders and Financial Regulations.)

RECEIPT OF BOOKS

When books and other printed material (excluding periodicals which are dealt with separately) come from the supplier they have to be submitted to various processes, firstly to ensure accountability and that audit requirements are satisfied, and secondly, to prepare them for public use and in so doing to make it possible to find any particular item in the minimum of time.

The first essential will be to check the items delivered, with the invoice and with the original order record, to make sure that the right item has been supplied and in the correct edition; that the price is correct, and, that the book or pamphlet has not been damaged. When this has been done the original selection/order slip (if this is the method used) will be endorsed to the effect that the book has been received and will be taken out of the order file. Its subsequent destination depends on the library's particular procedure. It could become part of another file 'supplied; awaiting processing'; it could be used as an entry in a shelf register (a list of books in stock, in the order in which they stand on the shelves) if such a list is kept; it could similarly be used as an entry for the accessions register; or, it could go into the catalogue as an indication that the book has been supplied and is in process—it would be removed when the catalogue slip is available. Thus it can be seen that one original record can become the basis of a second record or even more if it is triplicated or quadrupled when initially written out. With computerisation the initial input for the order record could be used with subsequent additional input for all the routines which the library has to carry out providing the system has been properly programmed in the light of the total requirements. This will be dealt with more fully later. If readers are allowed to suggest books and the practice is to inform them of the book's subsequent addition to stock, then the suggestion form can be one of the extra copies of the order or selection form which are provided, or the fact that the book is a suggestion can be programmed into the computer.

In describing the official order form, the point was made that each form was given a running number for the sake of easy reference and that this number had to be repeated by the vendor on all invoices relating to items on that order. The auditor, as was mentioned in Chapter 7, likes to satisfy himself from time to time that all goods invoiced and paid for have actually been taken into stock. In some libraries therefore he may insist that the order number is written on the back of the title page of each item so that it can be identified as being the copy supplied against a particular invoice, otherwise the safeguard is provided in the 'accessioning' process. Prior to this, however, the invoices will be checked for totals and the allowance for discount where applicable; they will then be stamped with a certification stamp which provides spaces to be initialled against headings such as: 'received by', 'items checked by', 'totals checked by', 'discounts checked', and a final heading 'certified by'. These headings, except for the last, will be initialled by the assistant carrying out the individual process but the final one must be done by the certifying officer mentioned on p 186.

The normal custom would be for the certifying officer to inspect the invoices in batches at regular intervals, probably weekly. He would not be expected to check for additions and duplicate the work already done but even a very quick perusal of invoices by an experienced librarian can often reveal some error. Being a different person from the one signing the original order he might also find some discrepancy between the terms offered by the bookseller and those allowed on the invoice, eg 10 per cent discount instead of 20 per cent discount for sale stock. If all is in order so much the better but in any event a conscientious approach by the certifying officer helps to promote systematic and careful work by subordinate staff. When the invoices have been checked and certified they will then be passed to the finance department for payment.

ACCESSIONING

There are different definitions of this term. In its broadest sense it is sometimes used to include all the processes through which 'books' pass from receipt until being placed on the shelves. Thus, it would include applying ownership stamps, collation (ie checking to ensure that the book is physically sound and has nothing missing from its contents and no damage—it is a process only normally employed with fairly expensive second-hand material, or costly new books especially those with many plates), it would also include equipping the book with library labels and stationery needed for the issue system, and providing the book with an identity, usually a unique number (see p 191). Another meaning embraces providing a record of the book's history from the date it is acquired until it is withdrawn and often implies a system which will provide a ready statistical record of the total stock and of annual growth. Whatever the definition, all of them involve giving each item taken into stock, whether purchased or donated, an individual and unique number which will identify it and which can be used for various other purposes.

Having given every item an identifying number the library can decide the purposes for which it is to be used and the extent to which it requires 'records'. At one time libraries used to keep very detailed accession records in beautiful leather-bound ledgers. The record was based on a consecutive sequence of numbers running from one onwards down the pages of the ledger on the extreme left-hand side. Against each number would be entered the author, title, published price, cost price, date of publication, date of purchase, vendor, and any other desired information, all the particulars being written across the page in ruled columns. When a book was withdrawn the entry in the accession register was neatly ruled through and the date of withdrawal entered against it. The number of books in stock at any time would be that of the highest number used minus the total of books withdrawn. A separate total of the latter would be maintained on a regular basis.

In the 1930s there was a strong reaction to accession registers in ledger-form as, with the growth in the use of libraries, so many books had but a short life and the registers became cluttered up with unsightly withdrawals. Instead 5 in × 3 in cards were used, thus introducing flexibility and the advantages of being able to extract entries for withdrawn books so easily. The withdrawn cards could also be filed separately as a withdrawal register. Then followed a period of reaction to all kinds of records and statistics. It was claimed that the latter were misleading and lent themselves to manipulation and misrepresentation, that they were of no significance in a library context and that the production of records merely served to take library staff away from more important functions. Thus it was asserted that accessions registers should be abolished and many librarians prided themselves on having done just that.

The claim to have discontinued the accessions register was however something of an over-statement. Certainly the leather-bound ledgers disappeared hurriedly from the scene and as a general principle librarians looked at their records and questioned their necessity. It thus often transpired that the number of records could be reduced and that librarians who kept both shelf registers and accessions registers for instance, could suffice with one only; the format too was changed and the card or sheaf took over from the book-form. Other librarians abolished the use of a formal register and substituted a file of duplicate invoices on which an accession number was written in against each item. This was still an accessions register of a kind but obviously saved a lot of work. It still enabled individual invoices to be checked against the books but apart from writing in the accession numbers on the invoices the library staff had nothing else to do in compiling such a register; in fact the majority persuaded their booksellers to do even this. As auditors are not normally very interested in library stock after the first twelve months, librarians often found that they could dispense with the duplicate invoices after this time and this practice of substituting invoices for the formal register became common. Most libraries employ it nowadays and even if they are not allowed to dispense entirely with a permanent record they do this by microfilming the duplicate invoices instead of preserving them indefinitely but whether even this form of rentention is really necessary seems very doubtful.

Whatever the conviction with regard to the need to perpetuate shelf registers, accession registers or some other substitute, the fact remains that some form of identification of individual copies of books and pamphlets in stock is essential and the running number is probably the most useful of all and the simplest to employ even though we now have ready-made identifiers for the vast majority of current books, eg ISBNs, or, the numbers given in the *British National Bibliography*. Unlike the independent running number however they indicate titles only and some additional device is needed to denote individual copies of the same edition of the same title. The identifier or accession number is still indispensable for audit purposes and although some auditors might be prepared to allow a certain amount of ephemeral material to go through without identification, rising prices and large-scale thefts from libraries tend to have had the opposite effect. Auditors are more anxious than ever to check that books purchased have actually been taken into stock. Most issue systems too, rely on the accession number as the basis for the arrangement of their files and although other methods can be used such as author, title and copy number, they are inferior and slower in use. Oddly enough the advent of computerisation has emphasised the importance of the accession number which has become the basis of most automated issue systems (though ISBNs are used by some libraries). Statistics too have become very fashionable, after years of condemning their compilation, librarians imbued with management zeal, welcome the many permutations which computers can provide from basic library statistics.

Regardless of the existence of a formal accessions register the accession number is almost universally used for the following purposes:

i it is written against the individual book's particulars on an invoice, either by the supplier or by library staff and on the back of the title-page of the book, for audit purposes and for general identification;

ii as the basis of the issue system especially those such as Browne, or computer (in most other systems even if the issue files are not primarily arranged by accession number it plays an important part in the loan record especially for indicating overdue books and securing their return, and for reservation);

iii it is the link between the catalogue and individual copies of any book;

iv it lends itself to easy recording for other processes, eg preparation of binding lists by accession number instead of writing down author and title, or as a means of stocktaking.

Where a library's stock includes a variety of materials it will probably have more than one sequence of accession numbers for it will be more convenient for administrative purposes to keep the records separate, particularly if statistics are kept. Thus pictures, gramophone records, local history material, microforms and other categories are likely to have their own sequences of accession numbers and will probably use some prefix before the number to identify the type of material. Periodicals are not normally accessioned until they are bound into annual volumes.

CATALOGUING AND CLASSIFICATION

The next administrative record of library stock will be the catalogue entries and these normally involve classification. The standard schemes of classification are usually employed but in some special libraries, and with some special collections, it may be considered necessary to draw up a classification scheme; the home-made classification scheme, however, is more normally used for small collections rather than whole libraries. Public libraries generally favour the

Dewey Decimal Classification, while university libraries in the United Kingdom employ Library of Congress, the University Decimal Classification and Dewey almost equally, with a small minority using Bliss. The needs of the special librarian may have to be satisfied with one of these schemes, probably with some amendment or he may devise his own. D. J. Foskett,[6] however, makes the point that the technical librarian may find none of them to his liking and looks to research to find a better answer to his problems in due course.

From the administrative point of view classification is important in bringing library stock into an order on the shelves which is appropriate to its exploitation and ready retrieval. The application of the notation of the classification system to the spine of the books and to the catalogue entries is a very neat shorthand device which places the book in its right position and guides the user from the catalogue to the shelves without any further explanation.

The catalogue, on the other hand, has a different function, or a series of functions, for it tells the user whether or not the library has a copy or copies of a certain book. Normally it will provide the answer whether the user consults the catalogue under author or subject but if so desired it can be drawn up to answer the question if the user looks under title, series or other headings. The HQ or the central library should have a union catalogue of all the libraries in a given system. This is compiled in a very simple bibliographic style—author, title, edition, date—then it will give the code letters or numbers of the libraries which have a copy. The union catalogue can be arranged by author or by classification; where it is compiled manually only one of these arrangements would be used for it would be too expensive of staff time to try to keep both author and subject sequences current. The union catalogue is the basis of inter-lending within the system, and is also used in checking order lists before despatch to the bookseller to ensure that no library already has a copy of the book, or alternatively which library might be in need of a copy. Until recently, it was the exception rather than the rule to supply a union catalogue in every service point in a system, not only was the cost of production expensive but it was even more expensive to maintain a series of union catalogues in up-to-date condition owing to the staff time involved in adding entries for new additions and deleting those for withdrawals. Recent progress with computerisation and in particular the advent of computer output microfilm (COM) makes it a simple matter to supply a union catalogue on microfilm or microfiche cheaply to each department on a regular basis with monthly up-dates (frequency can be geared to any desired interval). Thus, the reader at a small branch library can be placed in touch with the stock of a vast library system, or alternatively, the user of one subject department can find out whether any other department has books likely to be of use to him, without the need to move out of the department.

Catalogues are usually compiled according to the *Anglo-American Code Rules* of 1967, with or without modification. Their use is further encouraged by the fact that the Library of Congress/British National Bibliography Marc tapes also use them: many libraries subscribe to these and they can easily be modified to the computerised catalogue of the individual library.

Both author and subject entries are usually provided in library catalogues; these can be filed separately or can be combined. Where they are combined the subject entries are made under the *names* of the subjects and filed in one alphabetic sequence with entries for author. Additional entries can be made under titles, editors, etc, and references and cross-references are necessary. A catalogue in which all of these headings are combined in one alphabetical sequence is aptly called the 'Dictionary Catalogue'. When author and subject entries are kept separately the latter are normally arranged under the classification system and an index to subjects is also required. The author catalogue can be reinforced by additional entries under editor, translator, etc, and is then known as the 'Name Catalogue'. The ultimate choice of the form of catalogue is an administrative matter which will be based on the type of library and its users, the degree of use, the staff available to do the cataloguing, the size of the stock and other such factors. The physical form is also an administrative matter but the advent of the computer has materially affected the options open to the librarian.

Whereas a catalogue in book form has always been recognised as the simplest to handle, except for fairly small static collections, it has for many years been virtually impossible to use catalogues of this type because of the cost of production, and the speed with which such a catalogue becomes out-of-date. There is no satisfactory way of keeping a printed book-form catalogue current in respect of additions and withdrawals from stock because insertions and deletions on the printed page look unsightly and in time they come to outnumber the original entries. Loose leaves inserted for manuscript additions are almost equally unsatisfactory and do not allow insertion at the exact place in the alphabetical or other sequence; and the third alternative of supplements is not only time-consuming but like the original catalogue they are somewhat out-of-date even on the day of publication. They become a nuisance, especially when the stage is reached that the main catalogue has to be supplemented by a number of these volumes. It was because of factors such as these that the book catalogue was abandoned and its place taken by catalogues in the form of cards or sheafs. Both forms of catalogue however have the inherent problem of insertion of new entries or the abstraction of entries in respect of withdrawn books—a time-consuming job which staff find boring, and that leads to a great deal of innaccuracy. Fortunately, the computer has now provided a simple means for producing up-to-date catalogues cheaply and has entirely eradicated manual insertion and withdrawal of entries.

When computer catalogues were first introduced they were limited to listing a library's additions from the start of the new scheme; these were printed out at monthly intervals and cumulated every three, six, nine and twelve months and it was envisaged that there would ultimately be larger cumulations covering a period of five years or so until eventually most of the library stock (or at least the active part of it) would be catalogued in this way as the older material would have been withdrawn or placed into reserve. The print-outs for the appropriate periods were duplicated for as many libraries as required them and were displayed in binders for public use. It was a brave experiment which certainly paved the way for more extensive applications of computers for library housekeeping even though the bulky print-outs were far from satisfactory and the problems would have multiplied as the years went by and larger and larger cumulations became necessary. Fortunately, before this crisis arose, the idea of COM came to the rescue. There are administrative problems involved in its use but on the whole these have been surmounted very satisfactorily. The chief are as follows:

1 It involves the purchase of microfilm or microfiche readers in sufficient quantity to deal with users' needs in every library in a system and in every department; in busy departments at least two readers and two sets of microfilm or microfiche would be necessary. In justification it can be said that the cost of reading equipment is low as compared with the cost of staff time previously occupied in filing and abstracting entries, and as manual filing is no longer used the catalogues are much more accurate.

2 The public also has to be instructed in the use of cassettes or microfiches and their readers. Public dislike is another factor to be considered (but, in fact, public reaction has been very favourable and there seems to have been no real problem in this respect).

3 Security of cassettes and microfiches could present problems. The equipment should be installed in a position where it can be kept under reasonable supervision and a member of staff should be made responsible for periodical checking. If a cassette or microfiche does go missing the cost of replacement would be slight and reports to date do not indicate any great problem in this respect. One point to be decided at an early date is whether microfilm or microfiche is to be used; the former is the more popular at present but when library holdings grow the convenience of the microfiche is likely to reverse the relative popularity—the one factor most held against the micro-fiche appears to be that it could so easily be stolen but a cassette seems to be equally susceptible. In neither case would theft be to anyone's advantage.

Other factors involved in the sphere of cataloguing and classification include whether the work should be carried out in the same department as the other acquisition processes and if so the order in which the work should progress. It is obviously an advantage if all operations can be carried out in a logical order from receipt of books at the delivery point to their ultimate check out into the service points. Therefore, it is best if all the work can be done in one open plan room or at least a series of connected offices. This will keep handling down to a minimum, and also will ensure better security of material. Special classes of material require special treatment and would be best processed elsewhere, eg records and tapes in the Music Department; local history material in the Reference Library; pictures for loan in the Cultural Activities Department; periodicals in a separate Periodicals Department in a large library; patents in a Commercial Library; and so on with other such items which are likely to require separate accessioning, cataloguing and classification. Where subject specialists are responsible for classification in academic libraries a decision will have to be made whether they do this work in their own department or in the Acquisitions Department.

PROCESSING FOR USE

When books have been accessioned, catalogued and classified they have to be 'made ready for the shelves' to use the colloquial term. Not every item of a printed nature will actually go on to shelves however and the expression should really be reworded 'made ready for use by readers'. Part of the material is likely to be of a pamphlet nature, which is too slender and insufficiently stable to go on to the shelves as it stands. That of more substance might be suitable for a cheap binding if it is expected to have a few years' life and other material might be shelved in pamphlet boxes but these boxes are usually only suitable for items which form part of a series to which additions are made regularly. A very large part of the material will have but a short library life as it is bought only for the currency of its information which will soon go out-of-date or will be incorporated into more substantial works. This type of material is best classified and indexed only. The notation is written on the top right-hand corner and the pamphlets stored in drawers of a vertical file by notation. It must be checked at regular intervals and obsolete material discarded.

Items which are to be bound will either go away to the library's contractors or, in a few instances, the library may have its own bindery on the premises to which they will be despatched. The pros and cons of home binderies are discussed on pp 230–1.

Stamping. It is normal practice to stamp all printed material with a rubber stamp bearing the name of the library. This is usually impressed on the title-page, the first and last pages of text and then once or twice at random within the text. Some libraries also make a point of stamping plates to deter those who would tear them out; the same applies to maps, inserts, plans and the like. To what extent stamping is a deterrent is not known but at least it makes it possible to identify library property and helps borrowers to distinguish library books from others in their collection. Anyone who wishes to steal library books will find no real difficulty in erasing ink stamps if they are so determined. Many valuable books have been stolen and plates torn out regardless. The librarian is also faced with the fact that too much stamping ruins the appearance of a book and if books are of a really valuable nature some device other than the rubber stamp should be used, for instance a perforator which perforates the initials of the library or an embosser which gives just a raised impression of the library name without using ink. In some such way every piece of library property should be made identifiable.

In addition to the ownership stamp, libraries often use what is called an 'accession stamp' on the back of the title-page. In this is written the accession number and the classification notation for ready reference should the book go to binding or otherwise lose its identifying particulars. The accession number is usually also written at the top right-hand corner of the fly-leaf or on one of the book labels.

Labelling. It is common practice to label printed material which is made available for loan with a date label on which is stamped the date of issue or return. This might include very brief rules with regard to loan period, renewals and fines. Alternatively, in addition to the date label which is tipped in on the front fly-leaf, there may be a separate label pasted on the inside of the book, opposite to the date label. This gives the name of the library, and a brief summary of regulations but nowadays this kind of information is confined to rules of a static nature. Scales of fines, reservation fees, and even hours of opening are subject to change and the labels can thus become out-of-date within a very short time, involving the library in pasting revisions over the labels, or complete re-labelling, both of which are tedious and quite costly where a large stock is concerned. Depending upon the issue system used, additional or alternative stationery might have to be pasted into the front of the book, eg a pocket to hold a book-card with the Browne system, or to hold the transaction card with photo-charging, or a bar code with a computer system using the Plessey light pen. These are discussed further in the following chapter. Reference library books have a distinguishing label, indicating that they are not to be taken away, pasted on the inside front fly-leaf; stock belonging to other departments might also have special labels. Finally, the classification notation will be lettered in white, silver or gold on the spine of the book about 1in from the bottom, and used primarily for shelving. If plastic jackets are used then a small label has to be fixed on these or better still on the dust-jacket before it is covered with the plastic, the notation can then be written or embossed upon it. Most libraries preserve the original dust-jackets in this way; they improve the appearance of the book and add to its life and the information about the book which appears on the inside folds and reverse of the dust-jacket is retained.

Finally, the books should be checked by a senior non-professional assistant and despatched to the respective service points. If the library uses card or sheaf catalogues, it is a good administrative practice to have the cards or slips ready in time to go out with the books so that on arrival at their destination they can go straightway into the catalogues. If sending out entries with the books cannot be done, as with the COM catalogue, a 5 in × 3 in slip should be provided, giving details of author and title and accession number, as a temporary staff record—a duplicate of the order slip might suffice.

Books and other items which have been bought to satisfy urgent requirements or readers' suggestions should have an indication to this effect on the order slip or otherwise and be given priority on receipt. There is no reason why they should not be processed within twenty-four hours and the reader notified of their availability. Service of this nature is very helpful in establishing good public relations.

NON-PRINT MATERIAL

The foregoing paragraphs have dealt almost exclusively with printed material except for periodicals which will be dealt with separately, but all library stock needs processing for use either on or off the premises and to make it readily identifiable. Thus, gramophone records will have an accession number lettered on to the maker's label and some mark identifying library ownership. Record sleeves will also be marked in the same way, probably by affixing a label, and special cards will have to be made out in connection with the issue procedure. They will also need special shelving, either in browser units or by suspended vertical filing. Microfilms will arrive in metal containers which can be labelled as required, they often have cardboard boxes too which can also be labelled and special cabinets for shelving are available from the suppliers. Microfiche must also be labelled and made identifiable, special containers for these can also be purchased. Not only must readers be provided for both microfilm and microfiche but a reader-printer should be available for use when a readable copy of part of a microform is required for taking away. Pictures, films, cassettes, postcards, and all kinds of library material need to be accessioned in a way similar to books and substantial pamphlets but with ephemeral material this may amount to no more than application of the library ownership stamp.

PERIODICALS

Many administrative problems are involved in the selection and purchase of suitable periodicals. Further problems arise in using them to the best of advantage but this latter problem is dealt with in chapter eleven (see p 243-4).

Where the library buys only a very small collection of periodicals associated problems are slight and the local bookseller or newsagent will probably be able to supply most of them; a few may have to be ordered direct from the publishers. The larger the collection and the greater it is in depth, the more problems can arise; large collections are to be found in some special libraries, university and polytechnic libraries, and in very big city reference libraries. The first problem will be how to select two or three thousand titles, possibly more. Special and research libraries will rely on abstracts, union lists, indexes and other published guides but in addition will be able to enlist the aid of their special users; subject specialists will have a very important part to play in this connection; periodical agents also publish lists of periodicals available through them and the lists issued by other libraries are equally useful as are lists of publications of societies and government and semi-government departments at home and abroad. The emphasis will be on usefulness and it will be advisable to check at annual intervals whether certain periodicals are serving any useful purpose. This can be done by various means such as keeping the titles under survey behind the counter, and thereby making them available only on application, or, by affixing a slip to the front cover of selected titles with a request to readers to place a tick in the space provided, if they have used them. The views of research and academic staff would obviously be sought as a matter of course. Those responsible for selection must also keep themselves posted about new titles and if possible get on approval a copy of those which might be of interest.

Libraries providing large collections of periodicals acquire them from a number of sources. Local retailers will not be able to supply all of them, especially those published abroad, but for the sake of good relations they might be given the order for the more common journals which should offer no problems. A large proportion of the remainder will most likely be ordered through specialist agents such as Dawson's or Blackwell's. This relieves the library staff of a great deal of worry and means that periodicals once ordered can be forgotten except for routine receipt procedures, checking an annual account, and renewal of subscriptions. New titles can be ordered from the agents at any time but it saves trouble if the list is only amended once a year. Even where a library makes the utmost use of an agent there are still many titles which have to be ordered direct from the publishers or from their agents (eg for government publications), in this category are included periodicals issued by societies which issue their publications to members only. Other periodicals will be obtained by exchange if the library or its parent organisation has material of its own to offer. A certain amount of free material will also come to the library automatically from organisations anxious to have their journals made available on a wide scale. The librarian will need to exercise great discretion with regard to this, especially in public libraries, as much of the material offered is of little real worth to the library and some of it could definitely be classed as 'undesirable' or 'propaganda'. Any offer of the supply of a periodical free of charge should therefore be treated cautiously and copies should be submitted for inspection before any decision is made. Apart from any other consideration, every title taken involves some extra work in receipt and display, and if one is too generous in accepting such donations, a problem of display space can arise. One exception is locally published material which should find ready acceptance in the archives of any library which maintains a local history collection.

The expense of purchasing periodicals also calls for an examination of availability through inter-lending schemes in the case of lesser-used titles. It may be much wiser and cheaper to rely on borrowing, or more likely on paying for a photocopy of an article, in respect of periodicals which are used only on the odd occasion; it may also help to relieve a storage problem. A further possibility is the establishing of joint purchasing policies with other libraries in the local area. This is particularly effective where a group of academic libraries can combine with the public library, eg WANDPETLS in Wandsworth, or a group of industrial and scientific libraries with the public library as with LADSIRLAC in Liverpool, or SINTO in Sheffield, and numerous other such schemes. An undertaking to supply particular titles is likely to carry with it an obligation to retain some of them for an agreed period, sometimes indefinitely. It is vital, therefore, that any such arrangement should be implicitly honoured, particularly where the collection is listed in a union catalogue of holdings.

Having arranged a satisfactory acquisition system the next major problem will be to devise a method for accounting for the receipt of each issue of each journal and for drawing attention to copies which do not arrive on time. Any system used should record in one place all pertinent information regarding the treatment within the library of the individual periodicals, eg allocation to an individual department, or to an individual member of the staff; general circulation instructions; filing procedures, eg one month, three months, one year, or permanently; whether bound or disposed of in favour of a microform copy; if purchased as part of a co-operative arrangement this should also be shown. Naturally the record will show title, publisher, frequency, supplier and price and will be so devised as to show when each issue will be due and the date of receipt of individual issues. It should also show whether the publisher issues a title-page and index and the approximate date due. The system must be flexible to allow for the addition of further titles and for the deletion of those no longer taken. Periodicals are also prone to considerable change; new titles appear almost overnight and often disappear just as rapidly; titles change, as do frequency and publisher; mergers with other publications are by no means rare; and price increases occur only too frequently.

All the required features of a satisfactory periodicals record system can be provided for on a computer basis but to be of practical value for receipt and check-up this needs to be on a direct-access system capable of interrogation on-line. Inevitably, some of the problems associated with a manual system still remain and it is doubtful whether computerisation can be justified for what might be called the 'average large collection of periodicals' which can still be dealt with reasonably satisfactorily by clerical methods. Nevertheless, it has been demonstrated that computerised periodical records can be operated with efficiency and R. T. Kimber[7] gives a good account of some such applications in both the United Kingdom and the United States. Where computerisation is employed it can be justified not merely as a recording system but for the by-products that can be engendered such as selective listing of periodicals by subject, frequency, or by department to which allocated, and particularly for the publication of union lists. This work can be done in almost effortless manner and the lists can be kept right up-to-date.

Computerisation apart, the almost universal method of recording periodical holdings is by use of the visible index. With this system each periodical title is represented by a card on which all the particulars already enumerated can be listed. The cards fit into trays and each card lies flat on top of the others except that the bottom $\frac{1}{4}$in edge of each remains uncovered. On this edge is typed the title so that when a tray is pulled out of the cabinet in which they are all housed, the complete file of titles is immediately visible. What is more, by using a combination of colour codes, the frequency of publication is also immediately obvious; other kinds of signals can also be used for different purposes. The front of each card is ruled up in vertical columns in pairs, the first one is to be filled-in with the anticipated date of arrival, the second with the date received. The back of the card is reserved for all the information other than arrival and receipt. A cardboard or fibre hinge goes through the top of each card and holds it in position in the tray; it allows the card to be turned up by flipping over all those above it. At intervals the cards will have to be checked to verify receipt, and any non-arrivals will be noted and 'hastened' with the supplier. The use of the coloured frequency signals makes it easy to carry out this process daily, weekly, monthly, etc, for the respective categories of periodicals. No time should be lost in hastening non-arrivals as periodical stocks soon run out and it may be impossible to get another copy.

A large collection of periodicals does involve a considerable amount of work and this is by no means completed after the supply of all the titles has been satisfactorily achieved. There is a further task of filing back numbers for whatever period is decided. Where back-files are bound steps must be taken to ensure that none of the numbers goes astray and that all issues are complete, title-pages and indexes received, and that binding is carried out in systematic style and uniform colour for any sequence of a title. Alternatively, it may be decided not to bind some periodicals but to replace these by microform editions. These might be available commercially but if not the work may be done in the library's photographic department or put out to be reproduced commercially, and a policy must be established. Although periodicals may be distributed throughout the subject departments of a library, their acquisition, receipt and maintenance of the files is simplified if these processes are done centrally by a small staff engaged on this work only. It requires considerable patience, accuracy and experience rather than any professional expertise. The latter is required in selection, abstracting, indexing, inter-library loans, and other processes designed to make the best possible use of the collection, and should be left to the subject specialists.

References

1 University Grants Committee. *Report of the committee on libraries*, HMSO 1967.
2 Association of Teachers in Colleges and Departments of Education and Library Association. *College of education libraries: recommended standards for their development*, ATCDE/LA, 1967 (under revision).
3 See: Futes, E. *Library acquisition procedures*, Phoenix, Oryx Press, 1977.

4   Since this was written, the president of the Association of Assistant
    Librarians has echoed these sentiments. *see: Assistant Librarian,*
    July/August 1977, pp 118–20.
5   Scott, C. F. *Microform provision at Exeter university library,* Microdoc,
    Vol 13, No 3, 1974, pp 75–9.
6   Foskett, D. J. 'Classification', *Handbook of Special Librarianship and
    Information Work,* 4th ed, Edited by W. E. Batten, ASLIB, 1975.
7   Kimber, R. T. *Automation in libraries,* 2nd ed, Pergamon Press, 1974.
    Chapter 7, 'Serial accessory systems'.

10

Security—Circulation Control; Care of Stock; Library Rules

Where library material is freely made available to its membership certain measures have to be taken to safeguard it. These will vary to some extent from library to library and according to type of library but fundamentally all of them have a common objective—security and control.

CIRCULATION CONTROL

When books are made available for loan off the premises, it is necessary to make use of some formal system of control of both books and users. Whatever the methods decided upon the objectives are:

1 to ensure that books are borrowed only by those entitled;

2 that both the library and the borrower know when the book is due for return, and that the library should be able to send out overdue reminders;

3 to enable the library to trace books on loan, and know who has a given book so that if necessary it can be recalled, or 'stopped' on return, eg for reservations;

4 if so required by the library regulations, to limit the number of books in the possession of any one borrower or the number that he borrows at any one time;

5 to facilitate renewal without necessarily first having to return the book to the library.

Above all, the issue system should be one that commands respect and which the users believe to be foolproof; while no system is completely foolproof, both from the administrative point of view and that of borrowers it should be as free from error as possible and not one that can be easily by-passed.

The foregoing are the *essential* requirements of an issue system but certain libraries may have others which influence their decision on the method adopted, eg they might require detailed statistical information—not merely the totals of books issued and the numbers in each main class but details of the use of individual titles, information about the reading habits of individual borrowers, or the average length of time during which certain categories of books remain on loan. Then some libraries may have different loan periods for various groups of members, or types of books, eg fiction; non-fiction; text-books; short loan stock; and others might want to keep a record of the books that, some or all, of their members have read. It is also a frequent requirement that the issue system should be speedy and generally eliminate queues at both the 'in' and 'out' counters; this applies particularly in busy public libraries where use of the wrong issue system can result in very long queues, especially at peak periods. In special libraries on the other hand, this is not likely to arise; the more important factors will be 'recall' and possibly knowing what material a reader has already read. Thus, every librarian will have to choose his issue method in accordance with the conditions prevailing in his library. The chief methods in use are given below:

1 The duplicate slip. This is a very cheap and simple record which is used in some special, college and university libraries. It is based on the borrower filling in a slip with author, title and possibly accession number, and class number of the item required, together with name and residence or department; finally the borrower signs the slip. It is self-carboning so that two copies are automatically produced. The book has a date label and the assistant stamps the date of return on this and on the two slips. The latter are then separated by the library assistant and one is filed under author, the other under borrower's name, or alternatively under date due. If so required, three copies of the slip (or even more), can be written at the one process so that files could be kept under all three headings. This method is obviously very simple and transfers part of the work-load to the borrower but this has its disadvantages including inaccuracy, indecipherable handwriting, and deliberate falsification. It also involves the daily manual task of filing the sequences of slips which are not easy to handle; the more files kept, the further the filing multiplies. Slips must also be withdrawn in respect of items returned. On the other hand, costs are low and the books have to be equipped with nothing more than a date-label. Borrowers in turn need nothing other than a permanent membership card, not a number of tickets which will wear out and need replacement.

2 Bookamatic. Basically this is an elementary mechanisation of the slip system. Each reader has an embossed plastic membership card, similar to a Barclaycard, bearing his name, registered number and address. Each book has a plastic book-card, embossed with accession number, author, title and class number (if required). When a book is issued the two cards are fed into a manually operated Addressograph machine which transfers the details on each to numbered transaction slips printed in triplicate. These slips can be used in different ways— one copy will be put in the book pocket together with the book-card (the slip can be date-stamped in advance with date due for return or a separate date card or a date-label can be used); the second copy can be filed by transaction number within date guides, and the third by borrower's name, or by some other method if desired. Alternatively, the library could manage with one sequence only. While this system provides a far more legible record than the manually completed slip it still retains the inherent disadvantages of filing slips of paper and withdrawing them when books are returned, a slow and cumbrous procedure. If slips are filed by transaction number, not by accession number or author, then reservation-tracing is difficult and a visible index has to be used. Processing of books and issue of plastic membership cards may also rule out this system for the small college or special library, either of which may opt for the manual slips on the grounds of cheapness, and rely on staff scrutiny to reject those slips which are badly written. With a small issue, speed of operation would be of no great significance.

3 Browne. This system lends itself to use in a variety of libraries and until the mid-1950s was used in practically all public libraries. However, the larger the library and the greater the intensity of use at any one period the more the disadvantages outweigh the advantages. Browne is based on each book being equipped with a 4 in × 2 in book-card giving accession number, author, title and possibly class number, and a small pocket pasted on the inside front cover in which the book-card will be housed while the book is in the library. A date-label is tipped in the book on the front fly-leaf. The borrower is given a number of tickets according to the library rules, four is the average in public libraries but it may be double this number in college libraries. The ticket is made in the form of a pocket and has written on it the name and address of the borrower and date of expiry of the ticket. When a book is issued the date-label is stamped with date due for return and the book-card is extracted from the book and placed in the ticket. The combined ticket and book-card is referred to as a 'charge' and these are filed on the library counter in issue trays which hold about 300; they are arranged in accession number order, or if so desired by author or class number; each day's file of charges is preceded by a date guide which stands proud and is therefore readily scanned. When a book is returned the assistant looks at the last date on the date-label and the accession number written on the book-pocket and finds the relevant charge in the issue trays; the book-card is restored to the book and the borrower is given his ticket. Reservations are effected by tracing the accession number of the item required from the catalogue and scanning the trays of issue until this is traced and then a piece of coloured card or some other 'signal' is inserted in the charge to indicate 'reserved' so that the book can be stopped on return. Overdues readily identify themselves behind the relevant date guides and statistics can be recorded by a manual sort and count of each day's issue. The borrower will have either a full quota of tickets or books in his possession or of books and tickets corresponding to this quota.

The Browne system has the advantage of simplicity and meets most of the requirements of small and medium-sized libraries as it is *relatively* speedy for both issue and discharge but some libraries may reject it because it does not reveal what books any individual borrower has on loan nor what he has borrowed in the past. The work involved in processing the stock and in writing out numerous tickets is also likely to deter some libraries. In very busy libraries with a large flow of readers the system is likely to prove too slow on the return counter and cause long queues to form which can be a very serious disadvantage; it is also very much open to human error. Wrongly discharged books result in tickets being returned to the wrong persons with a subsequent build-up of further trouble when next used. Misfiling of charges, errors in writing book-cards and in writing accession numbers and other details in the books, and other such mistakes, can lead to much annoyance with borrowers and bring the system into disrepute, especially when overdue notices are received for books which have in fact been returned. Borrowers' tickets also wear out and have to be renewed, thus adding to the work and cost. In spite of all its disadvantages and the introduction of new methods, Browne still maintains majority support in many college and institutional libraries and in all but the largest public libraries.

4 Newark and other manual methods. There is a variety of simple manual methods which can be used, most of them being suitable for small libraries. They include other book-card systems such as Newark in which each book has a book-card as with Browne although this will probably be larger than Browne's. When a book is borrowed the assistant takes the card from the book-pocket and writes on it the borrower's name and address (a borrower's number system could be used instead). The assistant then stamps the card and the date-label with the date due for return. The cards are filed in whatever sequence is desired—author, accession number, or class number; they can be kept in one sequence or separated behind date-guides.

Another variant is for each book to be provided with two book-cards which are both marked up on issue with the borrower's particulars; the one card is then filed by accession number or author and the other by borrower's name. This is more likely to be used in special or college libraries than the Newark system which was originally designed for public libraries in America.

5 The Token System. This is another manual system but is worth discussion as a separate entity. It was originally introduced at the Charing Cross Library in Westminster to combat the terrific lunch-hour rush which overwhelmed the Browne system previously in operation; the provision of extra staff was found to be no real answer to this problem. Although it was designed to meet the special circumstances of this one library and although the then City Librarian, Lionel McColvin, warned other librarians of its very serious disadvantages, quite a number of public libraries did install it, especially for loans of novels which they regarded as being expendable.

The method is simplicity itself, indeed it has been criticised as being 'no method at all'. Each registered borrower is given a membership card which he retains and shows on each visit to the library and a number of small plastic tokens; four is the average. When a book is borrowed one token is surrendered and the date-label of the book is stamped with the date due for return. The library has no record of what books have been issued or to whom. The only control they have is that they know that each borrower has been issued with so many tokens and that at any time the number of books issued and tokens in the possession of each borrower should add up to the number of tokens issued. Membership is valid for one year and at the end of that period the borrower is required to account for his full quota of tokens; any that he fails to produce have to be paid for at a flat rate. The visible index has to be used for reservations and overdue notices cannot be sent out though at the end of the year those who have not renewed membership will be written to and asked for their tokens and/ or books. Without doubt this is a very speedy method and very economical of staff but the loopholes are numerous. With no ability to send out overdues, with no check other than the annual presentation of tokens and books, and with just a flat-rate charge for missing tokens regardless of the fact that a missing token might represent a borrower deliberately retaining a very expensive volume and willingly paying the charge for the token, there is virtually no safeguarding of stock and many auditors would not allow it. In the case of Westminster the circumstances were unusual but even then if the annual losses were revealed by stocktaking it might turn out to be a very expensive system in spite of its simplicity.

An alternative version of Westminster's method, used by some libraries has a better control built in. Each borrower is issued with a number of library tickets and when first borrowing he has to surrender a ticket for each book he takes away. When next he goes to the library he is given a token in respect of each book returned, if he takes no book then he is given a ticket back from the files. Thus, the borrower always has a fixed number of tickets or tickets and books. The colours of date stamps are changed periodically and readers are given their tickets back so that when they take a book out they surrender a ticket instead of a token as normally. These tickets are filed separately from the earlier sequence. After a time the tickets still remaining in the *original* file can be regarded as representing books which have become overdue since the new coloured date-stamp was used, and therefore overdue notices are sent out informing the borrowers that they have *a book* overdue and will they please return it. This is much better than complete inability to detect overdues but in these days of rising costs and heavy losses of library books it has little to commend it.

6 Photocharging. This was the only serious challenger to Browne in public libraries prior to the advent of computerised charging in the early 1970s. Its popularity was due to its speed of operation as compared with the former. The operational time for charging was 3·25 seconds compared with Browne's 4·72 seconds and on average 'four books could be discharged with photo-charging in the time taken to discharge one Browne charge'.[1]

The system is of American origin but it was improved and introduced in Britain in the Wandsworth Public Library in 1955. Each borrower is given a 'permanent' xylonite or plastic membership card and on the fly-leaf of each book at the top right-hand corner is written the accession number, author's surname and brief title. A series of punch-card transaction cards, pre-dated each day with date due for return, are used (each has a running number from one onwards and different colours are used for a series of packs of these cards, each colour denoting a new week, and the number being dependent on the frequency at which overdue cards are sent out; ten to 14 weeks is a fair guide). When a book is issued it is placed under a microfilm reader, open at the front fly-leaf so that a photograph can be taken on 16 mm film of the details about the book and of the borrower, the latter from his membership card which is placed alongside the book; the next transaction card in the sequence is also photographed with each book. The transaction card is placed in the book pocket and the membership card returned to the borrower. A film may take one day's issue or possibly a week's depending on how busy the library is; in due course it will be sent for processing but there is no hurry because there is no need for it for some weeks when the first overdue notice is sent. When a book is returned all that has to be done is to check for fines (the coloured transactions cards do this if a weekly fine system is used) and then take out the transaction card. Transaction cards are kept unsorted in batches by colour. After an agreed number of weeks, which depends on the number of weeks allowed to elapse before sending overdue reminders, the transaction cards are sorted into numerical order. Normally, busy libraries use forty-column punch cards and these can be put into a high-speed sorter where they are matched against a complete numerical sequence of cards (only one coloured sequence at a time is sorted). Where there is a gap in the sequence of returned transaction cards the sorter will throw out the corresponding card in the master pack. The numbers of these cards are listed and checked against the appropriate processed film. Details of book and borrower are noted and overdue cards posted off.

Photocharging is exceptionally economical in staffing, it eliminates much routine work, is cheap as a result of saving staff and is exceptionally speedy, almost eliminating queues, in fact delayed discharge can be used. The disadvantages levelled against it are that it requires a visible index for reservations and that it would not be of use in libraries generally other than public libraries. This is because it does not lend itself to instant recall of urgently wanted material, neither does it control the number of books any one person has on loan at any one time or reveal what books an individual has read in the past. Photocharging with its inherent freedom from borrowing controls also fails to measure up to the modern clamour for management information which the computer can promote. Nevertheless, it achieved a considerable popularity with many large public libraries from 1955 onwards and still is in use in many of them. It did, however, suffer a severe set-back in 1974/5 when forty-column ICL cards and their sorting-machines ceased to be manufactured. Some libraries have been able to keep going by having the punch cards made for them elsewhere and by having their sorters maintained by other agencies or buying up second-hand models; others who never did mechanise the sorting can still carry on with hand sorting or by 'needle' sorting with a more simple kind of punch card. The method is likely to continue in use in these latter libraries in particular for many years but larger libraries are gradually going over to a computer-based system. It is impossible and indeed unfair to compare photocharging with computer systems. The latter depends upon so many external factors.

7 Computer. Computer-based issue systems have increased with rapidity in libraries of all types since the early 1970s, though some libraries had made experiments in this direction even earlier, Southampton University and Aldermaston in 1966 and West Sussex County Library HQ in 1967, for instance. This increased popularity has been almost entirely dependent upon the parent organisation having its own computer and generally being anxious to realise its full potential. Thus, heads of departments within local authorities, universities, polytechnics and industry have been actively encouraged to consider various routines within their own departments which might lend themselves to computer processing. It follows, therefore, that it is in such situations that the librarian is most likely to be able to persuade the parent organisation of the desirability of a computer-based loan system otherwise the capital investment would be prohibitive; this apart, quite a large sum is involved in staff expenditure at the initial stage for programming, conversion of library stock, compiling the borrowers' register and probably re-accessioning. The librarian's case for conversion is also often simplified where he can show the new system can be used not only for loan recording, but also for accessioning, cataloguing and ordering—in a situation where library stock is being stolen on a fairly large scale, as seems common nowadays, then the backing of the auditors may also prove helpful. Normally one would expect a computer-based system to be employed only in large libraries but some industrial libraries and university and polytechnic libraries have them because the computer is there within the organisation and waiting to be used. It is difficult indeed to produce any satisfactory comparative figures of the costs of different charging methods, except within an individual library but from personal experience, taking into consideration capital investment and repayment charges, staffing, and all the necessary equipment, photocharging is the cheapest of all the systems which could reasonably be employed in a medium to large library. In a large library system the capital charge for a computer-based loan record will be high and will necessitate corresponding annual repayment charges; the rapid changes in computer technology must also inevitably entail regular additions to, or renewals of, equipment. Cost depends also on whether the system is simple batch-processing where the files are brought up-to-date at recognised intervals, perhaps daily or three times a week, or whether it is designed to be continuously up-dated on an on-line real-time basis which is much more expensive. The former is quite satisfactory for many libraries but where the provision of completely up-dated information is regarded as a necessity then the real-time system is needed. It is in the university field where this is most likely to be found so that the files can be interrogated at will to ascertain where a particular book is, but it would be equally useful, if it could otherwise be justified, in some special libraries. Real-time systems can also be programmed to give much greater control of borrowers and borrowing in other ways, such as providing for different loan periods and control of the number of books issued to any one borrower but unless the facility is already made available to the parent organisation it would be extremely difficult for the librarian to justify, however much he would *like* it. One possible answer to the problem is a hybrid system like that employed in the University of Lancaster and elsewhere. It was introduced at Lancaster after the university's computer department began to realise the extensive use of computer time which the library's issue system was occupying. With the hybrid system a mini-computer is used for storing those transactions which the staff will want to interrogate as and when necessary, such as recent transactions, issues from the short-loan and pop-loan (popular books) collections, and reservations, while the main computer is used for the main file up-dating and print-outs which need only to be employed on a daily basis. The method has been described in some detail by B. Gallivan.[2] D. A. Partridge[3] has also described a similar method employed in Havering Public Library.

One factor which must always be borne in mind when a library adopts a computerised system based on the parent organisation's computer is its dependence upon the central computer department. However urgent the librarian might think his issue requirements are the computer department may not be able to meet them, or the cost of storage facilities and equipment required for a real-time system. Even with batch processing there is always a danger that pressures of work from some other department may make it impossible for the computer department to provide print-outs with the regularity agreed in the first instance; any breakdown in the system produces equally adverse results.

When the computer-based issue system is devised in the first place the librarian will have to decide just what information he requires from it and have it programmed accordingly. All libraries will want it to show which books are on loan, who has a particular book, and the date all books are due for return. Additional feed-back with regard to the reading habits of individual borrowers and the number of books any of them have out on loan at any one time, and many other functions as outlined previously can all be provided if they are programmed but the more programming and the more sorting involved the greater the expenditure. As with all issue systems basic identifiers are required for both books and borrowers. It is usual to employ some kind of number in both instances. As books in most libraries have accession numbers these are frequently used, or alternatively a new sequence could be allotted which could have the advantage of bringing together all copies of the same title so that one reservation could apply to all copies; the disadvantage of this is that the other stock records would have to be amended. Another alternative but also having this same disadvantage, is to use the ISBNs, but this poses problems inasmuch as the library will have many books in stock published before the institution of ISBNs and will therefore have to devise

other numbers for these. With borrowers on the other hand, there is
no problem in giving each an identifying number from one onwards.
In any event they will all have to have new membership cards. The
computer itself will file the borrowers' register and can be asked for a
print-out as required but as borrowers have to fill in an application
form in the first instance these can be filed by identifying number at
the library for immediate consultation.

Each loan transaction has to be recorded by equipment which
registers the borrower's number against the numbers of all the books
he borrows at any one time; as with any other system the date due for
return must be incorporated into each day's issue record and stamped
on a date-label or card in the book. With a computerised system the
matching of book and borrower's number is electronically produced
on punch cards, paper tape, or magnetic tape, and then fed into the
computer. When books are returned the book identifier alone needs
to be 'captured' in similar fashion. At intervals of twenty-four hours
or longer with an off-line system the files will be up-dated to give a
record of all the books still outstanding. The more frequently the up-
dating is carried out the more accurate the record, but only the
on-line system will give a complete and up-to-date record at any
given moment. The computer can in turn be used to sort out the
overdue books, read the borrowers' register, print the overdue notices
and provide the library with a list of those sent. The batch loans
system can also be employed with a trapping store by which certain
details can be keyboarded in, eg identification of reserved books,
blacklisted borrowers or those whom the librarian wishes to see for
some other reason. When the books are returned or the borrower in
question next visits the library a warning light goes on to inform the
library assistant who can then take any action necessary.

There is a wide variety of equipment from which to choose. R. C.
Young[4] has listed eight types and very briefly described their main
features but there are others. Two of the most popular are the products of Plessey and Automated Library Systems (ALS). Both have
similar advantages though the method of input differs. The original
(Gurney) ALS system was first employed in April 1967 in the West
Sussex County Library headquarters. Plessey was first put into operation in a branch library in Camden in July 1972 though a demonstration of prototype equipment was given in the Earlsfield Branch of the
Wandsworth Public Library over a year earlier. Since these early days
both systems have been very much improved and options made

available to meet differing requirements. Librarians have been very much to the fore in co-operating and advising both manufacturers.

The ALS systems divide into label-based and card-based and both are available in off-line and on-line versions. The label-based system incorporates a special feature unique to ALS, ie a self-adhesive label which is non-magnetic and immune to wear and which is fixed inside the back cover of every book. This was first introduced in 1973 and contains aluminium dots which represent the identifying details of the book. The borrower's card, or 'badge' as ALS call it, is very similar. When a book is issued it is presented, back down and unopened, on a slope forming part of the library counter in which an electronic sensing device reads the label through the cover while the reader's 'badge' is placed in a badge reader at the top of the slope and the data from both book and badge are transmitted to a system centre where it is recorded on either magnetic tape, paper tape, or cassette magnetic tape for re-transmission to the computer. The label reader has a gate which normally allows books to slide on but remains up in certain circumstances, eg for reserved books or borrowers the librarian wishes to interview. This is done in conjunction with the trapping store into which the information can be fed. This trapping store, introduced in 1971, has been described by R. C. Young.[5]

The on-line system is based on a central mini computer within a network of libraries linked to it by Post Office telephone lines; an example of this is to be seen in the Derbyshire County Libraries in which Matlock is the system centre.

The ALS card-based system was first introduced in 1969 and has been in use since in several public and academic libraries. It employs 2in × 3in edge punch cards for books and borrowers, both being fed into an electronic scanner when a book is issued; only the book card has to be scanned when books are returned. ALS also have another system using eighty-column book cards. It is an on-line system to a medium capability computer and is arranged for full self-charging so that a borrower can complete an issue transaction and check the reservation status of books on loan without staff assistance.

Plessey as it is usually called, is based on self-adhesive *bar-coded* labels about 2in long × ¾in deep (the size can be varied). These consist of a series of thick and thin vertical lines representing the identifier (the number) of the book on the one hand and the borrower on the other (above the bar-code the number is also printed in plain language). Every book has a bar-code label stuck inside the front cover and every borrower's membership card has one attached to it too. The issue process is effected by the Plessey Library Pen which is light-sensitive and reads both labels direct on to magnetic tape cassette, which can in turn be automatically transmitted by telephone to the computer (out of hours if necessary) or can alternatively be transported to the computer department if conveniently sited. A peak traffic rate of issue by this system of 600 books per hour is claimed by the manufacturer. When a book is returned all that is necessary is for the light pen to be drawn over the bar-code in the book. Reservations can be keyed into a trapping store as can borrowers' numbers of defaulters. When the relevant books are presented at the counter, or the required individuals appear, an audio-visual signal will attract the attention of the library assistant. If so desired, a number of branch libraries within a limited geographical area can share the centralised equipment through on-line Post Office links by using the Satellite System modules.

With Plessey, counter procedure must follow a strict routine but once grasped it is simple enough:

1 The borrower's card is placed in card holder on issue terminal thus activating the 'Ready' lamp on the terminal.

2 The library pen is drawn across the bar-code on the borrower's ticket thus recording the number on the magnetic tape cassette of the Data Capture Unit.

3 The library pen is drawn across the bar-code labels on each book being issued to that borrower, thus recording the numbers on the cassette.

4 The date-stamp incorporated in the library pen is affixed to the date labels in the books.

5 The borrower's card is removed from the card holder thus causing an 'end of record' marker to be written on the tape and the terminal to be de-activated.

6 Any error in operation 2 above generates an error signal and a light comes on.

The composite terminal can be used for both issue and discharge of books and has a keyboard which can be used to input renewals and reservations (where a request has been received to renew a book which in fact has already been reserved, a visual indication is given so that the request can be refused) and for cases where a borrower has forgotten his membership card or where a bar-code label has been damaged and cannot be read by the pen. It should be pointed out, however, that library assistants should not be over-indulgent to persons who have 'forgotten' their membership card; this can soon develop into a regular habit.

As with ALS, Plessey also have a mobile unit that can be used for small branch libraries or in mobile libraries, or taken to the shelves for stocktaking purposes; alternatively it could be kept as a stand-by for emergencies. The models can be used both on mains and batteries.

Apart from printing overdue letters, computer-based issue systems can be programmed to produce statistics for management purposes, and various listings; they can be used for lists of books by particular author or subject; or others arranged by accession number; they can show what books a certain borrower has or which borrowers have more than a given number of books on loan. By giving various routines a borrower's card and special number, computer systems can be used in stocktaking, for listing books being sent to binding, or for listing withdrawals, etc. Providing the computer has facilities for on-line working most data collection equipment can be used on-line allied to visual display units.

The choice of any particular maker's equipment for data capture will depend on the circumstances of the individual library, the number of libraries within the system; the size of the stock and how much of it is on open access; the categories of user; loan periods; the computer facilities available within the parent organisation; the sum total of records required of the whole system (ie not merely loans but catalogues and accession records); servicing facilities offered by the manufacturer; delivery time; and of course, the total cost. Undoubtedly too librarians are influenced by the experience of their colleagues and no librarian is likely to go ahead with conversion before he has been to see systems in operation and sounded out the librarians. Once the system is installed good staff training is essential and a strict discipline of operation must be enforced. While the computer itself is free from error, it will not function properly if incorrectly programmed or if mistakes are made by the library staff; breakdowns are possible and there can be current failures so that a stand-by method is also needed. A computer-based system is claimed to save staff but this depends on comparison; certainly it should save as compared with the Browne system but in small libraries only a minimum staff is needed in any event; it is less economical of staff than photo-charging. However, it must again be emphasised that the case for computerisation rests on its efficiency and its management potential, not economy. Another factor in its favour is the psychological effect it has on borrowers and the air of efficiency and modernity it gives to the library; it has also introduced a new specialism into librarianship and opened up additional avenues of employment.

LOANS OF MATERIALS OTHER THAN BOOKS

As far as is possible it is advisable to issue similar kinds of material at the one counter and by the same method, thus for example pamphlets, periodicals, maps in pocket editions, and the like, can all be treated as books but other classes of material need different treatment for various reasons.

Gramophone records. As these can be easily damaged they have to be inspected by staff on return and by the borrower when taking them out so that it would be impracticable to be issuing these at the same counter as books, even in a library that was only moderately busy. The normal practice is to make out a special file card for each record, about 8in × 5in on which is recorded accession number, composer, and title, and other identifying information. On the card a circle is drawn, about 2in in radius to represent a record and on which can be roughly indicated any place where the record may be damaged or scratched. This safeguards the borrower who might otherwise be charged for damage which was already done when the record was issued. It also enables the assistant to mark any new damage that has been inflicted. As part of this process the record may be examined under a magnifying-glass on return but as this is a time-consuming business the examination can take place subsequently and the borrower charged next time he comes to the library; whatever the system every user of the collection should be made aware of the rules when first he borrows. The same card can also be used as an issue record by writing on it the borrower's number and date stamping; alternatively another card can be made out as with Browne and used in conjunction with pocket-type tickets. The cards would not be kept in the record sleeve but in a file(s) in the counter in accession number order. Very frequently an annual subscription or a fee per individual record is charged for the loan of records, cassettes, etc.

Loans of pictures from an *illustrations collection* can be dealt with quite simply by means of a ledger for all that is necessary is detail of borrower's name and address, number of illustrations borrowed, and broad subject(s), together with the date borrowed. The illustrations are usually issued in a large envelope printed with columns in which can be indicated the number of illustrations borrowed and the date due for return.

With *art pictures* a ledger system might also suffice for it would be unusual to allow more than one or two pictures to be borrowed at any one time; the borrower might also have to sign the entry in the ledger; the pictures will be accessioned and the accession numbers will form part of the ledger entry. More often than not a charge is made for each art picture borrowed, or an annual subscription levied; a deposit (refundable) may also be demanded on first registering as a borrower from the collection. The loan period is usually quite substantial, possibly three months.

Lantern slides are available for loan from some libraries and these again can be issued by the ledger system or on a special issue form on which the details are noted and the borrower's signature obtained. The slides may be accessioned in which case these numbers would be noted on the form but some libraries may be less formal and merely enter the total number of slides borrowed, with broad subject. As most slides of this nature represent special collections or are part of a local history collection, the first method is preferable. Slides should be issued in specially designed carrying boxes which guard against damage.

Confidential material can be issued in the normal way employed for books for the security emphasis is upon the status of the borrower. Thus it is essential that the assistant must have some means of checking which persons are allowed access to certain classes of material. This can be achieved by special tickets or by merely having a list at the issue desk of persons so qualified who would then be responsible if necessary for identifying themselves. Company rules might also make it necessary to keep separate records of this kind of material and if so special application forms, the ledger system, duplicate card or slip, and other manual methods may be used; signatures may be requested.

In open access *reference* libraries and in subject department libraries books are freely available on the shelves for consultation on the premises. There may be some proviso that books consulted are to be left on the tables (so that they can be counted for statistical purposes) but that is all. In some libraries there may also be a further control such as a turnstile, or a check-point at which cases and other belongings have to be deposited or inspected. Where security is tighter, then persons may have to be issued with a plastic token on entering the library and surrender it on leaving; alternatively, one of the electronic scanning devices mentioned on p 222 may be installed. Where the books to be consulted have to be fetched from the stack and particularly where valuable books are asked for, it is likely that the reader will have to fill in a request form giving details of the book and his name, address, and signature, before the book will be made available. In some cases, eg national and academic libraries, any user will first have to obtain a reader's pass, see p 223; valuable books may have to be read at special tables under the immediate supervision of the counter staff.

SECURITY

In an ideal world there would be no necessity for elaborate issue methods for either home reading or study on the premises. There would be no such thing as dishonesty and everyone would religiously abide by the rules and regulations. In consequence, a very considerable reduction in staffing costs could be achieved; however, in the absence of uniform honesty, the librarian has to exercise an 'acceptable' method of control and security of stock as cheaply as possible, having regard to the value of the different types of material being lent. This explains why some librarians are so very interested in the development of issue systems that can be reader-operated. Self-operation however, is not the only factor, if it were then some of the computerised systems available would solve it. *The crux lies in being able to introduce some other device which will ensure that borrowers cannot get out of the library without first having every book which is taken out properly issued* and that whatever the system it should be free from false alarms and detections. Such a system is certain to be invented in the long run and indeed its arrival must surely have been advanced in recent years by a number of methods invented to prevent 'illegal borrowing'. These are finding increased sale as the losses of books from all kinds of library continue to mount. In the early 1960s, in public libraries for example, an annual loss of books of 1 per cent to 1½ per cent was a fair norm but nowadays it is much higher and reports of 10 per cent annual loss are by no means uncommon, in fact they could be much higher because so many libraries do not carry out a stocktaking. This is by no means limited to public libraries, and the users of academic libraries seem to be equally ready to indulge in 'illegal borrowing' or outright theft according to Souter.[6]

The deterrent systems which are being employed are electronic and have the aim of detecting anyone walking out of the library with material that has not been properly issued. The devices can be applied to the stock of single departments of a library or to all departments. They depend on some sensory material being inserted into the books which will trigger an alarm system and close the library barrier when someone tries to take out a book which has not been de-sensitised. These systems have helped very much in combating 'illegal borrowing', for instance the University of Lancaster reported losses being reduced from a 10 per cent annual range to 1 per cent. Although it is not cheap to equip every book with the sensory device the individual system requires, where it has been installed the reduction in losses has justified the expenditure. Most of the methods do create some difficulties and a little embarrassment due to false alarms when the signal has been activated 'accidentally' but considerable improvements have been made since the early days. A number of the systems have been briefly described by Helen Davies[7]; obviously the extent of losses will be a deciding factor whether to opt or not for the installation of any one of them but with book prices rising alarmingly every year more libraries will be forced to improve security. It is ironical that libraries which have prided themselves on their ready accessibility and on the reduction of barriers between readers and stock, are now having to install methods such as these and reintroduce wicket gates and turnstiles but there seems little option. Allied with other security measures, such as not allowing bags and cases, or even any other books into the library, the electronic detectors make it possible to provide a fair degree of security for library stock.

Where mechanical methods are not considered justified, some additional security can be achieved by more constant supervision, relocation of staff and issue desks perhaps, and the employment of more janitors for patrol duties, or, a check-out man between the issue desk and the exit doors as practised in so many libraries in America. None of these methods is particularly cheap however and in the long run may cost more than the electronic devices. Other alternatives are mirrors or closed-circuit television but these are of psychological, rather than practical, value as they need constant observation to be effective. Even simple notices reminding users that 'illegal borrowing is stealing' may be effective for a time; press notices about legal action against offenders who have been caught are also helpful. On a more positive note, the provision of photocopiers, especially in academic and reference libraries must reduce illicit borrowing as it removes the need.

One of the most effective security checks open to all libraries is the strict scrutiny of all applications for membership. Whereas a stage was reached when public libraries gave up all checking of the veracity of the details given on readers' application forms for membership and academic libraries issued their tickets without too much formality, much more care is now generally taken. In public libraries the Register of Electors is again used as a check, or failing that, the applicant is asked to provide some proof of identity and address. If this cannot be supplied, instead of issuing tickets on the spot, they are posted to the address given on the application form. Academic libraries now often include a photograph of the member on his library card and national libraries required evidence of the individual's standing, etc. For instance the British Library Reference Division, Department of Printed Books stipulates that admission is by pass only and that proof of identity is required such as a document bearing a photograph, a banker's card or the like, or a letter of recommendation from an identifiable person of standing. If the evidence is satisfactory a photograph of the individual is taken in the Readers Admission Office and a pass, with maximum validity of two years and bearing the photograph, is issued. The use of some or all of these methods, according to the needs of the individual library should make it possible to keep losses down to a minimum; if someone is sufficiently determined he can usually find a way round most systems but it would be few library-users who would be so minded or, think it would be worthwhile.

FINES

The imposition of fines for books not returned within the permitted loan period and for other purposes is a security measure designed to ensure that books are eventually returned. It is also an economic measure inasmuch as books kept beyond the allotted spell and those never returned at all result in less books being in circulation. This in turn necessitates more books having to be purchased to maintain the selection on the shelves. Where damage is incurred to books or where they are lost, the fines are a small contribution towards their replacement although some libraries may charge the full cost of replacement.

The latter category of fines needs little comment for it seems reasonable enough to expect people to make some contribution towards making good loss or damage but fines for non-return are more debateable and the attitude in some kinds of library may be more tolerant than in others, eg academic libraries. While many academic libraries do have a fines system which they adhere to, a great deal of reluctance to charge fines is evident in others who maintain that: fines are self-defeating and can dissuade persons from returning books (this is true, but normally only after the fines have been allowed to creep up to large amounts); that they antagonise borrowers and give a bad impression of the library; and, that the imposition of fines and accounting for them can cost more than they are worth. In academic libraries the readership is almost entirely limited to the membership of the institution and it is therefore easier to contact offending borrowers; in the ultimate, outstanding books can be billed at replacement cost against the student and enforced by the institution. Where the latter is a degree-awarding body then there seems no reason why, if all other methods fail, the award of the degree could not be withheld until payment is made. In spite of the reluctance of the academic libraries to charge fines the provision of short-loan collections is a usual practice in university and polytechnic libraries. Coupled with the very restricted loan period is a very high fine which can be as much as 5p for every fifteen minutes the book is retained beyond the allotted spell which may be as short as three hours.

In public libraries on the other hand a system of fines is almost universal and local authorities deliberately raise them at annual reviews as a means of raising income and in opposition to the spirit of the Public Libraries and Museums Act, 1964 (see Chapter 7). Only a handful of libraries have no fines system but the majority exempt children as well as pensioners or alternatively have a lower scale for them. Children are exempted because fines are considered to be a disincentive to reading, and in any case it is normally the parents who pay and who in the end forbid their children to borrow any more books because of the fines. The pensioners are exempt because they make so much use of the library, and with their restricted finances may find that fines incurred, often through no reason of their own, but rather through illness, adverse weather conditions, and so on, may result in their having to forego one of their chief pleasures. When fines are levied in local authority libraries including college libraries, the authority will insist on a proper system of receipts and accounts or may otherwise accept the locked fines box into which the borrower drops the amount due.

OVERDUES

Whether or not fines are imposed, a procedure for chasing-up overdue books by means of printed postcards or letters is necessary and it is quite common for the cost of postage to be debited to the borrower. Where fines are charged there may be a maximum limit which operates after a certain number of weeks. If the borrower still fails to return the books after the final notice the library janitor or another member of the staff may be sent in person to retrieve the books. Should this fail there is no option but to write off the books as irrecoverable or resort to more drastic measures. These can include handing the matter over to the finance department who may have a collector of debts, or to the bailiff. The other alternative is to make a report to the legal department with a view to legal action. More local authorities are resorting to this method now that some courts have inflicted very heavy fines.

BLACKLISTING

Where borrowers default with library books or just fail to pay the fines due, the librarian may blacklist them, that is to say, add their name to a list of people who are no longer allowed to use the library. Where a computerised issue system is in operation the borrower's number can be fed into the trapping store so that should he try to use the library he will be detected; without this help the staff just have to rely on a list of names; providing the list is short this works well but in most libraries the number of blacklisted people is so large that trusting to memory is far from satisfactory especially where a group of libraries circulates lists of defaulters to each other, eg the London public libraries. On the other hand, blacklisting is reasonably easy to enforce in special libraries where numbers are small, and in some academic libraries.

STOCKTAKING

The practice of stocktaking is often belittled as a waste of time and because it reveals library losses after the event rather than preventing them. This is a misunderstanding of the purpose of stocktaking. Admittedly the ability to find out that 2,000 books are missing does nothing to retrieve them and stocktaking in itself is not a security device. On the other hand, apart from certain ancillary uses, it does inform the librarian whether serious losses are being incurred, and leads him to consider whether additional security measures should be taken. In any event, if the loss rate is considerable, as the manager of the library's resources, the librarian has a duty to inform the members of the governing body and advise them on security measures which might be taken. The onus for the decision whether the cost would be justifiable is theirs alone.

With the growth in size of libraries and often due to the lack of any satisfactory library record against which to check the book-stock (such as a shelf-register—a series of cards representing the books in the order in which they would stand on the shelves if they were all 'in') and due to the physical effort involved, stocktaking has been very much neglected. However, one important by-product of the computerised issue system is that by using a portable input recorder and by setting up a special borrower's number to represent the library, the books on the shelves can easily be recorded and fed into the computer along with the other loan records to be checked against the master file of library holdings. A list of missing numbers can be printed and the trapping-store can then be left to carry out the usual procedures while other possible sources are checked for the missing volumes. Where a complete stocktaking is not possible, or is a task so large as not to be lightly undertaken, it is at least possible to carry out a series of trial checks of various parts of the stock. These areas of stock can be selected—because they were bought in the last twelve months, because they were costly, or because they are the kind of books which people do steal, eg motor manuals, do-it-yourself books, well-known textbooks, and others of this nature. This should give some indication whether books are being purloined on a large scale. If so, it might prompt checking further selections, or a complete stocktaking in phases; in any event further security measures would need to be considered.

It is not only books that are stolen, losses of gramophone records, if on open-access, may be higher in proportion. As collections of this type of material are much smaller than those of books it should be easier to take stock regularly. As it is the most recent acquisitions which generally disappear, it should not be too difficult to check these at six monthly intervals to ascertain the extent of the problem. Solutions lie in the exhibition of the sleeves only; making only *part* of the stock open-access (in other words keeping the newer records in cupboards on request only); possibly re-siting the issue desk and/or exit barriers; and, more staff supervision as already indicated on p 222.

Apart from indicating losses of material, stocktaking has several other important advantages.

1 Having finally listed the books that are missing, a decision will be made as to which are to be replaced and which withdrawn.

2 Entries will be withdrawn or amended in the catalogue and other stock records as necessary.

3 In connection with (2) a certain number of clerical errors will be detected, such as wrong accession numbers, wrong lettering on books that have been bound, and wrong class notation.

4 While checking the shelves the opportunity can be taken to withdraw books in shabby condition with a view to binding, replacement or withdrawal. Seldom-used books will also be revealed and may be withdrawn or consigned to the stack.

5 Out-of-date material can be withdrawn.

6 Surplus duplicate copies can be consigned to the stack.

Finally, the point must be made that auditors today are more conscious of the loss of money represented by large-scale theft of books and other library material and may consequently regard stocktaking as part of good management procedures.

CARE OF STOCK

The conscientious librarian will try to maintain his stock in a clean and strong physical condition. Various factors are involved:

1 Some librarians have a policy of buying certain cheap fiction and non-fiction in paper-back and having these volumes bound commercially from the outset; they regard this as being more economical than buying the hard-back edition. It is a matter of

personal preference but is frowned upon by most publishers and is a practice they try to prevent. From a librarian's point of view it is questionable for it promotes the use of inferior publications of poor physical format and a degree of maltreatment is inescapable as in use the books have to be constantly bent back to keep the pages open. The economics are also doubtful but this must depend on the neighbourhood and the amount of rough handling the books receive.

2 Other books although published in hard-back, have poor joints which soon break down and then the sections begin to fall apart. These will either have to be bound or replaced if they are not to be withdrawn.

3 Some books get very badly handled, get stained and dirty, so that again a decision has to be made on binding or otherwise.

4 Another class of books are those which although well-used should not be bound because new editions are frequent, eg legal textbooks which are revised every two or three years and some travel books which come out in new editions every one or two years.

5 Some subjects are purely of topical interest; this dies down in less than twelve months and therefore binding would be a waste of money.

6 Other books may still be in good condition and will be required occasionally but do not justify retention on the open shelves. They should, therefore, be transferred to stack or possibly to another library in the system; in some cases the anticipated use may be so slight that the book could be offered to a co-operative storage scheme.

Generally, the aim will be to keep on the shelves the books that readers will expect to find there and to ensure good physical condition either by binding or buying replacement copies. Libraries are often being pressed to give their withdrawn books to hospitals and other institutions but there is a certain amount of opposition to this policy among librarians on the grounds that it is wrong to treat hospital patients or even prisoners as second-rate citizens who should be glad to read books which are regarded as not being suitable for general public use. However, where the library is withdrawing books simply because they have out-lived their day in that library or because, the initial demand having worn off, there are now surplus copies around, there seems no logical reason why these should not be given away for distribution abroad by the Ranfurly Library or to institutions at home. Library authorities are themselves becoming conscious that some withdrawn books may still be of value and are reaping financial reward by organising their own book sales.

Most libraries cover their books with plastic jackets which preserve the original book-jacket, or alternatively laminate the dust-jacket to the boards by a heat process which covers them with a transparent plastic material. Not only does this preserve the appearance of the books but they tend to last longer and remain clean, often until it is time to replace them. Other libraries also strengthen the publisher's cover or case and in particular have linen joints pasted over the inside of the original joints back and front. This is the part of the case which gets most wear. By methods such as these and by buying some books in 'reinforced editions' as frequently offered by library binders, it is possible to reduce very considerably the number of books which will need to be bound.

BINDING

Books which will have a long life on the open shelves will very often need to be bound, after a year or two in use; in some libraries there will also be a very considerable amount of binding of periodicals to be done each year. When long runs of periodicals are kept it is necessary to come to a decision whether to store them permanently as separate issues (probably in filing boxes); whether to buy an edition in microform or to have the library set converted to microform if not otherwise available; or alternatively whether to have them bound with index and title-page into annual volumes. Bound volumes are easier to consult than a microform and unbound individual issues have the very real disadvantage that it is very easy for copies to go astray. In favour of the microform on the other hand is the very considerable saving in shelf space which results. The solution is likely to be the employment of all three methods to some extent.

National, academic and special libraries, as well as large public reference libraries will inevitably have many periodicals to bind, they will also have a variety of other material including standard works of reference which get heavy usage—newspapers, government publications, patents, theses, local material, and any material in great demand which has to remain in circulation for a long time. Public libraries in particular will also have a large amount of relatively ephemeral material which will get very heavy use for three or four years, such as fiction and popular non-fiction; this will need attention if its life is to last as long as demand. Books in this class can be dealt with economically by merely 're-casing', ie stripping off the publisher's case, trimming the edges all round, applying an adhesive to the back and returning the pages to the old case if it is still sound, otherwise into new boards. The original dust-jacket is then replaced and a new plastic jacket fitted. Where this cannot be done, new boards will have to be covered with a suitable cloth and the title and author embossed on the spine.

Books intended for a long life and those with a large number of plates or printed on art paper, will also need their sections stitched before the boards are attached but books which are only to have a short life and are printed on a relatively coarse paper can be held together with a special adhesive and thus the expense of sewing is avoided—this is called 'perfect' binding. It is relatively cheap and is quite satisfactory for a large proportion of the stock of the average library. The general policy is to spend no more on binding a book than is justified by its anticipated life in the library. The vast majority of libraries send their books away for binding by recognised firms who specialise in library work and who have many years of experience behind them. They can be relied upon for good work and their prices are competitive. Commercial binding is particularly economical for books in the standard size ranges because this can be done by mass-production methods. On the other hand the prices for larger volumes, requiring individual treatment, are high and these books tend to be away from the library much longer than the others.

The Home Bindery. A few libraries have their own bindery including in particular university libraries where it can best be justified because of the large numbers of periodicals they have to bind and because these libraries are loath to allow material off the campus and thereby not being available for immediate use if so required, as well as the fact that they have a more than average amount of valuable material which should be kept on the premises for security reasons and which requires skilled treatment. A very limited number of public libraries also have their own bindery but even then they may send the mass-production work away to the commercial binder as the home bindery just cannot compete on prices. On the other hand, there are some distinct advantages of the home bindery:

1 It is very competitive not only in respect of periodicals but sheet music and all outsize material. It can deal with this particular type of work more quickly than when it is sent to outside firms.

2 It is unnecessary to write out binding lists and orders and there is no problem of transportation.

3 It provides a greater variety of styles and materials and standards can be specified.

4 On-the-spot control is made possible.

5 It can be used for making and fitting plastic jackets and for lamination, for mounting maps and photographs, for making filing boxes, lettering new books, and other odd jobs.

6 Some of the costs may be recovered by taking in work from other departments of the parent organisation; alternatively two or three libraries might combine.

One of the biggest problems of the home bindery is to provide it with a steady flow of work so that co-operation with other libraries in the vicinity or with other departments as referred to in item 6 above can be very helpful. In establishing a bindery, however, there will be a further problem of acquiring suitable premises if the library itself does not have spare capacity. It must also be equipped with the necessary machines and tools and must satisfy the factory regulations. The greatest difficulty of all is that of getting skilled staff, especially at the foreman-binder level. Without an enthusiastic professional and one with an ability to manage and handle subordinate staff the home bindery is likely to come to an untimely end. In estimating the economics of the home bindery versus the commercial binder one often finds that over-enthusiastic librarians tend to ignore loan charges on equipment, rents of buildings, heating, lighting and cleaning, and depreciation.

BYELAWS

In describing how libraries exercise control of the use of different types of stock and how they care for its physical condition, it has been expedient on occasion to refer to one or two rules enforced by individual libraries with regard to membership and return of overdue books. Without exception, however, all libraries have rules covering more than these two matters. Some libraries are content to use the word 'rules' but others prefer the more official-sounding 'rules and regulations' and in the case of public libraries there are byelaws too in addition to the rules and regulations. These are enacted by legislation, eg in England and Wales by the Local Government Act 1972, though byelaws enacted under earlier legislation are still valid (see Public Libraries and Museums Act, 1964). In Scotland the relevant legislation is the Public Libraries Consolidation (Scotland) Act, 1887 and the Local Government (Scotland) Act, 1973, and in Northern Ireland the Education and Libraries (Northern Ireland) Order, 1972. Byelaws generally concern misuse of library property and facilities and include specific penalties for their breach. Under certain circumstances they also give authority for the exclusion of offenders from the library premises. They need approval of the Minister of State, eg in England and Wales by the Secretary of State for Education and Science in which countries the byelaws provide for fines on summary conviction of up to £20 and a further £5 per additional day that the offence continues. The Secretary of State has issued a model set of byelaws which, with slight amendments most public libraries in England and Wales use. Byelaws are mostly framed in a negative fashion informing people what 'they shall not do' in the library, eg shall not, be unclean or offensive in dress; give a false name and address; bring animals into the library; take out books without permission; stay in the library after closing time; damage library property; be allowed to borrow more books after they have been blacklisted; behave in a disorderly manner; be a nuisance; obstruct an officer; eat, drink or smoke in the library; and so on. A very formal procedure is laid down in the legislation for the introduction of byelaws and a copy must be publicly displayed in the library.

The distinction between byelaws and rules and regulations, in the public library field, is that the former are enforceable by law and that penalties are prescribed. Rules and regulations on the contrary are not enforceable in this way. This does not necessarily mean that a breach of public library regulations could not be punished by law; the breach might be an offence against one of the byelaws or alternatively it might be an offence at common law in which case proceedings could be taken.

RULES AND REGULATIONS

It will be noticed that public library rules and regulations are not usually couched in the forbidding terms of the byelaws and that they are informative rather than repressive—they tell the library user what the facilities are and what he has to do to enjoy them to the full. They will include the general hours of opening and then the facilities offered by each department such as Adult Lending, Children's, Reference, Music and Records, and any other special department. The information will relate to membership, use of tickets and number of books which can be borrowed at one time, renewals, reservations, fines, loss of membership cards, notification of exposure to infectious or contagious disease, photocopying and copyright, inter-library loans and similar matters. While giving the library user certain privileges the regulations at the same time give support to the librarian; by laying down the rules within which the service operates they provide for uniformity of treatment for all library users and protect both staff and library property. They can always be referred to if any unfortunate argument should arise.

The regulations of the British Library Reference Division, Department of Printed Books are a kind of compromise between the public library's byelaws and its rules and regulations. The conditions for issue of a reader's pass have already been mentioned (p 223), in addition they include such matters as: opening hours; directions how to order a book; reservation of up to twelve books for two full working days; a request to return books fifteen minutes before closing time; responsibility for books being that of the person to whom they were issued; use of catalogues; and, a few other general rules with regard to facilities but also included are a host of prohibitions with regard to maintaining silence; eating, drinking and smoking; removal of material from the room in which it was issued; marking of books; tracing; introducing paste, bottles of ink, etc; use of cameras; and a warning that readers may have to submit to an inspection of their cases, handbags, and other objects they are carrying; it is suggested in very polite terms that they might prefer to leave their belongings in the cloak-room. Infringement of the regulations may involve withdrawal of the reader's pass. In addition certain special rules apply elsewhere in other rooms of the Reference Division, eg in the North Library where rare books must be read, the readers have to show their pass to the staff at the issue desk for security reasons. Other special regulations apply to the 'Rapid Copying Service' including placing of orders; payment in advance with the prescribed form; copyright; and the right of the librarian to refuse an application. The

Map Library too has special additional regulations including the necessity for readers to sign the register and to observe the special rules for the care and handling of maps displayed there. The Newspaper Library has a complete set of regulations of its own which are very similar to those of the Reading Room and so does the Department of Manuscripts. Naturally, apart from general conditions of admission, the regulations of this latter department are particularly concerned with the handling of manuscripts and forbid tracing, the use of ball-point pens and cameras. Borrowers are made responsible for the manuscripts until they are returned and their ticket recovered; other rules apply to general conduct and how to apply for manuscripts; there are also separate rules for the supply of photographs. The Department of Oriental Manuscripts and Printed Books also has its own regulations with emphasis on security, care of stock and control of readers. The general regulations of the Science Reference Library are brief but highly prohibitive—no bags or other impedimenta; no eating, drinking or smoking; no material belonging to the library to be taken off the premises; if a reader takes any books of his own into the library he must submit to having them examined by the staff before he leaves; books must not be damaged or defaced—*offenders will be prosecuted;* the staff are not authorised to accept written or verbal messages for readers. The only regulation not couched in prohibitive terms is that readers must write their name and address in the visitors' register every day. Thus it will be seen from the foregoing examples that the British Library's Reference Divisions rules and regulations are equally wide-ranging as the public libraries' byelaws and rules and regulations.

In academic libraries there appears to be quite a considerable difference of approach between one library and another but the term 'Regulations' is more often than not discarded in favour of 'Rules'. There is also a general attitude of discretion in publishing the rules; they are often tucked away unobtrusively in various guides to the library rather than in a separate pamphlet. Additionally while some universities may have as many as two dozen rules, others manage to convey the same information in a quarter of this number. University and other academic libraries provide in their rules for different borrowing privileges for undergraduates, postgraduates and members of the staff. Nearly all are concerned that bags should either be deposited in the cloakroom or be made available for inspection. A certain unwillingness to charge fines is evident except for short-loan stock. As with all other types of library, eating, drinking, and smoking, are frowned upon and emphasis is placed on handling material with care; silence is called for and special attention is drawn to the Copyright Acts with regard to photocopying. Threats are made very sparingly but where they are made they range from withdrawal of tickets to fines or penalties (unspecified) which may be imposed by the librarian or the library committee. Many of the university libraries include a rule for billing students leaving the university, in respect of any books not returned and further unspecified action is threatened in the event of such an invoice being ignored. The main emphasis of the rules in academic libraries lies in instructing the borrower in its facilities and how to make full use of them; at the same time borrowers are made very much aware of their responsibilities. It is noticeable that the prohibitive style is missing from the rules of this type of library but they have a membership which is limited to staff and students and they can, therefore, be contacted with relative ease and sanctions enforced if necessary.

In the special library field rules are again generally kept to a minimum for much the same reason as with academic libraries. Threats are rare as are fines but with a small closed membership, as is usually the case, the co-operation of most users can be taken for granted; if a persistent offender does emerge the parent organisation is usually in a position to take effective action.

References

1   Corbett, E. V. *Photo-charging*, J. Clarke, 1957, pp 58–60.
2   Gallivan B. 'University of Lancaster Hybrid Issue System', *Program*, Vol 9, No 3, July 1975, pp 117–32.
3   Partridge D. A. 'On-line circulation control in Havering PL', *Program*, Vol 9, No 3, July 1975, pp 115–16.
4   Young, R. C. 'United Kingdom Computer-based Loans System: a Review', *Program*, Vol 9, No 3 July, 1975, pp 102–114.
5   Young, R. C. 'University of Sussex Library', *Program*, Vol 5, No 1, January 1971, pp 8–11.
6   Souter, G. H. 'Delinquent readers: a study of the problem in university libraries,' *Journal of Librarianship*, April 1976, pp 6–10.
7   Davies, Helen. 'Security devices in the library', *Asst Libn*, January 1975, pp 6–9.

11

Library and User—Arrangement and Guidance; Co-operation; Public Relations

The most important fundamental in the context of the library service, the user, has been left for detailed consideration in this final chapter. The users are the *raison d'être* for the library; it is entirely on their behalf that the organisation and administration, described at some length in the preceding chapters, is necessary. It follows, therefore, that the maximum effort should be made to ensure that library users derive the utmost possible benefit from the service. The user has tended to be taken for granted and his satisfaction with the library service assumed by librarians until recently when several voices have been raised to question this conclusion and a certain amount of research carried out, such as the Hillingdon project (see pp 65–6).[1] Earlier work in this direction included that of Brian Groombridge[2] and Bryan Luckham,[3] and attention is also drawn to a little-known survey carried out in the Renfrew District Libraries in December 1975 'to assist the Chief Librarian and his staff in the work of book selection and provision of services'.[4] In the library context, this exercise in public relations must also be directed to establishing the best possible relationship with the parent organisation and ensuring its appreciation of the place the library holds in its particular community. This is an essential element in the continuous struggle to acquire an adequate income for providing a first-class library service, with a well-structured establishment and a staff imbued with a sense of pride and job satisfaction. Public relations in the library context also relates, not only to public opinion of the individual library, but collectively to the total library service of the country—the promotion of national goodwill towards the service is dependent, not only on the work of individual librarians and their own personal relationship with their public, but also upon professional associations and other bodies whose work has impact at the level of central and local government, and in the fields of education, industry and commerce. Indeed, international relationships between governments, associations and librarians are becoming increasingly important in influencing the domestic development of libraries: witness the United Nations Information System in Science and Technology (UNISIST), National Information Systems (NATIS) and Universal Bibliographic Control (UBC).

THE LIBRARY: ITS ARRANGEMENT AND EQUIPMENT

It is stating the obvious to say that every potential library user should know where the library is. It is a fact, however, that many people who might otherwise use the library do not know of its existence. Brian Groombridge[5] found that among those who did not use the public library 15 per cent did not know of the location of the nearest library, and a further 17 per cent had only a vague idea. This is scarcely likely to occur within a relatively small, self-enclosed institution such as a professional association or society, a college or a small firm, but where the library is part of a much larger organisation, for example in a huge factory or a public library in a large town, then quite a number of possible users may be unaware of its location and the services they are missing. Even in some universities it could take 'freshers' some time to find the library, and general members of the public who might be allowed to use its services could well find the library difficult to locate, and might give up the search. In the public library field especially, libraries often fail to announce their presence to the public. With a branch library serving a population living within a mile radius, good publicity is essential together with use of the standard street signs 'Library' liberally used to point out the way. Even the library building itself might fail to advertise its use, especially in the case of older buildings which were not deliberately designed, as are modern buildings, to reveal their identity at a glance. The first requirements, therefore, are adequate street signposting, and a clear indication of the name of the library on the building, adequately lit-up at night. Within the university campus the signs are equally necessary, and within other educational institutions, factories, office blocks, and the like the corridors should display adequate bold signs pointing the way to the library. In addition, where relevant, the telephone numbers and the name of the library should be inserted in bold type in telephone directories and *Yellow Pages*. Similarly, street plans, site plans, and general publicity literature should all clearly indicate the library location and copies of this material should be readily available in public offices, security offices, and enquiry desks, according to the type of library.

Having made sure that the library can be located, it is then necessary to take a close look at the library from the inside. The best advice is to go outside and assume the rôle of someone visiting the library for the first time. (It is as well to remember that some people can be very nervous in unfamiliar buildings.) On entering the library the first requirement is a plan showing the location of all its departments—the entrance hall is the best place for this. Once inside, the newcomer should find a sympathetic librarian ready to help and advise him on his special requirements and how to get the best use from the library but for the moment we will assume that the visitor by-passes the librarian. Assisted by the library plan he has had no difficulty in learning how the library is divided and what special departments are provided. The stairs, lifts and escalators should all have signs guiding library users to the facilities at different floor levels and at each level other guides should give further directions as necessary. The contents of each department should be arranged in a logical order, eg in a lending library the non-fiction by classification, the fiction in alphabetical order of author. If the department is large and contains a variety of special types of stock, each shelved separately, then a further plan of this department should be exhibited in a prominent place. All shelves, filing cabinets, periodical racks, and similar equipment should be clearly labelled with their contents. Books should have their classification lettered on the spine so that they can be properly replaced and found on the shelves. Catalogues to the entire stock should be displayed in a prominent position and a brief explanation of their arrangement and use supplied. Where catalogues are in microform then special instructions for loading and using the 'readers' will be needed. Where the library is on a number of floors it is likely that the catalogues of the *complete* stock will only be found at the entrance level but at each floor level there should be catalogues of the departments located there. Similarly, the issue of books is likely to be confined to one central desk at the entrance level with enquiry facilities available within each department. In smaller libraries these problems will not arise but in all libraries the need for clear shelf layout, the provision of catalogues and a bright and cheerful atmosphere are most important.

Lighting should be very good so that the titles of books on the shelves can be easily read or catalogues consulted, and special care should be taken in lighting all study and reading areas. Flooring should be comfortable, slip-proof, and noise absorbing (carpet being by far the best material available in these respects since it is also easy to maintain); the temperature of the rooms should be around 65°F (18°C); furniture should be well-built, comfortably designed, attractively covered and dirt-resistant as far as is possible; an attractive colour scheme for carpets, furniture and decorations adds much to the general appearance. Where prolonged study is catered for, study tables, offering a certain degree of privacy and large enough to take half-a-dozen books and writing materials, should be provided in adequate numbers. Where research is carried out, necessitating reference to books and other materials over a long period, carrels which can be locked by the reader will be a great boon enabling him to leave his materials there after each session instead of having to hand them in and have them re-issued later; the provision of typewriters in the carrels is also a very useful service. Similarly in special departments such as 'Periodicals' or 'Music', microforms and reading equipment, record-players, tape-recorders, and other special equipment must be made available together with adequate instructions as to use. In a learning resources library, film-projectors, closed-circuit television, tape/slide-projectors, videotape equipment, radio-receivers, programmed learning machines, and various kinds of copier will be required. In brief, whatever the department, access to it should be clearly indicated and the contents clearly labelled; proper facilities and equipment for consultation, selection and use must be provided.

STAFF AND LIBRARY USER

Within the library walls the most important element of the library/ user relationship is the staff. Where there is a distinct division of duties between the librarians, and the non-professionals, the library and its enquiry desks should be so planned as to give prominence to the fact that enquiries should be directed to the former unless of a purely routine nature. The attitude of staff at all levels towards users should always be both pleasant and efficient; library users should come to regard them as friends rather than bureaucrats: friends with knowledge and expertise to place at their disposal. Whether the professional members of the staff who come into contact with the library user at the enquiry desk, are called 'readers' advisers', as in many public libraries, 'subject specialists' as favoured in university and polytechnic libraries, or 'information officers' as in some industrial and other special libraries, or plain 'librarians' their duties have a common purpose and they will be the persons whom the new library user first approaches. It will be their function to explain briefly the facilities offered by the library and to ascertain in very broad terms at this stage, what are the user's particular requirements.

In public libraries it is normal to register new members of the lending library at the readers' adviser's desk. Here he is given a copy of the rules and regulations, and of the library guide. An explanation is given about the number of tickets allowed, period of loan, renewals, fines, and reservations. The catalogue is briefly explained as is the shelf arrangement—this is probably all that many such libraries do as a matter of course. Where the pressure on staff is not too heavy new members of the public might be asked if they have any special requirements. They can then be shown the appropriate place on the shelves but any more formal instruction in public libraries is more often than not limited to organised visits of students from local colleges or in the case of the junior library to schoolchildren coming in parties from primary schools. In the latter event a lesson on the catalogues and in finding books is also likely to be part of the visit with some practical test of ability in using books. Many schoolchildren also see a film on library services or, failing this, film-strips or slides. In further visits they are taught how to use the library for project work set by the teacher. College students may also have lessons in using the library for project work, literature searches, the use of bibliographies and indexes, basic reference work and local history, as well as a general introduction to the library facilities, catalogues and arrangement of stock.

In university and polytechnic libraries and in some colleges if staffing so permits, library instruction is a regular feature although it will vary in depth from one library to another. Nearly all of them make a point of giving an introductory talk to new students in the first week or two of term. It is usually the university or college librarian who does it, which has the added advantage of giving both parties the opportunity to meet. The talk can be illustrated with film, overhead projector or slides, and should include plans of the layout of the library and arrangement of material. Sometimes this procedure is replaced entirely or augmented by, videotape instruction. Where the library is large, covering several floors or separate buildings, subsequent guided tours for small groups may be arranged. Another part of the instruction of students at this level is introducing them to material relevant to their own particular studies and guidance in the use of the bibliographical tools but this will follow later when they have settled down to their courses. Practical exercises in library use may also be promoted but the difficulty lies in getting sufficient co-operation from undergraduates who might consider this beneath them. Postgraduates will need further instruction in the use of research material, abstracts, union lists, guides to theses, and the resources of special and national libraries. So far as the academic staff is concerned, one ought to be able to assume that the members have spent many years in close association with libraries and librarians but whether they have made the best use of this association is another matter. Again, while it can be assumed that a lecturer is competent to teach his subject, his knowledge of current literature in that subject may fall short. The relevant subject specialists have a function here to forge close links between lecturers and library; to promote better book selection; better reading lists for students; better use of material already in stock, current awareness of new books, periodical articles, reports, conference proceedings, statistics, and theses. University librarians have shown an increased interest in library user instruction in recent years and this has been accompanied by a desire to evaluate it as demonstrated in professional articles.[6]

The procedure in special libraries varies according to the size and nature of the institution. In some the introduction to the library will be on a personal one-to-one basis between librarian and new user when it will be possible to give a tailor-made outline of the library and its specific usefulness to that one individual. In larger organisations the initial talk about library facilities may be included in its induction course for all newcomers to that institution; again it will be accompanied by the distribution of a library guide and other current publications. At a later stage those who are going to make extensive use of the library should have an individual session with the librarian but where the library is serving the research needs of a firm the research staff should need no prompting to make use of the library/information facilities and to establish a two-way communication.

SELECTIVE DISSEMINATION OF INFORMATION (SDI)

This is a technique which can be employed in all kinds of libraries in varying degrees but it is used most extensively in large special libraries. The principle is to provide library users on a regular basis with information they may need in pursuing their research or everyday occupation, and to select only such material as *is likely* to be useful—in other words to save the user from having to search continually through a whole mass of literature, in the hope of discovering something which might be useful. Thus, the information officer/librarian saves the user from wasting time in the perusal of useless material. The information itself, obtained from a multiplicity of sources, can be stored quite simply by means of a card index or in a more sophisticated and more flexible manner by use of computer as is practised in larger firms and in some research institutions. The key to its successful exploitation lies in drawing up a precise profile of the library user who wishes to be kept informed in this way. It must be based on discussion between the user and the information officer/librarian and an appreciation by the latter of the user's position in the organisation and his particular functions; a proper understanding of the subject matter concerned is essential, hence the advantage of the graduate information officer/librarian with a degree in the appropriate subject field. It is not essential for profiles to be geared to individuals, they can be written for groups of workers within a department, or for the activities of a specialised department. The aim should be to define the user's interest with precision, this needs very careful interrogation in the first instance and further consultations at intervals to make sure whether the service is satisfactory or whether the requirements have altered since the last discussion. If the service is computer-based the profiles will have to be fed into the computer in a manner compatible with the organisation's data bank so that profile and data can be matched. The data can be derived from several sources—commercially published abstracts, participation in national or international data banks, and from the organisation's own abstracts, indexes, scanning of journals, reports and bulletins.

At a more elementary level special library users can be kept up-to-date by the circulation of periodicals, regular lists of abstracts, accession lists, house journals, and the like. This material would help to keep users in the picture and invite them to ask for further information, or to see a particular article, report or book as required. Bulletins, for instance, are often issued in such a way that required items can be ticked and the list returned to the library for supply, alternatively tear-off slips can be used. There is no reason why *personal* methods such as these cannot be used in any type of library but in public libraries, for example, it will only be in technical and commercial departments that information in depth would be often needed and the extent to which it would be practical to supply it depends on staffing and whether or not the library charges for such a service. In the average lending library there is, however, a need—usually unfulfilled—to provide the *purposeful reader* with information about new books and articles in specific fields in which he has an interest. In the academic world SDI can be developed between the teaching staff and subject specialists to their mutual advantage.

CIRCULATION OF PERIODICALS

It is a common practice in special libraries to circulate periodicals and it is also employed in academic and some other libraries to a more limited extent. Libraries and the requirements of their users differ so much that it is impossible to lay down any one uniform practice. Whilst it is apparent that it is simple enough to circulate periodicals in a small firm where only a handful of people may want to see any one particular journal, it is by no means only in small organisations that circulation is practised. Walford, for instance, remarks that the Ministry of Defence (Central and Army) Library 'circulates 1,054 copies of periodicals, with controlled circulation of periodicals other than weeklies and fortnightlies, to 3,090 recipients' and that 'it is fairly usual practice for a library circulating some 1,000 periodicals (including duplicates) to employ at least one full-time staff for that purpose.'[7]

Reasons in support of a policy of circulation of periodicals include:

1 the organisation is scattered and many people find it difficult or downright impossible to visit the library;
2 the time of technical, management and research staff is too valuable for them to waste in making journeys to the library;
3 the journals are basic working tools which need to be immediately to hand;
4 it is better to circulate journals than to leave them in the library displayed but unused for the most part.

On the other hand, there are many reasons against circulation including:

1 the time of library staff is wasted in circulating the periodicals;
2 those who receive them do not read them soon after receipt and may retain them for an excessive period thus making others wait;
3 unless the periodicals are passed on very quickly, readers at the

end of the line are going to receive them a long time after publication;

4 periodicals get damaged, lost *en route*, and purloined, so that separate copies may have to be purchased for filing or binding;

5 to achieve anything approaching a reasonable circulation programme, a considerable number of duplicate copies are needed, thus increasing expense;

6 contact between librarian and user is lost when he no longer has to come to the library to consult the periodicals;

7 where a periodical is in considerable demand in a department then that department should buy its own copies regardless of library provision—otherwise an excessive proportion of the library's income is spent on periodicals.

8 it is more satisfactory to circulate abstracts and then to provide photocopies of articles if so needed (alternatively, contents lists can be photocopied and circulated for scanning);

9 it is difficult for the library to keep check on the whereabouts of any one periodical at any time; the solution is generally reckoned to be that each user sends back the journal to the library after consultation so that this can be recorded and the copy then sent on to the next person on the list—a time-consuming occupation. An alternative is to paste a circulation slip to the front of each journal showing the names of the persons to whom it is to be sent and a column for date of despatch; *A* then forwards to *B*, *B* to *C*, and so on. Whatever method is employed they all depend on the co-operation of each individual recipient and his zeal in returning the journal to the library or otherwise sending it on its approved journey.

With regard to the practice of individual libraries, it is probable that as the circulation of weekly periodicals to more than two or three individuals is unlikely to work smoothly unless duplicate copies are bought, the policy employed will be to keep these and other popular journals in the library for an initial period at least. This would leave the less frequently published and the less popular periodicals for circulation; even so, where periodicals are subsequently bound it may be necessary to purchase separate file copies to guard against loss or damage. Another alternative is for a member of the library staff to scan the periodicals in advance and only circulate when something relating to a user's interest is discovered.

LIBRARY PUBLICATIONS

Almost without exception libraries produce a certain amount of publicity material guiding the user to the library as a whole or to special services. Foremost among these is the *Library Guide* which has already been mentioned as playing a vital part in the induction of the new library user. Without any doubt this is the most useful of all library publications and therefore warrants careful compilation and a good standard of production. It will get into the hands of many individuals and organisations other than existing library users and would-be recruits to the profession, and can therefore have a wide impact. The aim of the guide should be to give the reader a brief but accurate description of the library and the facilities that can be enjoyed. It should be written in a simple language and style and be well-printed with the possible inclusion of one or two photographs. It should contain a list of key telephone numbers, addresses of the different libraries within the system, hours of opening, and an outline plan of the main library if this can physically be accommodated. The procedure for becoming a member of the library and for using the different facilities should be included but rules and regulations as a whole are probably best dealt with in a separate pamphlet. A very brief description of the catalogues provided and the arrangement of the books on the shelves also form part of the guide but again this might be covered in more detail in a separate leaflet or in a framed notice on the catalogue stand. One important point to remember is that library guides often have to be produced in large numbers, especially in public, university and polytechnic libraries which have a large influx of new users. At the same time a well-produced publication is expensive so that the text of the guide should avoid the use of factual information which is likely to change, eg names of staff members; scales of fees and fines; numbers of books and other material in stock. Finally, the guide should make a point of welcoming readers' suggestions and requests for information or advice. The availability of readers' advisers or subject specialists should be emphasised.

Apart from the general guide a number of libraries issue a series of separate brochures describing in some detail individual services such as, the loan of records and tapes, local history or special collections, services to the disadvantaged, the mobile library, the short-loan collection, the request and inter-loan services, library rules, and in some cases a list of library staff arranged by department. The use of various publications in a current awareness service by special libraries has been described on p 241-2, but in addition they issue information bulletins, diaries of events, brochures about the organisation and developments in view, and contribute to, or oversee the publication of the house journal. Practically all libraries seem to issue lists of their periodical holdings, lists of new accessions, subject lists, guides to the catalogues, and a pamphlet about photocopying and photographic services; some also issue extensive catalogues of their special collections and make them available for general sale. Annual reports are published by many public and university libraries and the British Library, but it is rare in special libraries and colleges.

The Annual Report. It is a common fallacy among students that libraries (especially public libraries) have a statutory obligation to compile an Annual Report. This is not true for the United Kingdom, though the British Library Act, 1972 does require the Board to send the Secretary of State 'a report of the proceedings and activities during the previous twelve months'. The Secretary of State in turn has a duty to lay copies of the report before each House of Parliament. Public libraries, academic libraries and special libraries have no such obligation although the governing body of any one of them may make it a requirement that the librarian or his committee should draw up an Annual Report for submission to the full governing body, or to one of its constituent assemblies. Thus, a public library report may be submitted first to the controlling committee, and then to the full council, and in a university the report may go to the library committee, the senate and council. Even if there is no ruling that a report must be submitted, there is nothing to prevent the librarian of any kind of library from preparing one. It must, however, be borne in mind that many libraries of different kinds prepare no Annual Report of any description and in other cases it may be limited to a brief paragraph or two in the report of the whole institution which goes to the governing body, eg in a university the library would get a small mention, along with all other separate departments; it may mention little more than total stock, issues, book purchases, finances and any special problem such as the effects of limited accommodation. All these departmental reports would become part of the Vice-Chancellor's Annual Report to the Court. In local authorities where the library is part of a Leisure Department, the report on the library could be incorporated into one which deals with the omnibus department.

Another factor to be remembered is the difference between *preparing and submitting* a report to the governing body and *publishing it in printed form*. While many librarians adopt the former practice the number who publish for general consumption is much smaller. In the former instance the Annual Report remains in its original format as a typed committee paper. It goes first to the library committee and then to the full council in the case of a public library, and as all but confidential papers are accessible to the press further publicity and comment is usually provided by the local newspapers. In academic libraries too there is no compulsion to have any Annual Report printed for general distribution though the librarian often supplies his committee with a paper outlining the year's work.

A glance at printed Annual Reports of various institutions reveals wide disparities of practice; some of them are issued as the 'Report of the Librarian', others as the 'Report of the Library Committee'; some of these latter are nevertheless signed by the librarian while others are more appropriately signed by the chairman of the committee; others bear no signature whatsoever. Some are very formal in their presentation and introduction, eg the Annual Report of the Curators of the Bodleian Library has a preamble: 'The Curators of the Bodleian Library, having received and approved the following Report from the Librarian, present it to the Congregation . . .' (nevertheless, it is unsigned!); other reports are very informal, do not indicate to whom, or by whom they are being presented, and are obvious reprints of sections of a wider report. With printing costs being so high nowadays it is also by no means uncommon to find, within reasonably attractive printed covers, that the text of the report is a duplicate of the original typescript submitted to committee.

In discussing the *value of annual reports* it is therefore essential to have consideration of the purpose in each case. Where there is a requirement, or merely a long-established practice, that the librarian prepare an annual statement of his stewardship for the information of the controlling body then its value will be limited to its impact upon committees and councils if it is not made available for general consumption. In this event its effectiveness will depend upon the content and phraseology together with any introduction the chairman of the committee may make in presenting it to the members. Any additional publicity will depend upon the extent to which the press (including the organisation's own news-sheets or information sheets) care to use it. However, it must not be assumed that if an Annual Report is not subsequently printed and published it is of little value. Much depends upon the librarian, his forcefulness, his clarity of style, and his ability to underline both the strength and weaknesses of his library (in fact he should be even more willing to point out the latter than to seek praise for his achievements). Over a period of time, with the right liaison between chairman and librarian, the Annual Report assumes real significance with a committee which can employ it as an annual survey of the library service and as a taking-off point for development during the ensuing year(s). The committee can often use the report to good effect with other members of the controlling body and thus get support outside its own membership and from the community the library serves.

Where *maximum publicity* is required from an Annual Report then it must be printed and distributed on a wide scale. If the library is going to the expense of printing, then good-class work is called for—good-quality paper, pleasing and well-laid-out type, generous margins, a liberal use of headings, well-designed covers, and, if funds will permit, a few photographs. The use of colour is very effective, but probably too expensive for most libraries to consider. Sometimes when the Annual Report is to be published, the original version as submitted to the authority is edited and abridged, the aim being to convey information but at the same time to ensure readability. Whether this is done or not, it is very important that the Annual Report should in the first place be drawn up in clear and concise style; it should avoid jargon and terminology which is peculiar to the profession, and the text should be broken up into sections by dealing with various aspects of the library service separately.

It is usual to commence with a brief general introduction dealing with the highlights and trends of the year and then to deal in turn with each main department or special service and to indicate throughout where further developments or improvements might be made. The effects of any important decisions put into operation during the year should also be noted, eg computerisation; a new resources centre; increased fines; reduced book-fund or inflation; special purchases or gifts; new buildings; and book sales. As far as possible statistics should be kept to a minimum in the main text and printed as appendixes. A section should also be devoted to staffing—changes in personnel, examination successes, distinctions in other fields, service on professional committees, and retirements but there seems little need to print in full the names of all members of the staff as is a common feature of some academic library reports.

Distribution of the printed reports (which should have been scrupulously proof-checked for printing or any other errors) will depend on the nature of the library but the aim is to send copies to those organisations and individuals who have an interest in the library or who might be able to interest others, either in the library or the parent organisation. Thus the public library will send copies to all members of the council and chief officers; to the press; business firms and factories; doctors' and dentists' surgeries; local societies; neighbouring librarians; library schools; careers officers; chambers of commerce; Rotary and similar organisations. Some copies should be reserved for casual distribution to library users who may be directed to enquire for them by notices in the library. With university Annual Reports circulation would extend to all academic staff and senior administrators; lay members of committees; members of the court; local schools and colleges; firms; chambers of commerce; the local authority; other universities; benefactors of the university; the press and others, but the high cost of printing does make it sometimes necessary to limit the total edition published; postage costs too may tend to reduce the circulation list.

Thus, in summarising the value of an Annual Report, it must be admitted that judgment is mainly subjective and there is little of a quantitative nature to assist in its assessment. There is certainly a need for a regular review of the library service but outside the immediate parent organisation the effects of an Annual Report are cumulative rather than immediate. Certainly the report can be very effective within the parent organisation as has already been shown. In its wider application the expense of printing and distribution has to be weighed against the rather problematic advantages of giving the 'public' a sense of value for money, of educating non-users to some or all of the facilities which they have hitherto ignored, of influencing recruitment, and acquainting those engaged in the educational field of opportunities for use and co-operation. Occasionally it may induce gifts of money or materials (more likely in the case of an academic library), and it should help to foster esteem for the library both locally and nationally. As with all publicity methods however, some of the effect wears off when those at whom they are aimed become over-accustomed to them. One practical suggestion therefore would be to prepare every year a duplicated report for the controlling body only and in addition to prepare a printed five-yearly survey for general distribution. Great changes in a library in any one year are few; the five-year period would have the advantage of providing a broader view of progress and for assessing results.

EXHIBITIONS: DISPLAYS

A feature common to all libraries is the advertisement of their services by means of displays and exhibitions. The former can range from a simple arrangement of informative and illustrative material on a notice board to something far more substantial and employing glass display cabinets, display boards and other special fittings together with a variety of 'props' to attract the attention of the library user. Displays are normally designed to give prominence to some particular facet of the library's service with the aim of inducing people to make use of that service—to borrow books, reports, records, tapes; to use information services; to draw attention to special collections; or, they can be used to advertise services related to other departments of the parent organisation, eg family planning; town planning; smoke abatement; research; special products; international activities; adult education. While it can scarcely be claimed that all displays have the one purpose of inviting further use of the library, most librarians do seek to link the topics in some way with the library service.

The exhibition is in essence display work at a much more ambitious level but here again there is a wide disparity of size and wealth of contents between one exhibition and another. At the more modest level there are travelling exhibitions such as those provided by the Victoria and Albert Museum and other agencies, which can comfortably be accommodated in a room about 30 feet square (although these are small exhibitions, they are valuable and adequate security arrangements are necessary, together with insurance cover), and at the other end of the scale there are very large exhibitions like those staged by the British Library, and others. Public libraries sometimes mount quite large exhibitions either in the library, if there is sufficient room, or in other public halls belonging to the authority. These can deal with all manner of subjects but the most popular is the 'Children's Book Week', devoted to drawing attention to children's literature and the many facilities provided by the children's libraries. It is possible to borrow all kinds of 'props' from publishers and to enlist the personal help of authors of children's books in meeting the children, giving talks, demonstrating illustration processes, and just answering questions. Local history and career exhibitions are also very popular as are those demonstrating the work of adult education institutions in the area with material supplied from the colleges. Local art exhibitions, both adult and children's, are firm favourites and command good support as does the exhibition drawing attention to the work of the local societies in the area.

The choice of subjects for an exhibition is wide but no *large* exhibition should be contemplated without full recognition of the tremendous amount of work involved in planning, acquiring the necessary exhibits and supporting material, purchasing or borrowing adequate display equipment, arranging for speakers and stewards, preparing printed notices and labels for the exhibits, having guides to the exhibition compiled and printed, sending out invitations, having posters printed and distributed, and in holding meetings between all concerned. In some cases the preparatory work may begin a year or so before the date of the exhibition. All display work must be designed and executed to a high standard, there is no room for amateurism if the library image is to be promoted and it follows that adequate finance is needed, together with enough staff, not only to mount the exhibition but also to man it. The assistance of professionals in the field of display and design is highly desirable. Some libraries are fortunate enough to have one or two members of staff so qualified, in others there may be a public relations department of the parent organisation whose staff would expect to be called upon to advise and assist. With all the work that is involved any large exhibition ought to remain open to the public for at least a month, otherwise the work can scarcely be justified. Publicity needs the full co-operation of the press which can probably best be achieved by arranging an informal briefing session over a drink; both radio and television should be informed of the event. Even if the latter cannot help, the radio, especially local radio, will be glad to do so.

The Annual Report of the British Library for 1975/6 draws attention to the BL's public relations and how they have been improved by their exhibition programmes. These included the 'American War of Independence', followed by a 'Jane Austen' bi-centenary exhibition and concluded with 'the most comprehensive exhibition that has ever been mounted of the illuminated Qur'an'. Few other libraries are likely to have the privilege of having their exhibitions opened by such high-ranking personages. HRH the Prince of Wales opened the first of the exhibitions and His Eminence Dr Abdul Halim

Mahmud, the Sheikh Al-Azhar, the latter. Certainly much additional publicity is generated if an opening ceremony, performed by a well-known personality, can be arranged.

CULTURAL ACTIVITIES

Some local authorities and universities also have their own art centres in which exhibitions can be arranged but generally they go in for a much wider range of activities than the so-called 'extension activities' long-since practised by so many public libraries. The art centres have been established for the promotion of the arts and with the intent of encouraging the public at large to take an active, rather than merely a passive, interest. Like the local authority the university extends its facilities in this respect to the general public as well as its own students and staff. The arts centre will arrange dramatic events, films, lectures, concerts and exhibitions but one of its dominant features will be provision for the individual to participate in skills such as pottery, painting, photography, music, puppetry, wood-carving and other such forms of artistic expression. In the case of some public libraries the librarian may also be responsible for the arts centre and other cultural activities but the everyday administration and promotion will be in charge of someone specially qualified in this field, supported by an experienced staff. Certain public libraries such as Camden, Manchester, Luton and Bradford also have civic theatres built into the library complex and the librarian may have an overall responsibility, though the day to day administration would be left to a house-manager. Whatever the exact relationship of arts centres and other forms of cultural promotion there is usually a strong link between them and the library and each can help promote the other.

THE MEDIA

One of the most obvious ways of seeking library publicity is via the media and this has been touched upon in connection with exhibitions but wherever advertisement is required the co-operation of the local press should be the first resort; it is one of the cheapest and most readily available forms of publicity and certainly the most far-reaching, subject to the one proviso that the news item must be of local significance and newsworthy. Although it still seems to be a common belief among younger librarians that the local paper is always ready to publish lists of new additions to the local public library and similar routine information, that day is over. People *expect* the library to have new books on the one hand, and on the other, space is too valuable for the press to waste on the obvious. However, details of revised charges, amended hours of opening, proposals to close libraries or to open new ones, distinguished visitors, senior staff appointments or resignations, library weeks, amusing incidents, and the like, are usually welcome if written up briefly and in suitable form for publication. Local broadcasting will usually announce special events and news items and the librarian might be invited to talk about library developments of 'significance' but it is unlikely that TV will be able to assist except on outstanding occasions such as the introduction of unique equipment, visits of royalty, and on some other rare occasion when for some reason the library has made the national headlines or when the librarian as an individual may have some close contact with a subject of national concern such as Public Lending Right, or the statutory introduction of library charges.

POSTERS

Libraries will rely to a great extent on posters to advertise their respective facilities and events. These can be used both within and outside the library but it will be mostly public and national libraries which advertise externally in this way. The major difficulty lies in the acquisition of suitable sites; in a local authority the council will have some useful sites of its own but most likely resort must also be had to commercial notice boards and hoardings if adequate publicity is to be obtained and this is not cheap. Local shopkeepers, schools, colleges, factories, societies, etc, can also be approached with a fair measure of success but posters of good design are too expensive to send out indiscriminately without some promise in advance that they will be displayed. At national level the British Library uses 2,000 outlets in all (including libraries) and the underground stations too if an event so warrants, but they are in a privileged position. Once again it is emphasised that posters should be professionally designed and with a view to impact.

TALKS

Librarians of all types of library are called upon from time to time to give talks about their libraries to outside bodies or groups within the parent organisation. Again, it will be at the level of public and national libraries where this will mostly occur. At national level the talks will centre on international, national and regional conferences, study groups and seminars; at the public library level, while the individual librarian will also be called upon from time to time to speak at national and regional conferences and study groups, the major demands will come from local organisations—Townswomen's guilds, Rotary clubs, schools, colleges, youth clubs and church societies. In many cases the request may merely result from the desperation of the club programme secretary anxious to find a speaker to substitute for someone who has cried off at the last moment and in any event it is extremely unlikely that any great influx of new library users will result but it is good policy to forge links with local organisations. The time may come when they in turn can be of assistance to the library.

RELATIONS WITH OTHER LIBRARIES

No library, no matter how large and however well-endowed it may be, can operate entirely on its own; there is a long tradition of co-operation, both formal and informal, between librarians and libraries of all kinds, locally, regionally, nationally and internationally. The extent of such co-operation is one of the mainsprings of the library service in Britain and has for long been the admiration of other countries. Though at the centre, inter-lending and some other forms of library co-operation are now government sponsored via the British Library Lending Division, the amazing thing is that the vast web of co-operation which encompasses the whole of the United Kingdom sprang from voluntary measures initiated by far-sighted librarians. It is no part of this volume to outline the national and local schemes of co-operation at any great length except to show how well the user is served by them and the essential part they play in promoting public relations.

Inter-lending. Co-operation takes many forms. The best-known and the one which springs immediately to mind when the word is mentioned is inter-library lending through the several regional library systems which cover the United Kingdom and are supported by the British Library Lending Division. At regional level, public libraries in co-operation with some university and other academic and special libraries, agree to make their non-fiction stocks (with certain possible exceptions) available for outside loan when they receive a request from a member library for an item which it does not have in stock itself and either cannot, or does not want to, purchase. The normal procedure is for the requests to go to a central bureau in the region which has a union catalogue of all the holdings of the co-operating libraries and can thereby organise the loan. Furthermore, as the result of the initiative of the London and South Eastern Regional Library System (LASER) which first developed the union catalogue on microfilm in the regional library systems, it is now possible, in some of them, for a requesting library to consult its own microfilm copy of the region's resources and telephone or telex a holding library direct to effect a loan. Failing location of a copy of the required item within the region, the request is then passed on to the BLLD though in the case of university and special libraries in particular the request goes *direct* to BLLD at Boston Spa. The policy of the BLLD is to 'support' the individual library resources of the United Kingdom by an inter-loan and photocopy service and according to the Annual Report of the British Library for 1975/6 its holdings total 2,400,000 volumes; 1,500,000 microform documents; and 100,000 serials, current and dead. It acquires all significant periodicals, regardless of language and all monographs in the English language of a type and level likely to be required on inter-library loan. Thus, in terms of recent literature in particular, it is extremely well-placed to provide the material that the individual library cannot supply from its own resources. The stock also includes monographs in foreign languages on a selective basis except for Russian scientific works which are bought comprehensively, all EEC publications from 1973 onwards, all British official publications since 1962 and all Unesco publications since 1954.[8] The BLLD also lends to overseas libraries and in turn borrows from abroad if the material is not available in the United Kingdom. In all the BLLD receives about $2\frac{1}{2}$ million requests each year and claims a success rate of 93 per cent. This includes requests satisfied from its own stock and from certain major libraries at home who have agreed to act as back-up centres, as well as over 10,000 requests satisfied from overseas. The proportion satisfied from BLLD's own stock is 84 per cent. All kinds of library use its resources, 38 per cent academic, 45 per cent special but only 8 per cent public libraries because they make such heavy use in the first instance of the regional library systems and because they have fewer demands for periodical and report literature. Nine per cent of the BLLD requests come from overseas. The service is based on the use of pre-paid requisition forms, that is to say the borrowing library has paid for them. Normally the individual is not charged but there is no reason why the charge should not be passed on. With regard to borrowing from the BLLD one word of caution is necessary: it is not cheap and the cost of the forms has risen over the years; if a book is in print then the librarian should give serious consideration to purchase rather than loan. This apart, no matter what type of library, with the aid of the regional library systems and the BLLD the vast majority of requests can be satisfied. Of *all* the facilities offered by libraries this inter-lending procedure is the best known and needs no publicity; as a by-product it has had a remarkable effect in promoting general appreciation of library services.

Local co-operation. In view of such excellent regional and national inter-loan facilities it would seem that nothing further could possibly be necessary but there are numerous localised organisations involving different types of library in compact geographical areas. Two of the oldest and best-known of these are the Sheffield Interchange Organisation (SINTO) and Liverpool and District Scientific Industrial and Research Library Advisory Council (LADSIRLAC) but there are a few dozen of them nowadays all over the country and all with the common purpose of pooling resources with a view to the production of information in the shortest possible time and the loan of books and other material, virtually on demand (subject to any overriding consideration such as confidential information). These schemes normally link the public library with the university library, other academic and research libraries, and industry in a given town or county. A telephone call or a telex message, followed up by the library van is often all that is necessary to get information and material from one library to another. These local co-operative schemes can also be used for other joint ventures such as limited co-operative acquisition of books and periodicals, joint stores, union lists and staff training. In spite of all the co-operation already in being there is still room for more, especially in the rationalisation of services and resources of the different types of library. The difficulties in the way of achieving further co-operation are however very real indeed. Firstly, each library has a primary responsibility to its own membership and more important still, each type of library is funded differently. For instance although the libraries of universities, polytechnics, local education colleges and schools, together with public libraries, are all financed from public funds contributed by way of taxes and rates, the methods whereby the income of each is assessed and made available, are all different to varying degrees. The funds which are voted are also earmarked for specific categories of user and must be employed accordingly. (The public library is alone in that the users of all the other kinds of library also have an automatic right to use its services.) At the same time each of these libraries, with their large stocks of books and other materials, always has a major part of its stock standing unused on the shelves; they all provide accommodation for study, and at times much of this will also be unused; they all provide reference and information services which are very expensive; most of them have storage problems; nearly all provide and produce their own catalogues (some manually others by computer); and all of them have to spend time in training staff. To a certain extent, therefore, there is some duplication of services and effort. This being so it does not seem unreasonable to suppose that *there ought to be room for co-operation locally between different types of library* so as to make the joint provision more widely accessible and to obtain a greater cost-effectiveness. An encouraging lead in this direction was given by the Department of Education and Science in 1973/4 when it sponsored research[9] by the University of Sheffield Postgraduate School of Librarianship and Information Science into the possibilities of co-operation in the Sheffield area between different types of library. Although this was based primarily in support of higher education it points the way to future developments which commonsense and the economic situation would appear to dictate. One somewhat disturbing factor that did emerge from this report however was that more co-operation can only be achieved by the provision of additional staff to organise it. On the other hand, the advantages which might accrue in respect of depth of service and benefits to the public could probably not be provided as cheaply by any other means and in the long run more co-operation must save money.

Co-operative acquisition and storage. Where a number of libraries within a specific area all need copies of the same books and periodicals, which have only occasional rather than constant use, it seems sensible for their librarians to come to a common agreement to share the expense, particularly in the case of expensive publications. The best-known example of such an arrangement is the Metropolitan Special Collections Scheme (MSC) in the London public libraries. A copy or copies of every book should, ideally, be provided somewhere in London and should be kept permanently but without a co-operative arrangement there is a very real chance that some books may not be purchased by any of the public libraries and in other instances there may be too many. Thus, the MSC scheme divides the responsibility so that each library agrees to buy a copy of every book published and entered in the *British National Bibliography within a specific subject field*, above a certain price. They also agree to keep the book permanently so that a copy is always available in London, and to receive books within their field which have been withdrawn from the other libraries. Thus, co-operative storage of at least one copy of any title is achieved. The London libraries have a similar scheme for recorded music: Greater London Audio Subject Specialisation Scheme (GLASS); a Joint Fiction Reserve Scheme (MJFR) covers the purchase and retention of works of fiction, and another scheme covers the provision of play-sets which are mainly used by amateur drama groups. Devon County has a scheme for the co-operative purchase of sets of music scores and there are a number of other co-operative schemes of this nature throughout the country including, at national level, the Background Materials Supply Scheme and another for the provision of books for African Studies.

Periodicals seem an obvious field for co-operation in purchase and retention, but difficulties abound: the extensive number of titles; the fact that new periodicals come and others die with monotonous regularity; local considerations such as the need to reduce expenditure, which can result in a library's no longer being able to honour its commitments; and storage costs. There *are* schemes in existence but how strictly observed they are is a matter for conjecture; the London public libraries did make some attempt in this direction inasmuch as individual libraries were asked to take and preserve as far as they could a selection of periodicals within their MSC area. This has been done for some years to varying degrees but covers only a very small proportion of the nation's periodical literature. Some colleges of education have also drawn up local area schemes and the universities and other important libraries have contributed to important union lists of periodicals. The London and Home Counties Branch of The Library Association has also issued a union list of periodicals held by London public libraries but the work entailed in keeping union lists up-to-date is tremendous, and contributing libraries cannot be compelled to purchase or store any periodical indefinitely. With the excellent service provided by the BLLD and its back-up libraries, the need for co-operative arrangements for periodicals other than the purely local schemes has been considerably reduced.

Co-operative storage is a subject which appears regularly in the literature of librarianship but surprisingly enough not a great deal has been done on a large scale. It is not unusual in a single public library system for it to have one central store for copies of lesser-used material thus the branch libraries would keep very few books in their own stack; instead all books being withdrawn from the shelves would first be checked for number of copies within the system and where any copy was unique it would go to the central store (in some cases more than one copy would be kept). The MSC Scheme, already described, also includes dispersed co-operative storage; and nationally the regional library systems pursued a similar policy with a view to storing one copy of each title somewhere in the country.

London University has also had a library depository at the Royal Holloway College, Egham since 1961. This serves the needs of the constituent college libraries and the former National Central Library had a repository at Woolwich for which it was prepared to consider stock no longer required by other libraries. With the publication of the Atkinson Report attention has been sharply focused on co-operative storage by its suggestion that once a university's own reserve store is filled it should be expected to dispose of little-used books and periodicals to BLLD. A new building extension is anticipated to be completed at Boston Spa in 1979 and plans for future expansion are to be considered. If the BLLD is able to take on the vast quantities of material which other libraries, not only university libraries, will wish to offer, the result must inevitably be that some library users are going to have to wait longer till their requirements are met. Whereas there may be several copies of a particular book or complete files of periodicals in existence at the present moment in a spread of libraries, these may be reduced to a level too low to meet all demands if a policy of indiscriminate despatch to BLLD is pursued by all.

THE COMPUTER AND CO-OPERATION

It is in the realm of computer applications, fostered by the Bibliographical Division of the British Library and OSTI in particular that co-operation has provided some of the most outstanding recent results; results which no one library could have achieved in isolation and which have had a marked effect on the quality and depth of service to individual library users. They include schemes such as the Birmingham Libraries Co-operative Mechanisation Project (BLCMP) with its co-operative approach to cataloguing procedures by use of

Marc records; the South Western Academic Libraries Computer Project (SWALCAP), consisting of Bristol, Cardiff and Exeter universities, co-operating in the field of circulation systems; and the Scottish Libraries Co-operative Automation Project (SCOLCAP) embracing the National Library of Scotland, the universities of Dundee, Glasgow and Stirling, and the Edinburgh and Glasgow city libraries, with a view to the establishment of an on-line network for bibliographical processing in Scotland. Large advances too have been made in the information field by national and special libraries. Thus huge networks have been built up to which contributing libraries have access, eg MEDLINE at the US National Library of Medicine in Washington, DC, which can be tapped direct for medical information by libraries having their own terminal, or via BLLD which is the UK centre for the Medical Literature and Retrieval System (MEDLARS) or on British Library Automated Information Systems (BLAISE). Other examples are Information Services in Physics Electro-technology and Control (INSPEC); United Kingdom Chemical Information Service of the Chemical Society (UKCIS); and DIAL-TECH, the on-line service from the European Space Agency which is accessed by way of the Department of Industry Technological Report Centre. Use of some of these information services can, however, be very expensive, but the cost has to be assessed in relation to the benefits derived by the organisations which make use of them. At international level there is also the ambitious project EURONET which is to establish a data transmission network for scientific and technical information, and the many schemes projected under the umbrella of United Nations Information System in Science and Technology (UNISIST) which to quote J. S. Parker 'is considered to be one of the major programmes of UNESCO, and to which responsibility has been allocated for "all conceptual and operational activities relating to scientific and technical information and documentation services, whether financed by the regular budget or through UNDP funds".'[10]

THE LIBRARY AND THE PARENT ORGANISATION

At the outset of this chapter the point was made that public relations was an exercise not merely to be aimed at the library user but also at the parent organisation. This factor is often overlooked by students who think only of public relations in terms of everyday contact with the user and the employment of various publicity methods. In reality, the relationship between the librarian and those who provide the finance for the service is even more important. This fact is most evident to the librarian of an industrial firm who is only too conscious that there is no wasted sympathy in the business world—the library either produces tangible results or the librarian goes and is replaced by another: at worst the library is closed down. In other types of library such a situation does not occur except perhaps in the case of a small society which cannot continue to pay its way. Ignoring these circumstances therefore, it can be said that public relations are a permanent built-in duty of the librarian and that the financial support that his library receives will depend largely on his ability to sell the library to his governors. Consequently, the value of the library in the estimation of councillors, academic staff, and directors must directly affect the estimates which are finally sanctioned. It must inevitably be the responsibility of the librarian to ensure that these persons are well-served by the library, are suitably indoctrinated, consulted as necessary, and made aware of the rôle the library plays in the life of the community it serves. In the case of the academic library the very success of the students and of the academic staff and research workers depends upon a first-rate library service. Then in the public library field the librarian must impress upon his committee and other council members the many ways in which the library contributes to the intellectual and recreational needs of the community, not to mention its rôle as the provider of everyday information and the part it plays in the mental well-being of the population.

Where the library service is controlled through one or more committees then these committees are the librarian's most potent aid to the establishment of good public relations. This has become very evident in the public library context in recent years where the librarian's personal involvement with the library committee in particular has been reduced in some circumstances. The publication of the Maud Committee Report,[11] followed a little later by the Bains Committee Report[12] led many local authorities, which had previously placed responsibility for libraries with a library committee, to bring together such services as libraries, baths, parks and open spaces, entertainment, public halls, and possibly others, under one omnibus committee as explained in Chapter 3 and at the same time to give greater responsibility to the officers. From the point of view of senior officers such as the librarian, the explicit and extra authority was something they had long-since aspired to but they came to realise in due course that the new committee arrangement was not entirely to their advantage. Instead of a committee of about twelve to fifteen people, all reasonably interested in libraries and with some very enthusiastic members among them, including the chairman, they now had a committee which was larger but in which the interests of members were divided. Although with this new set-up the members were expected to make themselves 'experts' in all the leisure activities of the authority it was only natural that some were far more interested in facilities for outdoor activities, or in parks, swimming, or sports halls than in libraries (indeed in spite of all that has been said to the contrary, the strictly indoor and mentally centred activities of the library sit uneasily alongside the physical and outdoor activities of the other services). Instead of twelve or fifteen library enthusiasts on the council to work for the promotion of library services the librarians often found that perhaps no more than three or four were so-minded. Whatever may be said about corporate management, the truth is that libraries and other council services are in competition with each other for the attention of councillors and the provision of funds for both revenue and capital purposes. In addition the budget of the omnibus committee is now so large that it gets more careful inspection than did those of the services when operating independently and if the committee is labelled 'leisure', 'amenities' or 'recreation' it has little emotive appeal and is, therefore, more likely to be a target for cuts in adverse times. However, in these circumstances, the librarian must focus his persuasive powers on the director although if *he* is not a librarian he is less likely to be convinced of library priority over parks and swimming baths, or sports centres.

Apart from dealings with his committee, the librarian in his contacts with members of the council generally, should contrive to interest them either individually or collectively in the work of the library, to give them prompt service, be ready to offer to show them round the library or take them to see new libraries, send them copies of library programmes and publicity, find out their interests and provide them with relevant literature, use them to chair library activities, and try to establish a local government information service for councillors and senior officers. Another factor is that although some councillors may not be so very interested in the long-established services of the library, when it reaches out to serve disadvantaged groups (such as the housebound by means of a door-to-door van delivery service of books and records; patients in hospital with a fully-fledged hospital library service; old people's homes by regular deposit and replacement of static collections; those in prisons and other institutions with permanent libraries, supervised and well maintained from the public library; ethnic minorities by providing special collections in their native languages; or when it goes out into poorer areas of the district to take the library to the people, especially children), then a much greater body of support is likely to be forthcoming in view of the 'social service' aspect.

LIBRARIAN AND STAFF

The public relations exercise involves the governing body, the user and the staff. There is no need to deal with the rôle of the latter at any great length as this has been dealt with in Chapter 8. It is only necessary to repeat that an efficient and enthusiastic staff set the tone of any library and lead to good relations with the public; this can only be achieved if the staff is given a prominent rôle in decision-making, if its opinions are actively sought and if it is kept adequately informed. It must be appreciated that it is the staff in the departments, both professional and non-professional, which has the responsibility of contact with the public; prior consultation before the introduction of any radical changes in procedure can well obviate trouble or lead to better solutions of particular problems.

That the staff should be nicely spoken, pleasant, well-informed and neatly-dressed should need no emphasis.

PROFESSIONAL ASSOCIATIONS

To conclude the discussion on the wider aspects of public relations brief mention must be made of the work of the professional associations in this respect. The Library Association is the leading professional association and has a membership of about 24,000 including some 21,000 individual members. Its objectives are set out in the Royal Charter, granted in 1898, and can virtually be summed up as having the purpose of doing everything within its power to promote and improve libraries of all kinds by whatever means are considered practical; to promote the qualifications and the status of librarians; and to unite all persons engaged or interested in libraries. It follows therefore, that The Library Association has the major public relations responsibility in our professional work and it does this by means of its Council and officers and its geographical Branches and functional Groups. The Association celebrated its centenary in 1977 and can look back upon a century of continued and remarkable progress. Progress which was slow until 1929 but which has accelerated with increasing rapidity year after year since that date.

The nation-wide organisation of libraries today in this country is due to the work of thousands of dedicated librarians from all types of library and the efforts they have expended, both individually and through The Association, so that the professionalism of librarians, which is almost taken for granted today, has reached a stage that would have been thought impossible before the last war. All this has involved The Library Association in a mighty public relations exercise with government departments, particularly the Department of Education and Science and more recently the British Library, with academic authorities and educational associations, industrial firms, societies, local government, research bodies and the like, as well as international bodies such as United Nations Educational Scientific and Cultural Organisation (Unesco), International Federation of Library Associations (IFLA), the British Council, and the Commonwealth Library Association (COMLA). The Library Association was largely responsible for the creation of the latter. A glance at the files of the Annual Reports of The Association will readily reveal the diversity of its operations and contacts.

The Association of Special Libraries and Information Bureaux (ASLIB) established in 1924, has as its title indicates, a special concern with the work of special libraries, information science and research. Its membership is aimed primarily at the organisations providing libraries but includes individuals; it also has a wide-ranging membership in countries overseas. It has a close association with the government from whom it derives grant-aid. Well known for the work of its Information Department, its advice to organisations intending to establish libraries and information services, its short courses, its assistance with indexing and translation, its library of material on special librarianship and documentation, and its own publications, Aslib is particularly to the fore in its research work into documentation, indexing, classification, automation and abstracting. It has had a profound effect on the establishment of standards of service in the special library field and is equally well known for its work abroad through its contributions to international organisations and conferences.

In the world of university and national libraries, the main organisation, other than The Library Association, for advancing the views of professional librarians, is the Standing Conference of National and University Libraries (SCONUL). It was established in 1950, primarily to give the librarians an opportunity to discuss topics of interest to them as representatives of large learned libraries and to make known their views in whatever quarters might be thought necessary. They meet twice a year as a body during the year but meanwhile carry out much of their work through sub-committees. The organisation was prominent for instance, in giving evidence to the Parry Committee, the National Libraries Committee, and the Atkinson Committee. In addition SCONUL organises some courses and seminars and has a modest trainee scheme. The collective views of the leading librarians of these large research libraries must obviously have a considerable effect on library developments, both nationally and internationally.

Apart from the three organisations mentioned there are many others such as the University, College and Research, and the Reference, Special and Information, sections of The Library Association; the Council of Polytechnic Librarians (COPOL); the Association of London Chief Librarians (ALCL) which acts as an advisory body to the London Boroughs; the Association of British Library and Information Studies Schools (ABLISS); the Art Libraries Society (ARLIS); the Institute of Information Scientists; the Society of Archivists; the Society of Indexers; the School Library Association; the Scottish Library Association; the Welsh Library Association; the Northern Ireland Branch of the Library Association; and the Standing Conference of Librarians of Libraries in the University of London, to name but a few who have a regional or functional interest in librarianship and information work.

References

1 Totterdell, B. *The effective library*, LA, 1976.
2 Groombridge, B. *The Londoner and his library*, Research Institute for Consumer Affairs, 1964.
3 Luckham, B. *The library in society*, LA Research Publication 4, 1971.
4 Whatley, H. A. *Renfrew District Libraries: survey of library use and availability of library materials*, Department of Librarianship, University of Strathclyde, 1976.
5 Groombridge, B. *Op cit*, p 28.
6 Brewer, J. G. and Hills, P. J. 'Evaluation of reader instruction', *Libri*, 1976, Vol 26, No 1, pp 55–65. *And* Fjallbrant, Nancy, 'Evalua-

tion in a user education programme', *Journal of Librarianship*, Vol 9, No 2, April 1976, pp 83–95.

7 Walford, A. J. *Circulation, loan and inter-library loans*, in Batten, W. E., *ed, Handbook of special librarianship and information work*, 4th ed, Aslib, 1975, p 272.

8 See: British Library Third Annual Report 1975–76, for these and other statistics.

9 University of Sheffield, Postgraduate School of Librarianship, *Local library co-operation*, 1974, 2 vols.

10 Parker, J. S. 'International directions', *Prospects for British librarianship*, LA, 1976.

11 Ministry of Housing and Local Government. *Management of local government*. (Maud Report), HMSO, 1967.

12 Department of the Environment. *The new local authorities, management and structure* (Bains Report), HMSO, 1972.

Appendix I

LANCASHIRE COUNTY COUNCIL
AGENCY ARRANGEMENTS—LIBRARY SERVICE
(as approved by County Council—18th January 1974)

1. *Functions and Rights of the District Council*

   (i) The determination of opening hours of the libraries and keeping under review the effectiveness and convenience of any mobile library service operating within the District.

   (ii) Consistent with the efficiency of the Library Service, determining the use of library buildings when not open for library service purposes.

   (iii) The use of library buildings, materials and equipment, in the promotion or sponsoring by the District Council of cultural and recreational activities, or by other local agencies operating in this field.

   (iv) The enforcement of the County Council's Library Byelaws.

   (v) The provision, within revenue expenditure approved by the County Council, of supplementary items to promote the use of, and interest in, the library service, reflecting special local and historical interests. The District Council would submit annually, estimates of the revenue expenditure they would like to incur in the ensuing year under this heading.

   (vi) The right to receive from the District Librarian a quarterly report on book selection in relation to the Library Service within the District, the form of the report to be agreed between the Chief Executive of the County Council and the Chief Executive of the District Council, in consultation with the County Librarian.

   (vii) The right to put forward to the County Council suggestions on book selection.

267

(viii) The right to be involved in the appointment of the District Librarian of the County Council, at member or officer level, in accordance with a procedure to be settled by the County Council.

(ix) The submission of recommendations to the County Council's Library and Leisure Committee on any matter relating to the Library Service within the District.

2. *Provision to be made by the County Council*

(x) The County Council's District Librarian shall be available to attend meetings of the Committee of the District Council, charged with the exercise of the agency functions.

(xi) The resources made available to the County Library Service each year by the County Council for the purchase of books shall include a sum which shall be expendable on books selected by the District Librarian to reflect special local needs as identified by the District Council.

(xii) District Librarians shall be entitled to submit to the County Librarian recommendations on books to be purchased within approved annual estimates.

(xiii) The County Council shall convene a meeting annually between representatives of the County Council and each District Council to review the Library Service within the District.

3. *Conditions of the above-mentioned arrangements*

(xiv) The exercise by the District Council of the functions, and their rights, under 1 above shall be subject to the overall financial and general policy control by the County Council.

(xv) The arrangements shall operate for a period of five years, subject to review by the County Council in consultation with the District Council at the end of the fourth year.

[Quoted by permission of the County Librarian.]

Appendix II

NEW LEICESTERSHIRE COUNTY COUNCIL

REPORT OF THE COUNTY LIBRARIAN AND THE DIRECTOR OF MUSEUMS AND ART GALLERIES

CONSULTATION WITH DISTRICT COUNCILS IN RESPECT OF THE COUNTY LIBRARY AND INFORMATION SERVICE AND THE MUSEUMS AND ART GALLERY SERVICE

1. *Introduction*

1.1. The Library and Information Service and the Museum Service (which for the sake of brevity are referred to below as 'the County Service') have links with County Council services and with some services of District Councils and are services in which the District Councils will take considerable interest. The experience of the present County Council has shown the value of the present District Councils as an additional channel of communication for local views and opinion on the Libraries Services and the Secretary of State, in paragraphs 20–22 of Circular 5/73, has urged the new Counties to establish ongoing arrangements by which they can benefit from the local knowledge of particular needs and interests and which will enable District Councils to contribute to the development policy for the library service of the whole county.

1.2. The County Council has established a joint County Conference with the District Councils as a first step towards achieving a reasonable degree of liaison between itself and the Districts, and has agreed that each service should adopt appropriate arrangements for additional consultation.

1.3. This report makes recommendations for the establishment of an effective system which will contribute to the management of the

County Service. The recommendations have been considered by the Chief Officers Management Team and have their support.

2. *The objectives of consultation*

2.1.   The objectives of consultation are:

2.1.(1)   To inform the District Council of the functions, objectives, and programmes of the County Service as a whole, to discuss them and to ascertain the views of the District Councillors.

2.1.(2)   To obtain the opinions and suggestions of the District Council on the working and progress of the County Service in the District.

2.1.(3)   To obtain the opinions and suggestions of the Districts on the future development of the County Service in the District.

2.1.(4)   To assist in the co-ordination of relevant County and District activities and services (e.g. in public information and the Arts).

2.1.(5)   To facilitate contact and communication between County and District officers.

3. *Consultative arrangements for the new County*

3.1.   It is suggested that the Libraries and Museums Committee appoints a Consultative Panel of 6 members including the Chairman, Vice-Chairman and Shadow Chairman to visit each District Council, meeting at their offices. The District Council representation would be at its discretion, for example by its Chairman, other members and Chief Executive, by a specially appointed committee, or by one of its Standing Committees, and by non-members with relevant special interests co-opted for the meeting. The County Councillors for the electoral divisions in the District would be informed of the meeting and could attend if they wished. Special arrangements, possibly in the form of a rota, could be made for the Leicester District as there are so many (32) County Councillors involved. This might also be necessary for some of the other larger Districts.

3.2.   The County Council and the District Council representatives would receive in advance of the meeting papers prepared by the County Librarian and Director of Museums and Art Galleries covering the County Service in the District, and in each community, the standard of provision, public response and the long term requirements.

3.3.   The frequency of meetings of the Consultative Panel should be discussed with each District Council bearing in mind the experience of the present County Council that an annual meeting enabled leading members and senior officers of both District and County Councils to attend and to concentrate discussion on local problems in the context of policy and progress in the County as a whole.

3.4. Because a close working relationship with District Council officers would assist in co-ordination of the County Service to the public it is intended to allocate to members of the Library and Information Service staff responsibility for officer level liaison with each District, and it is hoped that the Chief Executives of the Districts will be able to involve them in relevant officer working parties etc regarding them as the librarian and information specialist in the District.

[The paragraphs of the report with respect to Museums and Art Galleries have not been reprinted. *Author*]

1.12.73.

[Quoted by permission of the County Librarian]

Index

compiled by Audrey Bamber
according to the provisions of BS 3700: 1976

In this Index the method of alphabetisation is word by word; acronyms and other abbreviations are grouped at the beginning of the initial letter. Page numbers in italics refer to the lists of references at the end of the chapters. For the sake of clarity the heading 'Librarians' has been used to indicate chief librarians by whatever title they may otherwise be known. Entries relating to the less exalted will be found under the heading 'Staff'.

ABLISS, 265
ADP, *see* Computer applications
ALCL, 265
ALS, 215, 216
ARLIS, 265
ASLIB, 264
Academic libraries
  book-selection committees, 53
  fines for overdue books, 224
  government influence, 8
  growth of facilities, 3–4
  history, 1
  objectives, 71
  organisation, 90–2
  rules, 235
  see also College libraries;
    University libraries
Accession numbers
  allocation, 189, 190
  uses, 192
    in computer issue systems,
    214
Accession stamps, 197–8
Accessioning, 189–92
Accessions lists, 246
Accessions registers, 190–1
Accounting methods, 122
  commitment procedure, 185
  see also Finance
Ad hoc committees, 37

Administrative Staff College, 4
Advisory committees, 37, 39
Advocates' Library, 19
African studies, co-operative
    purchase scheme, 258
Agency arrangements
  in Lancashire, 33, 267–8
  in Leicestershire, 33, 269–71
Aldermaston (UKAEA) Library,
    212
American Library Association
  Standards, *78*, 89, *99*
  work on standards, 66, *143*
Anderson, Ursula, *171*
Anglo-American Code, 194
Annual reports, 246–50
  contents, 248–9
  distribution, 249
  purpose and value, 247–8, *249*
Appraisal of staff, 158–60
Approved auditors, 128, 129
Arts centres, 252
Arts Libraries Society, 265
Association of British Library
    and Information Studies
    Schools (ABLISS), 265
Association of London Chief
    Librarians (ALCL), 265
Association of Research Libraries,
    72, *78*

Association of Special Libraries and Information Bureaux (ASLIB), 264
Association of Teachers in Colleges and Departments of Education, *203*
Association of University Teachers, *59*
Atkinson, Professor R., 90
Atkinson Report, 10, 11, 90–2, 119, 259, 265
Audio-visual material, *see* Non-print material
Auditors
 attitude to stocktaking, 227
 duties, 128–30
Audits, 123–31
 external
  non-public libraries, 130–1
  public libraries, 127–30
 internal, 189, 191
  non-public libraries, 126–7
  public libraries, 124–6
Author catalogues, 193, 194
Automated Library Systems (ALS) issue systems, 215, 216

BLAISE, 260
BLCMP, 259
Background Materials Supply Scheme, 258
Bagley, David, 83–4
Bains Report, 43, 52, 59, 261, *266*
Balliol College Library, 1
Bancroft, Richard, Archbishop of Canterbury (1544–1610), 1
Batten, W. E., *266*
Berriman, S. G., 93, 97, 98, *99*
Bibliographical services
 control of stock acquisition, 179
 from British Library, 14
 in subject departments, 95
 induction of new professional staff, 162
Binding, 229–31
 bases for decisions, 227–8

costs, 103
home binderies, 230–1
pamphlets, 197
'perfect', 230
periodicals, 203, 229
Birmingham Central Library, 81
 subject departments, 93, 98
Birmingham Libraries Co-operative Mechanisation Project (BLCMP), 259
Blacklisted borrowers, 225
Board of Education, 77
 see also Department of Education and Science; Ministry of Education
Bodleian Library, 57
Bone, L. E., 67, *78*
Book catalogues, 194
Book funds
 allocation in public libraries, 178–9
 allocation in university libraries, 180–1
 central accounting methods, 185
Book losses, 222
 revealed by stocktaking, 226
Book prices, 103
Book reviews, 176
Book selection, *see* Stock selection
Bookamatic issue system, 207
Bookseller, The, guide to book prices, 103
Booksellers, 186
Borrowers, *see* Users
Bourdillon Report, 11, 30, 66, 89, 143
Bradford Central Library
 subject departments, 93, 98
 theatre, 252
Brandwein, L., *171*
Brewer, J. G., *265*
British Council, 264
British libraries
 history, 1–5
 influence of central government, 6, 7–15
 international status, 1

planning on national basis, 7,
64
policy objectives, 9
post-war growth, 3
British Library, 5–6
accommodation problems, 80
advisory committees, 39
annual reports, 246
Bibliographical Services
Division, 17
Board, 17–19
calls for further development,
36
co-operative computer schemes,
259
exhibitions, 250, 251
external audit, 131
financial control, 122
internal audit, 126–7
involvement in research, 10, 13
Lending Division, 10, 13–14, 17
accommodation, 80
effect on requests of extended
storage, 259
holdings (1976), 255
of foreign publications, 255
links with Science Museum
Library, 21
overseas requests, 255
support for regional library
systems, 254–5
users' needs, 86
new building, 13, 80, 120
organisation problems, 79–80
Reference Division, 2, 13, 16
accommodation, 80
departments, 16
regulations, 233–4
security procedure, 223, 224
users' needs, 86
revenue estimates, 114
takeover of Library Association
Library, 23
British Library Act (1972), 5, 8,
13, 17, 28
British Library Automated
Information Systems
(BLAISE), 260

British Museum Act (1963), 21
British Museum Library
need to replace premises, 13
role as national library, 5
taken into British Library, 16,
80
British Museum (Natural History)
Library, 21
British National Bibliography
as stock selection tool, 175, 184
basis for co-operative purchase
schemes, 258
Marc tapes, 194, 260
numbers used as identifiers,
191
taken into British Library, 5
Browne issue system, 207–9
Buckingham University College, 3
Buildings
effect on organisation, 80–1
effect on staff provision, 141–2
financing in universities, 119
maintenance costs, 104
Burkett, J., 36
Burnham salary scales, 154
Byelaws, 231–2

COM catalogues, 95, 193–4, 195
COMLA, 264
COPOL, 265
Cambridge University Library, 57
Camden, London Borough of, 215
library theatre, 252
Canterbury Cathedral: Chapter
Library, 1
Capital estimates, see Estimates,
capital
Capital expenditure
effect on revenue estimates, 118
estimates, 100
related changes in revenue
expenditure, 104
Career prospects, according to
level of qualification, 147–8
Carlyle, Thomas, 2
Carnegie, Andrew, 28
Carrels, 239
Cassettes, see Non-print material

Catalogue cards, 198–9
Catalogues, 193–6
  COM, 95, 193–4, 195
  Marc tapes, 194, 260
  physical form, 194–5
  position in library, 238
  provision in subject
    departments, 95
  published guides, 246
  regional holdings in microform,
    255
  types, 194
Cataloguing, 193–5
Certifying officers, 186, 189
Charges, 36
  as source of income, 133–5
  fines, 223–5
    exempted borrowers, 224–5
  for interloans, 255–6
  for loan of gramophone records,
    220
  in estimates, 105
  permissible categories, 30,
    133–4
Chartered Institute of Public
    Finance and Accountancy,
    102
Chetham, Humphrey, see
    Humphrey Chetham Library
Chicago Public Library survey,
    68–9, 77
Children's Book Weeks, 250
Circulation
  of periodicals, 243–4
  of special library stock, 182
Circulation control systems,
    205–21
  Bookamatic, 207
  Browne, 207–9
  computer-based, 212–19
    ALS, 215, 216
    Plessey, 215, 216–18
  duplicate slip, 206–7
  Newark 209
  photocharging, 210–12, 213
  stock preparation, 198
  token, 209–10
Civic theatres, 252

Civil Service Commission, 139
Classification
  notation on spines, 198
  of pamphlets, 197
  schemes, 192–3
    functions, 193
Classified catalogues, 193, 194
Closed-circuit television, 223
Cobham, Thomas, Bishop of
    Worcester (d. 1327), 1
Collation, 189
College libraries, 4
  committees, 39, 57–8
  effect of DES influence, 12
  finance and administration, 26
  instruction in library use, 240
  organisation, 92
  revenue estimates, 111–13
  staffing, 112
  standards and objectives, 74,
    143
  stock requirements, 173
  stock selection policy, 174
  see also Academic libraries;
    University libraries
Committees
  purpose, 38–9
  Redcliffe-Maud proposals, 42–3
  types, 37–8
  see also College libraries:
    committees; Polytechnic
    libraries: committees; Public
    libraries: committees;
    University libraries:
    committees
Commonwealth Institute Library,
    21
Commonwealth Library
    Association, 264
Communication channels, 167–70
  indirect, 169–70
  oral, 168
  written, 168–9
Complaints procedure
  against public libraries, 30–1
  in Northern Ireland, 35
Comptroller and Auditor General,
    131

Computer applications
  accessions records, 191–2
  accountancy records, 104
  ancillary uses of issue systems,
    218
  book orders, 188
  British Library involvement, 17
  catalogues, 194, 195
  COM catalogues, 95
  considerations on introduction,
    47–8
  co-operative schemes, 259–60
  cost-benefit, 213
  DES involvement, 9
  issue systems, 212–19
  library routines, 212–13
  periodicals receipt records, 202
  related to staff provision, 142
  Selective Dissemination of
    Information (SDI), 242
  stock ordering, 183
  stocktaking, 226
  use of Post Office lines, 216,
    217
Computer output microfilm, see
  COM catalogues
Conditions of service, 75, 136,
    153–4
  effect on staffing levels, 140–1
  in public libraries, 46
  in university libraries, 53
Confidential material, 220–1
Contracts of employment, 153,
    154
Contracts of Employment Act
    (1972), 153
Co-operative schemes, 254–9
  acquisitions and storage, 257–9
  as economic necessity, 10, 36
  computer applications, 259–60
  DES involvement, 9
  local, 256–7
  periodical circulation, 201
  Sheffield Report, 10, 65, 257
  study in USA, 7
  see also Interlending schemes
Co-option of committee members,
    41

Corbett, E. V., 77, 78, 171, 235
Corporate management, 47–8
Corruption, avoidance of, 123
Cotton manuscripts, 2
Council for National Academic
    Awards, 4
Council meetings, attendance of
    Librarian, 45
Council of Polytechnic Librarians
    (COPOL), 265
Council on Library Resources,
    72
Cultural activities, 252

DIALTECH, 260
Dainton Committee Report, 5
Date labels, 198
Davies, Helen, 222, 235
Defaulters, 225
Department of Education and
    Science, 15, 77, 99
  control function, 7–12
  funding British Library, 114
  Library, 21
  responsibility for public
    libraries, 9
  standards for service points, 89
  see also Board of Education;
    Ministry of Education
Department of (the) Environment,
    59, 266
Department of Health and Social
    Security Library, 21–2
Department of Industry Library,
    21
De Prospo, E. R., 78
Derbyshire County Libraries, 216
Detector systems, 222
Development programmes, 81
Devolution, possible effects on
    libraries, 36
Devon County Library, co-
    operative purchase of scores,
    258
Dictionary catalogues, 194
Disciplinary action
  shown on staff records, 164
  use of appraisal forms, 159, 160

Discounts on stock purchases,
187, 189
Displays, 250
District auditors, 128, 129
Downes, R. B., *15*
Duplicate slip issue system, 206–7
Durham Cathedral: Dean and
Chapter Library, 1
Dust-jackets, 198
laminated, 229
Dutton, B. G., 156, *171*

EEC publications, 255
EURONET, 260
Eastlick, J. T., *78*
Eccles, David McAdam, 1st
Viscount, 18
Ecclesiastical libraries, 1
Edinburgh University Library, 1
Editing stock, 176, 177, 227
Education and Libraries
(Northern Ireland) Order
(1972), 34
appointment of library
committees, 41–2
provision for Byelaws, 232
Edwards, Passmore, 28
Edwards, R. J., *171*
Employment Protection Act
(1975), 165, 170
Equipment in special
departments, 239
Esdaile, Arundell, 16, *36*
Establishment, *see* Staffing
Establishment departments, 138
Estimates, 100–20, 261
capital, 117–19
national and government
libraries, 120
public libraries, 117–19
university libraries, 119–20
defining spending limits, 104
of income, 105
passage through committees,
105–6
in universities, 110–11
relationship to Rate Support
Grant, 102, 106

revenue
college libraries, 111–13
national and government
libraries, 114–17
public libraries, 101–7
society and professional
libraries, 113–14
special libraries, 113
university libraries, 108–11
scrutiny, 60
transfers between votes
in public libraries, 105
in university libraries, 110
typical example, 107
vote numbers, 104
European Economic Community
publications, 255
European Space Agency, 260
Evans, E., 77, *78*
Executive committees, 37
Exhibitions, 250–2
Expenditure, *see* Estimates;
Finance

Fawcett Society, 58
Finance
book fund
allocation in public libraries,
178–9
allocation in university
libraries, 180–1
central accounting, 185
checks on expenditure, 123
committee approval, 44–5
control, 121–3
in government libraries, 121
in polytechnics, 122
in public libraries, 121–2
in universities, 122
cuts, 100
effect of 'pervasive' committees,
46
effect on staff provision, 143
effect on stock selection policy,
174
for capital projects, 117
for colleges, 112
for exhibitions, 251

278

for research in librarianship, 10
grants-in-aid from DES, 9
income from charges, 133–5
influence on objectives, 76–7
limits of officers'
    responsibilities, 122
of college and polytechnic
    libraries, 26
of government libraries, 22
of Northern Ireland public
    libraries, 35
of university libraries, 23, 25,
    53–4
problems of learned societies
    and associations, 58
provisions of 1850 Act, 2
Rate Support Grant, 8, 64, 102,
    106, 112
scrutiny of estimates and
    expenditure, 60
sources, 100–1
see also Charges; Estimates
Fines, see Charges
Fines boxes, 225
Fire precautions, 165
Fjallbrant, Nancy, 265
Flippo, E. B., 77
Flooring materials, 239
Foreign publications, 178
Foskett, D. J., 193, 204
French, W., 144, 171
Fugitive material, acquisition,
    173, 178
Furnishings for libraries, 239
Futes, E., 204

GLASS, 258
Gallivan, B., 214, 235
Gardner, Frank, 65, 78
General Rate Act (1967), 108
Goals, see Objectives
Government influence on
    libraries, 6, 7–15
Government libraries, 4–5, 20–2
    capital projects, 120
    estimates, 114
    financial control, 8, 121
    grades of staff, 147

ordering from HMSO, 185
parent bodies, 22
staffing, 22
use of staff appraisal, 159, 160
Government publications, 255
    acquisition, 177
Graduate staff, 147–8
Gramophone records, see
    Non-print material
Gray's Inn Library, 2
Greater London Audio Subject
    Specialisation Scheme
    (GLASS), 258
Greater London Evaluation
    Scheme, 156–7
Groombridge, Brian, 236, 237,
    265
Group selection techniques, 151–2
Guides to library services, 240, 245
Guiding, 238

HMSO, 22, 177, 185
Haak, J. R., 74, 78
Hailsham, Lord (Quintin
    McGarel Hogg), 29
Handicapped people, library
    services to, 4
Harleian manuscripts, 2, 16
Havering Public Library, 214
Health and Safety at Work Act
    (1974), 164–5
Her Majesty's Stationery Office,
    22
    publications acquisition, 177
    supplying government libraries,
    185
Hereford Cathedral Library, 1
Hillingdon project, 65, 68, 77, 78,
    236
Hills, P. J., 265
Hinks, J., 142, 171
Home binderies, 230–1
Hookway, Harry Thurston, 7, 18
Hospital libraries, 4
Hours of service, 233
    effect on staffing, 140
Humphrey Chetham Library, 2
Hurstfield, Joel, 11

IFLA
  conference (1974), 6, *15*
  liaison with Library
    Association, 264
  on acceptability of standards,
    85
  Standards for Public Libraries,
    70–1, *78*, 89, 99, 143
INSPEC, 260
INTAMEL, 89
ISBNs, 184, 191, 192
  use in computer-based issue
    systems, 214–15
Illegal borrowing, 221–2
Imperial College of Science and
  Technology, 20
Imperial War Museum Library,
  21
Indexing special library stock,
  182
Induction courses, 160–2
Inflation
  effect on estimate preparation,
    102, 103
  effect on university
    quinquennial submissions,
    109
Information bulletins, 242
Information retrieval, 36
Information Services in Physics,
  Electrotechnology and
  Control (INSPEC), 260
Inner Temple Library, 2
Institute of Chartered Surveyors
  Library, 23
Institute of Information
  Scientists, 265
Institutes of Education libraries,
  90
Insurance, 123, 131–3
Inter-lending schemes, 254–6
  cost, 255–6
  participation by special
    libraries, 5
  periodicals, 201
  union catalogues, 193
  with foreign libraries, 255
  see also Co-operative schemes

International Association of
  Metropolitan Libraries
  (INTAMEL), 89
International Federation of
  Library Associations, *see*
  IFLA
International Standard Book
  Numbers, *see* ISBNs
Interviews, 151–3
Inventories, 125
Invoices, 189
  use as accession records, 191
Ipswich, 2
Issue systems, *see* Circulation
  control systems

Jamaica Library Service, 6
Jarrow, monastic library, 1
Job analysis, 146, 155
Job classification, 156
Job descriptions, 145–6, 156
Job evaluation, 146, 155–8
Job specifications, 146
Johnson, Gerald W., 66
Joint Fiction Reserve, 258

Kenyon Report, 61
Kimber, R. T., 202, *204*
King's Library, 16
Knight, D. M., *78*

LADSIRLAC, 201, 256
LAMSAC
  job evaluation scheme, 157–8
  report on library staffing, 11,
    64, 143
LASER, 255
Labels, 198
Lambeth, 143
Lambeth Palace Library, 1
Lancashire
  agency arrangements, 33
  text, 267–8
Lancaster University
  detector system, 222
  hybrid computer issue system,
    213
  Library Research Unit, 77

Lanchester Polytechnic, 84
Layout of library, 238
Learned society libraries, 23
  committees, 58
  estimates, 113–14
  history, 1–2
Leeds Library, 2
Legal action under Byelaws, 232
Legal deposit libraries, 19
Legal libraries, 2
Legislation
  British Library Act (1972), 5,
    8, 13, 17, 28
  British Museum Act (1963), 21
  byelaws, 231–2
  Contracts of Employment Act
    (1972), 153
  control function, 8
  Education and Libraries
    (Northern Ireland) Order
    (1972), 34, 41–2, 232
  Employment Protection Act
    (1975), 165, 170
  General Rate Act (1967), 108
  Health and Safety at Work Act
    (1974), 164–5
  Local Government Act (1972),
    8, 40, 41, 121–2, 128, 232
  Local Government Act
    (Northern Ireland) (1972),
    34
  Local Government
    (Boundaries) Act (Northern
    Ireland) (1971), 34
  Local Government (Scotland)
    Act (1973), 33, 34, 41, 232
  Offices, Shops and Railway
    Premises Act (1963), 164
  Public Libraries Acts (1850,
    1855, 1919), 2–3, 28, 61
  Public Libraries and Museums
    Act (1964), 3, 8, 28, 29–31,
    62–3, 133, 224, 232
  Public Libraries Consolidation
    (Scotland) Act (1887), 33, 34,
    232
  Public Libraries (Scotland) Act
    (1955), 33

see also Byelaws; Rules and
  regulations
Leicester, 2
Leicestershire, 142
  agency arrangement, 33
  text, 269–71
Librarians
  appointment in Northern
    Ireland, 42
  appointment in universities, 53
  attendance at Council meetings,
    45
  ineligibility for election to
    employing authority, 41, 44
  professorial level in universities,
    155
  relationship with source of
    library finance, 261
  role in committee (public
    libraries), 18, 43–5, 55–6
  status comparison, public v.
    university, 55
Libraries, see Academic libraries;
  British libraries; College
  libraries; Government
  libraries; Learned society
  libraries; Polytechnics:
  libraries; Special libraries;
  United States of America;
  University libraries
Library Advisory Councils, 63, 89
Library Association, 171, 204,
  263–4
  case for free public library
    service, 135
  guide to book prices, 103
  guidelines on public library
    service structure, 89, 143
  liaison with international
    organisations, 264
  Library, 23
  on need for separate library
    committees, 43
  proposals for post-war
    development, 29
  Sections, 265
  standards for college libraries,
    74, 143

Library Association. London and
Home Counties Branch, 77
see also Public Libraries
Research Group
Library Licence Agreement, 187
Library of Congress/BNB Marc
tapes, 194, 260
Library publications, 245–50
Library Research Unit, see
Lancaster University
Library schools, DES
involvement, 9, 10
Lighting in libraries, 238–9
Lincoln's Inn Library, 2
Liverpool and District Scientific
Industrial and Research
Library Advisory Council
(LADSIRLAC), 201, 256
Liverpool City Libraries, 93, 143
Loan periods, 206
Local authorities
control function, 7
financing capital projects, 117
'pervasive' committees, 46
precepting authorities, 108
Local Authorities Management
Services Advisory Council,
see LAMSAC
Local Government Act (1972), 8
appointment of library
committee, 40, 41
external audit provisions, 128
financial control provisions,
121–2
provision for byelaws, 232
Local Government Act
(Northern Ireland) (1972), 34
Local Government (Boundaries)
Act (Northern Ireland)
(1971), 34
Local government reorganisation
effect on public libraries, 3,
31–3, 35–6, 67
committee status, 43, 261–2
reframing of library objectives,
77
in London boroughs, 81–2
reviews of structure, 82–3

Local Government (Scotland) Act
(1973), 33, 34
appointment of library
committees, 41
provision for byelaws, 232
Local newspapers, 252–3
Local radio, 251, 253
Location of libraries, 237
London and South Eastern
Regional Library System
(LASER), 255
London boroughs, 81–2, 87
Management Services Unit, 156
London Library, 2
London University Library, 57
depository at Egham, 259
Standing Conference of
Librarians, 265
Luckham, Bryan, 236, 265
Luton library theatre, 252

MbO, 71, 74, 76, 81
MEDLARS, 17, 260
MEDLINE, 260
MJFR, 258
MSC, 257–8, 259
McAnnally, A. M., 15
McColvin, Lionel, 3, 209
McElderry, Stanley, 6, 7
McKay, J. R., 145, 171
MacKenzie, Graham, 77, 78
Management by Objectives
(MbO), 71, 74, 76
in planning Birmingham
Central Library, 81
Manchester
Humphrey Chetham Library, 2
library theatre, 252
Marc tapes, 194, 260
Martin, Lowell, 68–9, 77, 78
Mason, Don, 71, 78
Maud Report, see Redcliffe-Maud
Report
Medical certificates, 166
Medical examinations, 153
Medical Literature and Retrieval
Systems (MEDLARS), 17,
260

Merton College Library, 1
Messenger, M., *171*
Metropolitan Special Collections
  Scheme (MSC), 257-8, 259
Microforms
  in university libraries, 181
  of periodical files, 203, 229
  reader-printers, 199
  use in COM catalogues, 195-6
  see also Non-print material
Middle Temple Library, 2
Ministry of Defence (Central and
  Army) Library, 243
Ministry of Education, *15, 36, 77,
  99*
Ministry of Housing and Local
  Government, *59, 266*
Mirrors (security), 223
Monastic libraries, 1
Montagu House, 2
Morris, R. J. B., *15*
Mourse, E. S., *78*
Moys, Elizabeth M., *71, 78*

NATIS, 237
Name catalogues, 194
National Board for Prices and
  Incomes, *171*
National Central Library, 5, 259
National Information Systems
  (NATIS), 237
National Joint Council salary
  scales, 154, 155
National Lending Library for
  Science and Technology, 5,
  79
National libraries, 5-6, 16-20
  British Museum Library
    established, 2
  capital projects, 120
  control functions of Boards, 7
  estimates, 114-17
  government influence, 12-13
  see also British Library;
    National Library of
    Scotland; National Library
    of Wales
National Libraries Committee,

15, 265
National Library of Scotland, 5,
  19
  estimates, 117
National Library of Wales, 5,
  19-20
  estimates, 117
National Maritime Museum
  Library, 21
National planning for library
  services, 7, 64
National Reference Library of
  Science and Invention, 5, 16
Net Book Agreement, 187
Newark issue system, 209
Newcastle upon Tyne Central
  Library, 98
Newnes, Sir George, 28
Non-print material
  accession numbers, 192
  acquisition, 177
  co-operative purchase, 258
  issue systems, 219-21
  processing, 199
Non-professional posts, 146-8
  induction courses, 161-2
  recruitment procedure, 149
Non-recurrent estimates, *see*
  Estimates: capital
North East London Polytechnic,
  84
North Staffordshire Polytechnic,
  84
Northern Ireland
  appointment of Chief
    Librarians, 41
  appointment of library
    committees, 41
  libraries linked with education,
    8
  Library Boards, 34
  library finance and
    administration, 35
  public library legislation, 3, 34
  public library staffing, 35
Northern Ireland Branch of the
  Library Association, 265
Norwich, 2

OSTI, *see* Office of Scientific and Technical Information
Objectives
  Chicago study, 68–9, 77
  demystification, 75
  effect on staffing, 139
  international expression, 69–70
  of academic libraries, 71
  of issue systems, 205
  of library policy in UK, 9
  of public libraries, 61–71
  of special libraries, 71
  of university libraries, 72–3
  organising to achieve, 79
  regular review, 76–7
  related to standards, 75
  related to user needs, 85
  setting priorities, 75–6
Office of Scientific and Technical Information (OSTI), 5
  co-operative computer schemes, 259
  Manpower Project, 145
Office of University Library Management, 72, *78*
Offices, Shops and Railway Premises Act (1963), 164
Official order forms, 184–6, 188–9
Old people's homes, 4
Open University, 3
Oral communication, 168
Order procedures, 122, 183–6
  official order forms, 184–6
  use of union catalogues, 193
Ordinances, 37, 53
Organisation
  by subject departments, 93–8
  effect on staffing, 139
  limitations of inherited systems, 80–1
  of academic libraries, 90–2
  of library systems, 79–98
  of new library systems (1974), 83
  of polytechnic libraries, 83–4
  pattern in county areas, 88–9
  pattern in London boroughs, 87–8

review in London boroughs (1965), 82
  use of job analyses, 146
Organisation and Method investigations, 144
'Outreach' programmes, 143
Overdue books, 205
  in Browne system, 208
  legal proceedings, 225
  not traceable with token system, 210
  tracing in photocharging systems, 211
Overdue fines, *see* Charges
Overdue reminders, 225
Ownership stamps, 197
Oxford
  Bodleian Library, 57
  University library, 1

Pamphlet files, 197
Paper-back editions, 227–8
Parish libraries, 2
Parker, J. S., 260, *266*
Parry Committee Report, 3, 5, 72, 90, 109, 174, 180, 265
Partridge, D. A., 214, *235*
Paterson Committee Report, 43
Penny rate, 108
'Perfect' binding, 230
Performance measurement, 67–8
Periodicals
  accessioning, 192
  acquisition, 199–201
  agents, 200
  binding *v.* microforms, 229
  circulation, 243–4
  expenditure in university libraries, 173
  files, 203
  in subject department organisation, 94, 97
  in university libraries, 181
  lists of holdings, 246
  price fluctuations, 103
  problems of co-operative purchase, 258
  records of receipt, 201–3

union catalogues, 201, 202
visible indexes, 202
Periods of loan, 206
Personnel, *see* Staff
Personnel specifications, 146
Photocharging systems, 210–12, 213
Photocopies
from BLLD, 255
reducing illegal borrowing, 223
Pictures, *see* Non-print material
Plans of library layout, 238
Plessey issue system, 215, 216–18
Plessey Library Pens, 217
Police College, 4
Political parties, operation in local authorities, 48
Polytechnics, 4
financial control, 122
influence of government policies, 12
internal audit, 127
libraries, 26, 28
committees, 57–8
organisation, 92
problems of split sites, 83–4
standards, 74
stock requirements, 173
sub-committees, 39
role of governors and local authority, 26–8
type of clientele, 86
Pope, Elspeth, *171*
Post Office lines, 216, 217
Posters, 253
Precepting authorities, 108
Press, admission to committee meetings, 51
Priority assessment, 75–6
Prison libraries, 4, 89
Probationary period, 158, 162
Processing books, 189, 196–9
Professional association libraries, *see* Learned society libraries
Professional associations (librarianship), 263–5
Professional posts, 146–8
further training needs, 162–3

recruitment procedures, 149–50
Profiles of users, 242
Public Lending Right, 9, 135
Public libraries
annual reports, 246–7
capital estimates, 117–19
committees, 40–53, 261–2
agendas, 49–50
appointment in England and Wales, 40–1
in Northern Ireland, 41–2
in Scotland, 41
approval of estimates, 105–6
chairman's role, 48–9
conduct of meetings, 49–52
co-option, 41
formation of sub-committees, 52–3
relationship of Librarian, 18, 43–5, 55–6
size, 41
terms of reference, 45–7
entitlement to book purchase discounts, 187
external audit, 127–30
extra-mural services, 4
finance and administration, 29–36
fines on overdue books, 224
forerunners, 2
grades of staff, 148
history, 2–3, 28
internal audit, 124–6
linked with leisure services, 8
objectives, 61–71
standards, 8, 29
Bourdillon Report, 11, 30, 66, 89, 143
statutory requirements, 8
stock selection policy, 174
stock selection procedures, 174–80
Public Libraries Act (1850), 2, 28
lack of book provision, 61
Public Libraries Act (1855), 2, 28
Public Libraries Act (1919), 28, 61

Public Libraries and Museums
Act (1964), 3, 8, 28, 62–3
fines provision, 224
main provisions, 29–31
provision for byelaws, 232
provisions relating to charges,
133
Public Libraries Consolidation
(Scotland) Act (1887), 33, 34
provision for byelaws, 232
Public Libraries Research Group,
report on standards, 64, 65
Public Libraries (Scotland) Act
(1955), 33
Public relations, 236
in local authority
administration, 45
oriented towards parent body,
260–3
Publications by libraries, 245–50
Publicity
for exhibitions, 151
talks, 253–4
through the media, 252–3
Publicity material, 237
accessions lists, 246
posters, 253
Publishers' Association, 187

Ranfurly Library, 229
Rate Support Grant, 8, 64
related to departmental
estimates, 102, 106
Rate Support Grants (Pooling
Arrangements)
Regulations (1967), 112
Rateable values, 108
Rates, 106, 108
Reader-printers, 199
Readers, see User studies; Users
Recommending committees, 37
Records (administrative)
accessions, 190–2
book orders, 183
following receipt of stock, 188
of book fund expenditure, 179,
185–6
periodicals, 201–3

staff, 163–4
see also Circulation control
systems
Records (discs), see Non-print
material
Recruitment, 149–50
Redcliffe-Maud Report, 42–3, 52,
59, 261, 266
References (for job applicants),
151
Regional library systems, 14,
254–5
Renewing loan of books, 205
Renfrew District Libraries, 236
Reorganisation, see Local govern-
ment reorganisation
Reporting committees, 37
Reports
annual, 246–50
Atkinson, 10, 11, 90–2, 119,
259, 265
Bains, 43, 52, 59, 261, 266
Bourdillon, 11, 30, 66, 89, 143
Dainton, 5
Hillingdon project, 65, 68, 77,
78, 236
Kenyon, 61
Parry, 3, 5, 72, 90, 109, 174,
180, 265
Paterson, 43
Redcliffe-Maud, 42–3, 52, 59,
261, 266
Roberts, 29, 61
Sheffield, 10, 65, 257
Wheatley Commission, 33, 43
Requests, see Reservations
Research
British Library involvement,
10, 13
by ASLIB, 264
Research workers' requirements,
86, 141
Reservations
fees, see Charges
from overseas libraries, 255
locating books on loan, 205
rapid processing, 199

tracing
   in Browne issue system, 208
   in computer-based systems,
      216, 217, 218
Reserve stocks, 228, 259
Resources libraries, equipment,
   239
Revenue estimates, *see* Estimates,
   revenue
Roberts, Sir Sydney, 29
Roberts Committee Report, 29,
   61
Royal Botanic Gardens Library,
   21
Royal College of Physicians
   Library, 2
Royal College of Science, 20
Royal Commission on Local
   Government in Scotland, 59
Royal Geographical Society, 23
Royal Institute of British
   Architects Library, 23, 58
Royal Library, 16
Royal Society Library, 2
Rules and regulations, 232–5
Rules labels, 198
Russian library service, 6
Russian scientific literature, 255
Rutgers University, 67

SCOLCAP, 260
SCONUL, 265
SDI, 241–3
SINTO, 201, 256
SWALCAP, 260
Safety at work, 164–5
St Andrews University Library, 1
Salaries and wages, 136
   as percentage of library
      expenditure, 136–7
   college library staff, 112
   effect of job evaluation, 157
   estimates, 102
   in university libraries, 109
   national scales, 138, 139
   local application, 154
Schofield, J. L., 156, *171*
School libraries, 4

School Library Association, 265
School visits, 240
Science Museum Library, 20
Science Reference Library, 16, 17
Scotland
   appointment of library
      committees, 41
   effect of local government
      reorganisation on libraries, 33
   library legislation, 3, 33–4
   National Library of, 5, 19, 117
Scott, C. F., 181, *204*
Scottish Central Library, 19
Scottish Development
   Department, *59*
Scottish Libraries Co-operative
   Automation Project
   (SCOLCAP), 19, 260
Scottish Library Association, 265
Security, 221–3
   criteria for systems, 221
   in British Library, 233–4
   in open access reference
      libraries, 221
Selection of staff, 150–3
Selective Dissemination of In-
   formation (SDI), 241–3
Sergean, R., 145, *171*
Serial publications, 177
Service points, standards, 89
Sewell, Philip H., 32, 64, 75, *78*
Sharr, F. A., 66, *78*
Sheffield Interchange
   Organisation (SINTO), 201,
   256
Sheffield Report, 10, 65, 257
Sheffield University:
   Postgraduate School of
      Librarianship and
      Information Science, *15, 78,*
      257, *266*
Shelf registers, 188, 191
Shelving provision in subject
   departments, 95
Shimmon, R., *78*
Short-loan collections, 182, 224
Sickness leave, 166
   effect on staffing provision, 141

Sikorsky, N. M., 6
Single-copy orders, 178
Sion College Library, 1
Slides, *see* Non-print material
Sloane, Sir Hans, 2
Sloane Collection, 16
Society of Archivists, 265
Society of Indexers, 265
Souter, G. H., *235*
South Western Academic
     Libraries Co-operative
     Automation Project
     (SWALCAP), 260
Southampton University Library,
     212
Special collections
   in university libraries, 172–3
   published catalogues, 246
Special libraries, 4–5
   classification problems, 193
   contribution of ASLIB, 264
   external audit, 131
   function and finance, 22–3
   government influence, 8
   grades of staff, 148
   limited clientele, 86
   objectives, 71
   organisation, 92
   periodicals, 200
   rules, 235
   stock requirements, 173
   stock selection policy, 174
   stock selection procedures, 182
   use of SDI, 241–2
Staff
   appraisal methods, 158–60
   balance of grades, 136, 141
   channels of communication,
     167–70
   conditions of service, 75
     in public libraries, 46
     in university libraries, 53
   dealing with personal problems,
     166
   for home binderies, 231
   ineligible for election to em-
     ploying authority, 41
   probation, 158

records, 163–4
recruitment and selection,
     149–53
relationship with users, 239–41,
     263
subject specialists, 96–7, 98
union membership, 169–70
welfare, 164–6
Staff committees, 169
Staff libraries, 183
Staff management, 137
   involvement of new staff, 163
Staff manuals, 169
Staffing
   college libraries, 112
   DES involvement, 9
   establishment, 139–44
   in subject department
     organisation, 95, 96–7
   LAMSAC report, 11, 64, 143
   of government libraries, 22, 147
   of public libraries in Northern
     Ireland, 35
   requests for additional staff in
     universities, 109
   standards, 64
   structure related to numbers,
     142–3
Stamps
   accession, 197–8
   ownership, 197
Standards
   acceptability, 84–5
   American formulations, 66
   effect on staffing, 140
   effect when imposed from
     without, 91
   guideline status, 63
   IFLA *Standards,* 70–1
   public libraries, 8, 29
     Bourdillon Report, 11, 30, 66,
       89, 143
     PLRG report, 64, 65
   published, 89, 143
   related to objectives, 75
   staffing, 64
   see also User studies
Standing committees, 38

Standing Conference of National and University Libraries (SCONUL), 265
Standing orders (for stock), 177
Standing Orders (for committees), 37
Statistics, 192
  from computer-based systems, 218
  from issue systems, 206
  limited value, 61
  see also Performance measurement
Statistics and Market Intelligence Library, 21
Statutory requirements for public library authorities, 8, 30, 63
Stock
  co-operative acquisition and storage, 257–9
  disposal of withdrawn copies, 228–9
  editing, 176, 177
    in conjunction with stocktaking, 227
  losses, 222, 226
  physical condition, 227–9
  receipt procedures, 188–9
  reinforced editions, 229
  related to user needs, 172
  reserve stores, 259
  selection, 173–83
    filling gaps, 175
    policy, 173–4
    procedure in public libraries, 174–80
    procedure in special libraries, 182
    procedure in university libraries, 180–2
  suppliers and terms, 186–8
  types, 172
  see also Non-print material
Stocktaking, 226–7
Street direction signs, 237
Study leave, effect on staffing provision, 141
Study tables, 239

Stueart, R. D., 78
Subject catalogues, 193, 194
Subject departments, 93–8
  advantages and disadvantages, 94–7
  in public libraries, 93, 97–8
  in university libraries, 93, 97
Subject indexes, 194
Subject specialists, 96–7, 98
  exploiting periodicals, 203
  involvement in classification and cataloguing, 196
  involvement in stock selection, 180, 181
  links with lecturers, 241
Subscription libraries, 2
Supervision of open access areas, 222–3, 227
Sutton, London Borough of: subject departments, 93, 98

TRC, 260
Talks to local organisations, 253–4
Technological Reports Centre (TRC), 260
Telephone directories, entries in, 237
Temperature in libraries, 239
Text-book provision, 181–2
Theatres, 252
Theft of books, 222
Thompson, James, 15, 97, 99
Thompson, V. A., 144, 171
Token charging system, 209–10
Tomlinson, N., 32
Totterdell, B., 78, 265
Trade unions, 169–70
Trainee posts, 146, 148
Training, 136, 160–3
  for information workers, 17
  use of job analyses, 146
Training officers, 138
Translation services, 17
Trapping stores, 216, 217, 225, 226
Tynemouth, W. A., 98, 99

UBC, 237
UKCIS, 260
Unesco
  liaison with Library
    Association, 264
  Public Library Manifesto,
    69–70, 135
  publications held by BLLD,
    255
UNISIST, 237, 260
Union catalogues, 193
  of periodicals holdings, 201, 202
    in London public libraries,
    258
United Kingdom, see British
  libraries
United Kingdom Chemical
  Information Service, 260
United Nations Information
  System in Science and
  Technology (UNISIST),
  237, 260
United States of America
  government involvement in
    libraries, 6–7
  library standards and
    objectives, 66–9
  National Commission on
    Libraries, 69
  'Outreach' programmes, 143
  role of university libraries, 72–4
  staff management, 137
  standards, 89
  use of staff appraisal, 159
Universal Bibliographic Control
  (UBC), 237
University Grants Committee,
  15, 78, 99, 120, 203
  control function, 7
  effect of government policies,
    11
  funding departmental libraries,
    90
  quinquennial submissions,
    108–9
  terms of reference, 24
  Working Party, see Atkinson
  Report

University libraries
  advertising location, 237
  annual reports, 246
  clientele limited, 86
  committees, 53–7
    agendas, 56
    effect of other committees, 57
    powers and duties, 53–4
    relationship of Librarian, 54
    size, 54
  departmentalism, 90
  estimates, 108–11
  external audits, 130
  finance and administration,
    23–6
  financial control, 122
  grades of staff, 147–8
  history, 1
  home binderies, 230
  internal audit, 127
  library instruction for students,
    240–1
  non-recurrent expenditure,
    119–20
  objectives, 72–3
  organisation, 90–2
  Parry Committee terms of
    reference, 72
  post-war growth, 3
  rules, 234–5
  salaries related to academic
    staff, 155
  short-loan collections, 182, 224
  status within university, 3
  stock requirements, 172
  stock selection policy, 174
  stock selection procedures,
    180–2
  subject departments, 93, 97
User needs
  effect on staffing provision, 141
  related to objectives, 85
  related to stock acquisition, 172
User studies, 65–6, 236
  in USA, 67–8
  see also Standards
Users
  blacklisting, 225

group visits, 240
introduction to library facilities,
240, 245
profiles, 242
registration, 215, 223, 240
relationship with staff, 239–41,
263

Vertical files
for gramophone records, 199
for pamphlets, 197
Victoria and Albert Museum
exhibition service, 250
Library, 20, 21
Viewdata, 36
Visible indexes
for periodical records, 202
for reservations, 207, 210, 212
Visual display units, 218
Vote numbers, 104

WANDPETLS, 201
Wages, *see* Salaries and wages

Wales
National Library of, 5, 19–20,
117
Walford, A. J., 243, *266*
Wandsworth Public Library, 201
photocharging, 211
Plessey demonstration, 215
Wearmouth, monastic library, 1
Welfare of staff, 164–6
Wells Cathedral Library, 1
Welsh Library Association, 265
West Sussex County Library, 212,
215
Westminster City Libraries, 209
Whatley, H. A., *265*
Wheatley Commission Report,
33, 43
Williams, James G., *171*
Winchester College: Warden and
Fellows Library, 1
Withdrawn books, disposal, 228–9
Working conditions, 164–5
Written communications, 168–9

Young, R. C., 215, 216, *235*